# EMERSON HANDBOOK

# Emerson Handbook

*By*

FREDERIC IVES CARPENTER
*University of California*

NEW YORK
HENDRICKS HOUSE, INC.

Copyright, 1953, by Hendricks House, Inc.

*All rights reserved. No part of this book may be reproduced in any form, by mimeograph or any other means, without written permission from the publisher.*

Reprinted 1967

228788

Manufactured in the United States of America

# CONTENTS


Preface . . . . . . . . . . . . . . . . . . . . ix

Chronological Table . . . . . . . . . . . . . . . . xiii

PART I: EMERSON'S BIOGRAPHY

Problems and Interpretations . . . . . . . . . . 1

The Two Sides of the Face . . . . . . . . . . 1

Heredity and Original Genius . . . . . . . . . . 3

From Weakness to Strength . . . . . . . . . . 6

Beyond Tragedy . . . . . . . . . . . . . . 10

The Problem of Vocation . . . . . . . . . . . 13

Loves and Friendships . . . . . . . . . . . . 21

Reform and Anti-Slavery . . . . . . . . . . . 35

The Chief Biographies . . . . . . . . . . . . . 41

*Bibliography:* Part I: Bibliographies . . . . . . . . . 45

Biographies . . . . . . . . . . . . . . . 45

Biographical Articles . . . . . . . . . . . . . 49

PART II: EMERSON'S PROSE AND POETRY

The Prose Works . . . . . . . . . . . . . . . 51

The Unpublished Manuscripts . . . . . . . . . 72

Method and Style . . . . . . . . . . . . . . 74

The Poetry . . . . . . . . . . . . . . . . 79

Aesthetic and Poetic Theory . . . . . . . . . . 90

*Bibliography:* Part II: Text . . . . . . . . . . . . 102
Textual Criticism and Aesthetic Theory . . . . . . . 104

PART III: EMERSON'S IDEAS
The Ideal and the Real . . . . . . . . . . . . . . 108
Transcendental Idealism: Mysticism . . . . . . . . . 113
Transcendentalism . . . . . . . . . . . . . . . 124
Romanticism . . . . . . . . . . . . . . . . . 136
Optimism and Evil . . . . . . . . . . . . . . . 143
"The American Dream" . . . . . . . . . . . . . 153
Yankee Realism: Pragmatism . . . . . . . . . . . 164
Experience and Nature . . . . . . . . . . . . . 178
Politics and Individualism . . . . . . . . . . . 186
Puritanism and "The Moral Law" . . . . . . . . . 194
The Genteel Tradition . . . . . . . . . . . . . 200
*Bibliography:* Part III . . . . . . . . . . . . . 203
The Background of Emerson's Ideas . . . . . . . . 204
Critical Studies of Emerson's Ideas . . . . . . . . 205

PART IV: EMERSON AND WORLD LITERATURE
Sources: The Ancients . . . . . . . . . . . . . . 210
The Moderns . . . . . . . . . . . . . . . . . 217
Influences: America, Nineteenth Century . . . . . . 225
American Reputation . . . . . . . . . . . . . . 234
America, Twentieth Century . . . . . . . . . . . 235
England . . . . . . . . . . . . . . . . . . . 238
France and Belgium . . . . . . . . . . . . . . 241
Germany . . . . . . . . . . . . . . . . . . . 244
Other Countries . . . . . . . . . . . . . . . . 250
Conclusion . . . . . . . . . . . . . . . . . . . 252
*Bibliography:* Part IV . . . . . . . . . . . . . 254
INDEX . . . . . . . . . . . . . . . . . . . . . 261

# PREFACE

In his famous *Decline of the West,* Oswald Spengler lists "Compendium Literature" as one symptom of the "Extinction of Spiritual Creative Force" which accompanies the decay of every great civilization. And surely the publication of a series of handbooks for the major American authors might seem to confirm his diagnosis. But in the present state of American literature, handbooks can do no more than describe the incompleteness of scholarship and the differences of the interpretations of their subjects. Therefore, they must point the way to further investigations while suggesting tentative solutions. Professor Allen's *Walt Whitman Handbook* suggested new approaches, not only to the interpretation of Whitman, but of American literature. And the study of Whitman's "master," who proclaimed himself an "opener of doors to those who come after" must attempt to do likewise.

Indeed an *Emerson Handbook,* in the traditional sense of the word, is a contradiction of terms, for Emerson's thought perpetually escapes systematization. "I am too young yet by some ages to compile a code," he said. Like Whitman, his world view remained aggressively and purposefully unsystematic, answering closely to Spengler's definition of the "Springtime" of a Civilization: "Earliest mystical-metaphysical shaping of the New World Outlook"; rather than to his definition of its "Decline." Like those other mystics, Plotinus and Eckhardt, whom Spengler lists as spokesmen of the early, "springtime" period of other "Civilizations," Emerson sought to foreshadow some new ideal. Indeed, his was the recurrent dilemma of American idealists, who have struggled to realize their dreams of a new, equalitarian democracy, at the same time that they have found themselves involved in the traditional patterns of a privileged aristocracy. By temperament and by philosophy Emerson prophesied that American dream which no handbook can codify.

But if an *Emerson Handbook* cannot finally summarize its subject and define his philosophy it can point some of the problems and suggest some of the alternatives. If, like many Americans, Emerson lived in an ideal democracy, at the same time that he clipped his coupons and paid his taxes to the existing state, it can describe this dualism. If his America did not and could not answer exactly to his dreams, neither did it quite fit the patterns of the past. If he wrote more passionately of his visions than of his politics, it is important to relate the visions to those of Plotinus and of Eckhardt on the one hand, and the politics to those of Charles Sumner and of Colonel Forbes on the other. Because he lived in two worlds and because he still triumphantly escapes definition, it seems all the more important to summarize what we do not know about him in order, perhaps, to prove Spengler wrong.

But a handbook, by definition, must destroy the imaginative fusion of dream and reality which constituted Emerson's greatness and must itemize his life, catalogue his books and analyze his techniques as well as attempt to describe his different ideas and to suggest the impact of his writing on our modern world. It must present both facts and interpretations. And so, in the following chapters, Emerson the citizen and Emerson the technician must be packaged into sections separate from Emerson the mystic and Emerson the idealistic dreamer.

In this book the facts about Emerson come first, in the traditional order. But the reader interested primarily in Emerson's ideas will find it easy to begin with Part III. Some fresh interpretations of Emerson may be found in Parts III and IV, which deal with his ideas and with his influence on the modern world of today. In addition, part of Part I, which describes some of the psychological problems of Emerson's biography, and that section of Part II which discusses his aesthetics, may also prove of general interest. The other chapters are intended primarily for the student.

Every writer of handbooks owes an unpayable debt to all those critics, professors, and students who have written on his subject before him. To Professor Bliss Perry, who first introduced me to Emerson, I owe most because the debt goes beyond the formal words which he has written and published to his personal teaching and inspiration. To Mr. Van Wyck Brooks—like Emerson, a friend and aider of those who would live in the spirit—I owe a similar, intangible debt for encouragement. To other scholars and critics, my debt can be acknowledged formally in footnotes and bibliography. Wherever I have not mentioned my source in the text itself, I have tried to suggest it in footnotes.

More than is customary, however, I have drawn upon the ideas and the formulations of the many graduate students whose doctoral dissertations on Emerson remain in university libraries, unpublished. Often these studies have seemed to me far better than others which have been published, and I have borrowed from them freely. Since they are not protected by copyright, and are not familiar to readers, I have emphasized them perhaps too much. And since I have not been able to consult all such studies, I have certainly been partial.[1] But I have attempted always to indicate my indebtedness and my partiality in the text. I can only hope that many of these theses may be published in the future.

Finally, the Bibliography[2] of this *Handbook* is more selective and more critical than most. When I have not discussed an important book or article in the text, I have attempted to describe and to criticize it in the Bibliography. The criticism, of course, has also been personal and therefore partial, but here I have attempted as far as possible to summarize the critical judgments of other readers.

In writing this *Handbook* I have always remembered the by-line of a familiar columnist: "Aut Scissors, Aut Nullus." A handbook must be critical and selective or it becomes merely a handful.

1. In general, I have consulted those dissertations which have been particularly recommended, and those which have dealt with subjects of particular interest.

2. For convenience, the Bibliography has been divided into four sections, one at the end of each Part of the *Handbook.*

# CHRONOLOGICAL TABLE

## SIGNIFICANT EVENTS IN EMERSON'S LIFE

| | |
|---|---|
| 1803 | Born May 25, at Boston, fourth child of the Reverend William and Ruth (Haskins) Emerson. |
| 1811 | His father, William Emerson, died. |
| 1812–1817 | Attended the Boston Latin School. |
| 1813 | First surviving letter (to Aunt Mary Moody Emerson). Began his first ambitious poem "Fortus." |
| 1814 | Verse on naval victories in the War of 1812. |
| 1817–1821 | Attended Harvard College. Began keeping journals. |
| 1821–1825 | Taught at brother William's "school for young ladies." |
| 1822 | Published first article, in *The Christian Disciple*. |
| 1825–1826 | Studied divinity at Harvard. Occasional school-teaching. |
| 1826 | Licensed to preach. Threatened with tuberculosis; sailed for Charleston and St. Augustine. |
| 1827–1829 | Occasional preaching. |
| 1828 | Nervous breakdown of his brother, Edward. |
| 1829 | Ordained pastor of Second Church, Boston (March). Married Ellen Louisa Tucker (September). |
| 1831 | Ellen died (February). |
| 1832 | Resigned pastorate; preached farewell sermon (September). Sailed for Europe (December). |
| 1833 | Traveled in Italy, France, and England. Visited Carlyle at Craigenputtock (August). |
| 1834 | Edward Emerson, brother, died. Occasional preaching. First series of lectures. Moved to Concord. |
| 1835 | First met Alcott and Margaret Fuller. Married Lydia Jackson (September). |
| 1836 | Charles Emerson, brother, died (May). *Nature* published (September). First meeting of the "Transcendental Club." Waldo, his first child, born (October). |
| 1837 | Friendship with Thoreau. "The Concord Hymn" (July). Phi Beta Kappa address on "The American Scholar" (August). |
| 1838 | "Divinity School Address" (July). |
| 1839 | Four poems published in *The Western Messenger*. Ellen, his first daughter, born. |
| 1840 | *The Dial* first published, including Emerson's *Address to the Reader*. |
| 1841 | *Essays*, First Series (January). Edith, his second daughter, born. Brook Farm founded. |
| 1842 | Waldo, his son, died (January). Lectured on "The Transcendentalist." Met Horace Greeley and Henry James, |

Sr. on New York lecture tour (March). Assumed editorship of *The Dial* (July). Hawthorne moved to Concord.

1843 Alcott's *Fruitlands* (June). Lectured in Philadelphia and Washington.

1844 Edward, his fourth child, born (July). Address on "Emancipation in the British West Indies" (August). *Essays,* Second Series (October).

1845 Thoreau to Walden (July 4).

1846 *Poems* (December; dated 1847).

1847 Sailed for England (October). Second visit to Carlyle in London. Lectured in England and Scotland, 1847-1848.

1849 *Nature; Addresses and Lectures* (September). *Representative Men* (December; dated 1850).

1850 First journey west (St. Louis and Chicago). Margaret Fuller Ossoli died (July).

1851 First address on "Fugitive Slave Law."

1852 Edited *Memoirs of Margaret Fuller Ossoli.*

1853 Lectured through the West. His mother died (November).

1854 Thoreau's *Walden.*

1855 Whitman's *Leaves of Grass* (July). Met Whitman in New York (December).

1856 *English Traits.*

1857 "Days" and "Brahma" published in first issue of *The Atlantic Monthly.* John Brown in Concord.

1859 First speech on "John Brown."

1860 Lincoln elected. Talk with Whitman in Boston. *The Conduct of Life* (December).

1861 Civil War (April).

1862 Lectured in Washington, met Lincoln. Thoreau died (May); Emerson's funeral address published (August).

1863 Celebrated the Emancipation Proclamation with "The Boston Hymn."

1864 "We buried Hawthorne in Sleepy Hollow." (May)

1865 Address on "Abraham Lincoln."

1866 "Terminus" written. LL.D. from Harvard

1867 Lectured to St. Louis Philosophical Society. *May Day* published (April). Elected overseer of Harvard.

1870 *Society and Solitude.* Gave course of fourteen lectures at Harvard.

1871 Trip to California.

1872 "House burned" (July). Trip to Egypt (October).

1873 In France and England. Third visit with Carlyle.

1875 *Letters and Social Aims.*

1879 Read lecture at first meeting of the Concord School of Philosophy.

1882 Died April 27, at Concord.

# EMERSON HANDBOOK

# *PART I*

# EMERSON'S BIOGRAPHY

## Problems and Interpretations

Emerson's life is interesting chiefly for the light which it throws upon his writings, but this light can be modulated and focused in many different ways: both Emerson's life and his writings have proved extraordinarily complex. The facts and the texts have been established, but the interpretations of the different biographers have varied.[1] Perhaps the best approach to Emerson's biography, therefore, lies through the study of the different problems of his life.

His life has suggested complex problems of interpretation. First, how can the radical conflict between the Yankee and the mystic elements of his character be reconciled? Then, more specific problems (roughly in chronological order) have arisen: of heredity as opposed to original genius, of constitutional weakness as opposed to self-reliant strength, of recurrent personal tragedy as opposed to optimistic philosophy, of retirement from the "proud world" as opposed to an increasing round of lectures and activities, of an alleged "coldness" toward friends as opposed to an actual wealth of social contacts, and finally of a rejection of reform as opposed to an increasing devotion to the reform of anti-slavery during the latter part of his life. These problems are not equally simple, nor equally possible of solution. But taken together they suggest the fascination of Emerson's biography.

### 1. *The Two Sides of the Face*

From Lowell's early characterization of:

> A Greek head on right Yankee shoulders, whose range
> Has Olympus for one pole, for t'other the Exchange,

1. For summary and criticism of the biographies of Emerson, see pp. 41 ff., "The Chief Biographies," and "Bibliography."

. . .
A Plotinus-Montaigne, where the Egyptian's gold mist
And the Gascon's shrewd wit cheek-by-jowl co-exist.[2]

to the latest biography and critical essay, observers have emphasized the dualism of Emerson's personal and intellectual life. As Woodberry phrased it: "Emerson leaves a double image on the mind that has dwelt long upon his memory. He is a shining figure on some Mount of Transfiguration; and he was a parochial man."[3] But Bliss Perry was perhaps the first to emphasize the actual embodiment of this dualism in the physical lines of Emerson's face:

> His features were slightly asymmetrical. Seen from one side, it was the face of the old school, shrewd, serious, practical. . . . Seen from the other side, it was the face of a dreamer, a seer, a soul brooding on things to come, things as yet very far away. I once asked Daniel Chester French, the sculptor of the statue of Emerson now in the Concord Public Library, if this well-known characteristic of Emerson's features did not increase the difficulty of the sculptor's task. Not at all, he replied: all that he had to do was to project the planes of each side until they met at a point beyond the face itself.[4]

That Emerson's character embodied two contradictory elements is well known. The problem is: how to reconcile and to integrate these paradoxical opposites? Do the planes of his face actually meet if projected to a "point beyond the face itself?" What does each of these planes truly represent? Which one was dominant—the dreamer, or the parochial man? Does that "centre of integrity," which Woodberry described, lie within the mind, or outside and "beyond the face itself?" Was the integration inward, and psychological; or outward, projected upon "things to come?" Was Emerson "The prophet of modern America," or merely a dreamer of old dreams? And was his parochial side expressive of a narrow, New England gentility, or of a broadly human sympathy?

The answers to these questions depend upon the critic's point of view—both literally and figuratively. Bliss Perry's sympathetic interpretation, for instance, led him to choose for his frontispiece an unfamiliar portrait of Emerson in profile, which pictures the left, or parochial side of Emerson's face, as it smiles sympathetically toward some friend. And his description also emphasizes "the

2. From *A Fable for Critics* (1848).
3. G. E. Woodberry, *Emerson*, p. 1.
4. Bliss Perry, *Emerson Today*, p. 1.

quiet, friendly white house on the outskirts of the village." But other portraits[5] show the left side of Emerson's face as stern, or even grim.—And similarly, some of those portraits which emphasize the right, or dreamer's side of the face show it smiling serenely into the future. But others show the right corner of the mouth drawn down, as if remembering the phrase, "though He slay me, yet will I trust in Him."

There are not only two sides to Emerson's face and philosophy, but also two (or more) interpretations of each side. The best biographies are those which recognize and describe this dualism, without falsely simplifying its complexity. And the best criticisms are those which recognize and describe this complexity, without imputing it either to conscious duplicity, or to a foolish inconsistency. Some "biographies," like his son's *Emerson in Concord*, and Phillips Russell's *The Wisest American*, emphasize primarily the parochial, Yankee side. Others, like Régis Michaud's *La Vie Inspirée d'Emerson* (translated *The Enraptured Yankee*), emphasize the mystical side. Some critics, like Van Wyck Brooks in *The Flowering of New England*, have celebrated Emerson as the apotheosis of an earlier America. Others, like Yvor Winters, in *In Defense of Reason*, have simply condemned him as "a fraud." There are almost as many different interpretations as there are different points of view. His face, and his life, embodied many of the conflicts and complexities of the modern world.

## 2. *Heredity and Original Genius*

To begin at the beginning—Emerson was born into a world in transition. Not only was all Western civilization changing with the industrial revolution, but America was developing from an adolescent nation with a "colonial complex" to an independent nation with a literature of its own. And in New England, Puritanism, with its theocracy of stern authoritarianism, was giving way to Unitarianism, with its more democratic and individualistic spirit. By ancestry Emerson belonged to the earlier America and to the older religion, but by education and by personal choice he belonged to the new. Yet because he derived from the old, his biographers have tended to emphasize it.

Oliver Wendell Holmes, who had earlier described "the Brah-

5. The biography by Phillips Russell reproduces eight portraits.

min Caste in New England,"[6] sought to identify Emerson with it, introducing his biographical study with a further description of "the Academic Races," and a geneology emphasizing "a long succession of clergymen." Moreover, when he finally got down to "Ruth Haskins, mother of Ralph Waldo Emerson," he characterized her as "a woman 'of great patience and fortitude, of the serenest trust in God,'" making no mention of the fact that her father, John Haskins, had been a "cooper and distiller," and even in his youth the member of the crew of a privateer. But, on the other side, it is true that the bluff John Haskins had also been a pious church member, while the earlier ministerial ancestors of Ralph Waldo had also fought against the Indians, and taken part in the Revolution: the grandfather, William Emerson, had died as a chaplain of the Revolutionary army near Ticonderoga.

The point is that the dualistic conflict between ministerial piety and secular commercialism did not loom so large in those days as it does now. Like Milton's Satan, the puritan minister had been the leader of revolt, and the enterprising merchant, his natural ally. Emerson recognized both the pious and the pioneering elements of his ancestry and accepted both. But unlike his friend Holmes, he chose (especially in his early life) to minimize the ministerial heritage and to emphasize the pioneer.

In Emerson's early journals for 1825 he recorded his quiet rejection of the merely hereditary:

> It is my own humor to despise a pedigree. I was educated to prize it. The kind Aunt whose cares instructed my youth (and whom may God reward) told me oft of the virtues of her and mine ancestors. They have been clergymen for many generations, and the piety of all and the eloquence of many is yet praised in the Churches. But the dead sleep in their moonless night; my business is with the living.

But forty-seven years later he had come to identify himself with these ancestors, as pioneers, and to argue against Bret Harte that "I also spoke from Pilgrim experience, and knew on good grounds the resistless culture that religion effects."[7] The conflict in Emerson's mind, therefore, was not so much between the religious and the secular, as between the hereditary and the living experience.

The natural dependence of youth on paternal authority was

6. In the first chapter of his novel, *Elsie Venner.*
7. *Journals,* October 18, 1872.

lessened in Emerson's case by the death of his father in 1811, when he was only eight years old. The family was left in poverty, dependent largely upon the charity of friends and parishioners; and Mrs. Emerson's energies were sorely taxed by the task of raising five sons and by taking in boarders. The place of the father was taken not by any male guardian, but by "the kind Aunt whose cares instructed my youth"—the famous Mary Moody Emerson.

Even at the age of eight, Ralph Waldo seems to have welcomed this Aunt Mary with a combination of appreciative affection and humorous detachment. Her enthusiasm kindled his love of reading and of serious discussion, but her orthodoxy and ancestor-worship failed to carry authority. And the same was true of his step-grandfather, the Reverend Ezra Ripley of Concord, with whom he often visited during his youth, in the "Old Manse." He observed:

> Dr. Ripley prays for rain with great explicitness on Sunday, and on Monday the showers fell. When I spoke of the speed with which his prayers were answered, the good man looked modest.[8]

The symbols of ancestral authority and of religious orthodoxy were too distinctly related to Emerson's person and experience to be taken very seriously. Throughout his life paternal authority—the psychological basis of all authority—remained surrogate.

So Emerson grew up under the discipline, not so much of his parents, as of the community in general. And the Bostonian community of the time was more progressive than conservative. It remembered vividly the Revolution. It had chosen Emerson's father to be chaplain of the State Senate, where he had delivered the fourth of July oration the year before Ralph Waldo's birth. It feared invasion by the British in the War of 1812, when the young boy, together with his schoolmates, was asked to help throw up earthworks in Boston Harbor for defense of the city. And its population was in a constant state of flux, with the old Yankee stock thinned by migration to the West and by sailing "before the mast," while new immigrants from Europe gradually took possession of the ancestral city.

And beyond Boston was Concord—a symbol both of the country

8. *Journals*, August 17, 1838.

as opposed to the city, and also of the frontier as opposed to the older, more settled, civilization. The modern joke about the Bostonian tourists who planned to drive to California by way of Dedham would not have seemed so silly in those days, when Concord, like Dedham, was truly a country town, and had fairly recently been a frontier community. There Emerson's earliest ancestors had settled: the Reverend Peter Bulkeley, who having fled from Anglican persecution, founded the town in 1635, and named it in honor of his peaceful relations with the Indians; and the Reverend Daniel Bliss who welcomed the revivalist preacher, Whitefield, there in the eighteenth century. From there Emerson's grandfather had gone to join the Revolutionary army, and there his step-grandfather, Ezra Ripley lived. So, naturally now, Mrs. Emerson often visited Concord with her sons; and Ralph Waldo himself moved there permanently in 1834. When he wrote "Goodbye, Proud World, I'm Going Home," he was bidding goodbye to Boston, and going "home" to Concord. Also, in a sense, he was going West to a farming community where religion had not become genteel, nor society stratified.

So in 1884, from Boston's Beacon Hill, the urbane "Autocrat of the Breakfast Table," could look through the wrong end of his binoculars and see, stretching backwards, the long line of ministers from whom Emerson had sprung. But from the same Boston, in 1822 and 1823, Emerson had looked West and seen magnified "the deserts and forests of the interior of this country"; and had dedicated his journal to "the Spirit of America. . . . With a spark of prophetic devotion, I hasten to hail the Genius, who yet counts the tardy years of childhood but who is increasing unawares in the twilight and swelling into strength."[9] It was Emerson's humor to despise a pedigree, because the community of his time was looking toward the future, rather than toward the past. But he could quote his "pilgrim" past, when he wished.

### 3. *From Weakness to Strength*

Besides the pilgrim tradition, Emerson inherited from his ancestors a week constitution. His father died of tuberculosis at the age of forty-two, an elder brother and a sister died in early childhood, and his two brilliant younger brothers, Edward and

9. *Journals* I, 160, 247.

Charles, died in their late twenties. Granted that the death rate was much greater then than now, and that "the academic races" have seldom been robust, the Emerson stock was physically below par. Ralph Waldo was constantly threatened with the family malady of tuberculosis during his twenties. His struggle to overcome this weakness, and his success in doing so, undoubtedly exerted a profound effect upon his philosophy.

The problems of heredity and individual genius, and of physical weakness and self-reliant strength both find illumination in the comparison of the lives and temperaments of four Emerson brothers: William, Ralph Waldo, Edward, and Charles. William, the oldest, became an able and successful, but not outstanding, lawyer; Ralph Waldo, in youth the least promising of the four, became world famous. But Edward and Charles, both of whom were brilliant and successful as young men, died early of consumption—aggravated in each case by some obscure psychological "consumption" of the will to live.

William had always been hard-working and dependable. But Ralph Waldo had seemed a disappointing boy. In Harvard College, although a scholarship student, he had not done well in his courses and had graduated below the middle of his class. He had been chosen "class poet" only after six other men had declined the honor. His chief remembrances of college had been of a few friends, of occasional non-academic reading, and of desultory strolls along the Charles River and Fresh Pond. But his younger brother Edward graduated triumphantly at the head of his college class, and Charles later graduated a close second, after four years of intense competition with his rival, and with the added reputation of being a brilliant orator, universally beloved.

After graduation all four brothers took their turns teaching school in order to help the family finances—none enjoyed special privileges or exemptions. The younger three all suffered from ill health, and threatened with tuberculosis, took trips to the South for rest and recuperation. But Edward, befriended by the great Daniel Webster, still struggled intensely to live up to his friends' expectations in the law, and Charles also sought to drive himself against his nature; while Ralph Waldo, of whom less was expected, rested, let nature take its course, and in time recovered and even improved his health.

The manuscript journals, both of Edward and of Charles reveal deep inner conflicts. Edward confided to his journal: "I tho't to find [God] in the hurricane of ambition—but He was not there. . . . Faint and weary, I have fallen prostrate."[10] And shortly afterward he suddenly lost his reason. Although he recovered it, he remained to the end a victim of "melancholy and a morbid conscientiousness."[11] Similarly Charles, the most universally admired of the Emerson brothers, also felt himself driven: "Charles says the nap is worn off the world," his brother noted. And sadly contrasting himself to Ralph Waldo, Charles privately wondered if, "perhaps, all minds are racked as mine is with doubt and self accusation."[12] In his effort to realize his father's exhortation: "For shame! O Emerson! Arise to industry! To glory!"[13] Charles fell victim, like his brother Edward, to an accusing conscience and a consuming ambition.

Although he inherited the physical weakness of the family, Ralph Waldo was protected from its psychological weakness partly by an instinctive sense of "humour," and partly by a more conscious sense of proportion. He observed to his journal:

> It is a peculiarity (I find by observation upon others) of humour in me, my strong propensity for strolling. . . . I do not know a creature that has the same humour, or would think it respectable. . . .
>
> When I consider the constitutional calamity of my family, which, in its falling upon Edward, has buried at once so many towering hopes—with whatever reason, I have little apprehension of my liability to the same evil. I have so much mixture of *silliness* in my intellectual frame that I think Providence has tempered me against this. My brother lived and acted and spoke with preternatural energy. My own manner is sluggish; my speech sometimes flippant. . . ."[14]

This combination of self-conscious humour, which he had earlier deprecated as "a propensity to laugh, or rather, snicker,"[15] with a more sure self-knowledge formed the psychological basis for his philosophy of self-reliance. It was at bottom an assertion

10. Quoted by Rusk, *Life of Ralph Waldo Emerson*, p. 127.
11. J. P. Cabot, *Memoir*, p. 221.
12. Quoted from ms. journal by Rusk, *Life of Emerson*, p. 156.
13. *Ibid.*, p. 1.
14. *Journals*, 1828, undated, II, 244-245.
15. *Ibid.*, April 18, 1824.

of the individual's right to see himself in proportion to other men, and to act—or to refuse to act—accordingly.

Two elements of this psychological self-reliance need emphasis. First, this humour did not lead Emerson to value his own weakness or to call it strength; he condemned heartily his own "signal defect of character," as perhaps an "absence of common sympathies," or a "frigid fear."[16] And repeatedly he accused himself of coldness—"I shiver in and out; don't heat to the good purposes called enthusiasm a quarter so quick and kindly as my neighbours."[17] He emphasized merely that, since this was his nature, he must make due allowances for it.

Second, his self-reliance did not really reject the ambition or the conscience which were his heritage. The individual's defects of character, having been observed and compensated, were to be cured as far as possible, like his defects of physique. So later he remembered the warm-hearted virtues of his two brothers and of his first wife, purposefully.

> I ask now, why was I not made like all these beatified mates of mine, *superficially* generous and noble as well as *internally* so? . . . Well, O God, I will try and learn from this sad memory to be brave and circumspect and true henceforth and weave now a web that will not shrink. This is the thorn in the flesh.[18]

Progressively Emerson actually did correct the faults of his psychological nature, as of his physical nature: he became more social as he became physically stronger. But he became strong and successful not by driving himself against his will. Mr. Van Wyck Brooks has pointed out that Emerson's psychology was one which always emphasized the unconscious, and deferred to it. He struggled always to make his "superficial" self express his "internal" nature, rather than the reverse. "Not consciousness but the unconscious, not the will but the involuntary, not mechanics but dynamics, not argument but intuition was the way of health."[19] And Professor Eduard Lindeman has considered Emerson primarily a psychologist: "Since there were no professional psychologists, Emerson became one. . . . Psychological

16. *Loc. cit.*
17. *Ibid.*, September 28, 1826.
18. *Ibid.*, March 4, 1838.
19. Van Wyck Brooks, *Life of Emerson*, p. 51.

facts constituted for him the given data from which generalizations were to be drawn."[20] The Emerson family's weakness was so great that Ralph Waldo became a sort of physician in order to cure himself.

### 4. *Beyond Tragedy*

The thoroughness of the cure which he accomplished upon himself, and the strength of mind and serenity of soul which he finally attained, have suggested to many biographers and critics the myth of an ignorance of suffering and an inexperience of soul which the facts of his life utterly belie. So Woodberry exclaimed: "There was . . . no storm and stress; he was born free from all that. . . . His youthful journals show . . . no friction, no disturbance, no unrest."[21] And so, in later times, Barrett Wendell used Emerson as an example of our "national inexperience," Henry Adams called him "naif," and James Truslow Adams spoke of him as lacking in "depth of experience."[22]

The facts disprove this myth. In the first place Emerson himself lived for ten or more years in what Van Wyck Brooks describes accurately as "the House of Pain": "years of illness, frustration, false beginnings, of calamity and confusion."[23] Threatened constantly with tuberculosis, he also suffered sporadically from failure of the eyes and from rheumatic pains. From 1825 to 1835 he had constantly to guard himself, and often after efforts of preaching suffered intense pains in the chest. Not until after his long and leisurely first trip to Europe did he begin to feel safe from physical breakdown.

Second, and more important, he suffered such a succession of personal tragedies during these years and after, as seldom falls to the lot of one individual. In 1828 his brother Edward suddenly went insane: "there he lay, Edward, the admired, learned, eloquent, striving boy, a maniac." "We are born to trouble," he wrote to his brother William, and described "the state of feeling produced by watching him being utterly wretched."[24] After six more years of intermittent sickness, Edward finally died.

20. E. C. Lindeman, "Emerson's Pragmatic Mood," in *The American Scholar*, XVI, 57-64.
21. G. E. Woodberry, *op. cit.*, pp. 25, 31.
22. All quoted in Bliss Perry, *Emerson Today*, pp. 102-103.
23. Van Wyck Brooks, *op. cit.*, p. 40.
24. Quoted from *Letters*, I, 236.

Next in 1829 he happily married his first wife, Ellen; but in 1831, a year and a half later, she too died of tuberculosis. All his *Journals* and *Letters,* and all the observations of his friends and relatives bear witness to the depth of his love for her. Long after her death he walked every morning to visit her tomb. It is said that on one of these visits an uncontrollable impulse caused him to open her coffin.[25] And yet he afterwards constantly accused himself of coldness of feeling for her also. He felt that he could not have loved her enough.

Then, after Edward had died in Puerto Rico in 1834, his brother Charles died suddenly in 1836. Because of his extraordinary love and admiration for Charles, he was struck by this new loss more almost than the others. As he stood at his brother's grave he let "compressed nature" break through in a *laugh*—and an ejaculation "dear boy."[26] And later he wrote that he could "gather no hint from this terrible experience," but only groped "in greater darkness."[27]

Almost ironically, it seemed, his first son, Waldo, was born shortly after Charles' death. For less than six years later, the death of "this boy, in whose remembrance I have both slept and awaked so oft,"[28] climaxed his series of personal tragedies, and put the greatest strain on his faith. His *Journals* chronicle his despair once more:

> I comprehend nothing of this fact but its bitterness. Explanation have I none, consolation none that rises out of the fact itself; only diversion; only oblivion of this, and pursuit of new objects.[29]

And among the last words he uttered, at the very end of his life, was the exclamation: "Oh, that beautiful boy!"

This series of tragedies and the series of emotional disturbances which accompanied them amply attest the fact that Emerson was not inexperienced in suffering, whether physical or mental, and that he had felt at first hand "the slings and arrows of outrageous fortune."—Why, then, the myth of an inexperience of soul and a "fatally easy life?"—Partly, of course, because he later

25. Quoted in Rusk, *op. cit.*, p. 150.
26. Quoted from a letter by Elizabeth Peabody, by Rusk, *op. cit.*, p. 230.
27. *Letters,* II, 25.
28. *Journals,* Jan. 30, 1842.
29. *Ibid.,* March 20, 1842.

won through to a serenity beyond tragedy. But the problem is more complex than that. Negatively, Emerson shared the New England temperament which represses its own emotions and denies them articulate expression; at the opposite extreme from Rousseau and Byron, he made no public pageant of his bleeding heart. And further, he also shared the New England habit of self-deprecation, and condemned himself publicly for not feeling those tragic emotions which—although he did feel—he did not culivate or publicly parade. To put it differently, his psychology —even though it celebrated the subconscious—was pragmatic rather than romantic; it sought to heal the scars of tragedy by a life of action, rather than to cultivate them for purposes of artistic exploitation.

This New England habit of repression and self-deprecation worked to the harm of his reputation. If Emerson had been content merely to forget the tragedies of his life or even to confine his self-accusation to his *Journals*, the public might have forgotten, too. But the death of his son moved him so deeply that he could not forbear punishing himself for not being able to realize his sorrow articulately. Although he did succeed to some extent in doing this in his poem, "Threnody," he castigated himself for a lack of feeling in his famous essay on "Experience." This, perhaps the most biographically important of his essays, needs analysis.

Essentially Emerson's "Experience" meets the problem of personal tragedy head-on, seeking to give voice to his own "temperament without a tongue," and then to answer it. "Every roof is agreeable to the eye until it is lifted," he wrote; "then we find tragedy and moaning women and hard-eyed men. . . . There are moods in which we court suffering," he admitted, but added, "the only thing grief has taught me is to know how shallow it is. . . . In the death of my son, now more than two years ago, I seem to have lost a beautiful estate,—no more. I cannot get it nearer to me. . . . It does not touch me, but falls off from me and leaves no scar." (Yet his dying words remembered his tragedy; clearly, in this first part of his essay, Emerson was punishing himself or, in psychological language, was "over-compensating.")

But then he went on to remember the death of his brothers also: "Very mortifying is the reluctant experience that some unfriendly excess or imbecility neutralizes the promise of genius. We see young men who owe us a new world . . .; but they never acquit the debt, they die young and dodge the account."—The experience of tragedy and grief, that is, not only failed to satisfy Emerson emotionally, but also produced a feeling of emptiness and of being cheated by life: young men of genius "dodge the account."—Thus far, the negative experience of bitterness and loss prevailed.

But tragic experience presupposes the positive value of life, so that death and failure can merely subtract some "bad debts" from the total account. Evil is "merely privative, not absolute," and each tragic loss is the deprivation of a given good.—And here Emerson's heritage of Puritan discipline and Yankee thrift provided the positive part of his "Experience":

> I compared notes with one of my friends who expects everything of the universe and is disappointed when anything is less than the best, and I found that I begin at the other extreme, expecting nothing, and am always full of thanks for moderate goods. . . . If we take the good we find, asking no questions, we shall have heaping measures.

Emerson therefore was happy; having been disciplined by the experience of poverty and suffering, he had learned not to expect perfection in life. Beyond tragedy and loss lay the peace of accepting the world as it is. "Blessed are the poor in spirit; for theirs is the kingdom of heaven." Unlike Byron, or Nietzsche, physical weakness and personal tragedy led Emerson to a self-reliant acceptance of life's limitations—not to a romantic escape, or to a philosophy of the superman.

## 5. *The Problem of Vocation*

But for a time it seemed as though his own illness and the tragic death of his first wife had destroyed the very foundation of his career and driven him to romantic escape. Some time before his first marriage he had become minister of the Second Church (Unitarian) of Boston; but six months after his wife's death he resigned this pastorate, sought rest and diversion in a long trip to Europe, and, on his return, retired to Concord without any regular position or apparent vocation. Earlier he had written his defiant "Good-bye" to the proud world. It was small wonder that the world in its turn washed its hands of him. In 1840, ex-president John Quincy Adams wrote in his diary:

> A young man, named Ralph Waldo Emerson, and a classmate of my lamented son George, after failing in the everyday avocations of a Unitarian preacher and schoolmaster, starts a new doctrine of transcendentalism, declares all the old revelations superannuated and worn out, and announces the approach of new revelations and prophecies.[30]

From 1832 to 1842, Emerson seemed clearly a failure to the eyes of the world (which included many of his own family). Therefore he felt the need, both ideally and practically, of justifying himself.[31] Of course he never bothered to argue whether he had "failed" in the vocation of minister. But he did feel obliged to give some account of his idleness. Practically, he demonstrated his ability to succeed in the very difficult "vocation" of popular lecturer.[32] And, ideally, he defined his personal vocation of "American scholar," or "man thinking." Incidentally, almost, he became a writer, but his early contemporaries knew him chiefly as a lecturer and thinker.

The reasons for Emerson's seeming failure as a minister are worth noting, for he had actually been a popular success, with very minor qualifications. For a minister must be both a preacher, and a pastor or personal counselor to his flock; and as a preacher, Emerson had always enjoyed an unqualified success, for he had always wholeheartedly desired to preach well. In his early Journals, for April 18, 1824, he had admitted his own defects, both social and intellectual, but on the other hand he had noted his "passionate love for the strains of eloquence," and his possession of "those powers which command the reason and passions of the multitude." From the age of twenty-one to the end of his life, his love of eloquence and command of the attention of the multitude increased.

But in this same early passage of self-examination he also noted his apparent "absence of common sympathies," and his lack of

30. *The Diary of John Quincy Adams, 1794-1845*, ed. Allan Nevins (New York, 1928), p. 511.

31. See Henry Nash Smith, "Emerson's Problem of Vocation," *The New England Quarterly*, XII (March, 1939), 52-67.

32. W. N. Brigance, ed., *A History and Criticism of American Public Address*, II, 501, Chapter on Emerson by H. A. Wichelns.

social "address"; and as he advanced in the ministry, this social inhibition or awkwardness caused him embarrassment. Many amusing stories survive of his lack of unction at prayers, funerals, weddings, and ritual ceremonies. And this disinclination for the pastoral part of his vocation apparently led to his resignation.— But, emphatically, Emerson's resignation was his own idea; his congregation remained enthusiastically in his favor, and even when he refused to administer the rite of the Lord's Supper, a large minority still favored keeping him on his own terms. After his resignation he remained a popular guest preacher, both in his own former church and in others. And later he refused the ministry of another church which offered to free him from the duty of administering the sacrament. His lack of skill in his pastoral duties was not decisive, and even his lack of inclination was probably not the major factor in his resignation.

Emerson resigned from the ministry primarily because, in the changing world, the profession of the ministry itself was becoming narrower and less influential than it had been in the days of his fathers. In his spiritual crisis before his resignation, he had written that "in order to be a good minister, it was necessary to leave the ministry,"[33] and that "Religion . . . is not a form. It is a life."[33] In the manuscript of an earlier sermon he had even implied that his own profession had been chosen for him "against his inclination, or before he was acquainted with the character of his own mind."[34] The ministry was one of those hereditary forms which Emerson, as the spokesman of nineteenth-century liberalism, sloughed off.

But in abandoning the profession of the ministry, he did not abandon the ideal of the religious teacher, nor did he abandon the practice of eloquence which the preacher had formerly monopolized. He merely redefined the religious teacher more broadly as the American scholar, and spoke with eloquence from the lecture platform instead of the pulpit. Emerson failed as the minister of a small parish of a minor sect, in order that he might succeed as a minister to all serious and thoughtful people throughout America and Europe. Although his resignation was

33. *Journals,* June 2 and July 6, 1832.
34. A. C. McGiffert, ed., *Young Emerson Speaks,* p. 251.

partly motivated by his personal disinclination and unfitness for pastoral duties, it was more deeply motivated by the progressive secularization of the modern world.

Emerson's ideal vocation of American scholar will be considered later as an ideal; but his practical vocation of lecturer formed part—and a large part—of his biography. From November, 1833, a few weeks after his return from Europe, when he began in Boston his first series of lectures, to the end of his active life, he lectured constantly, both in order to earn his living, in order to test and to popularize his ideas, and in order to fulfil actively his duty as "American scholar." The story of his progressive success as a lecturer has never been fully told.

The vocation of the popular lecturer (as contrasted to the religious preacher and to the political orator) was just beginning to be recognized in America when Emerson began his career. Taking the place of the twentieth-century adult education speaker, newspaper columnist, and radio commentator combined, the nineteenth-century popular lecturer purveyed ideas, information, and even amusement to the serious-minded public of the time.

The American lyceum, founded in 1826 in Millbury, Massachusetts, boasted 3,000 affiliated town lyceums by 1834;[35] and to these lyceums and their successors Emerson lectured throughout his life. Moreover, innumerable local Literary Societies, Mechanic's Institutes, Societies of Natural History, and Young Men's Mercantile Library Associations supplied large and appreciative audiences both in America and in Great Britain. If Emerson had occasionally to compete with such dubious celebrities as "Doctor" Spurzheim, lecturing on phrenology, and Lola Montez, the world-famous mistress of Ludwig I of Bavaria, lecturing on whatever she chose, he also had as colleagues orators, reformers, and literary celebrities like Horace Greeley, Henry Ward Beecher, Wendell Phillips, Susan B. Anthony, John Greenleaf Whittier, and, from England, Charles Dickens.[36]

Emerson's first lecture was delivered at the Masonic Temple, to the Boston Society of Natural History, before an audience of "sev-

35. W. N. Brigance, ed., *op. cit.*, I, 121.

36. W. Thorp, "Emerson on Tour," in *Quarterly Journal of Speech* (Feb., 1930), XVI, 19-34.

eral hundred" who "seemed highly gratified with the address"; although one of the audience could see "on retrospect very little of it that is tangible."[37] But brother Charles Emerson thought that "Waldo lectured . . . to a charm," and "was glad to have some of the stump lecturers see what was what and bow to the rising sun."[38] Prophetically these first criticisms emphasized the large audiences, the appreciative attention of the majority, but also the complaints of a minority concerning the intangibleness or obscurity of what he said.

Many eminent men also remembered in later years the excitement of these early lectures by the ex-preacher. Lowell recalled how "we used to walk in from the country to the Masonic Temple, I think it was, through the crisp winter night, and listen to that thrilling voice of his, so charged with subtle meaning and subtle music."[39] And George William Curtis, writing in *Harpers Magazine*, remembered:

> Many years ago 'the Easy Chair' used to hear Ralph Waldo Emerson lecture. Perhaps it was in the small Sunday-school room under a country meeting-house, on sparkling winter nights, when all the neighborhood came stamping and chattering to the door. . . . At the desk stood the lecturer and read his manuscript, and all but the boys sat silent and inthralled.[40]

Meanwhile, as Emerson's fame grew, other reports of his lectures reflected other opinions. A *Hartford Times* reporter in 1851 judged that "half the audience were disappointed in him," but admitted that "the intelligible parts of his address I admired in common with everyone."[41] A Cincinnati reporter "remained long enough to hear him utter one unmistakable absurdity and left,"[42] although agreeing on Emerson's skill as a public speaker. And William Cullen Bryant's *New York Evening Post* emphasized Emerson's excessive vagueness and abstraction, even while praising his "great powers of language, great felicity of illustration

37. Dr. Moses A. Curtis, botanist, as quoted in B. Perry, *op. cit.*, p. 46.
38. Ms. diary of Charles Emerson, quoted by Rusk, *op. cit.*, p. 201.
39. J. R. Lowell, "Emerson the Lecturer," *My Study Windows*, pp. 375-84.
40. G. W. Curtis, "Emerson Lecturing," *From the Easy Chair* (New York, 1891), I, 21.
41. Quoted in W. Thorp, *op. cit.*
42. Louise Hastings, "Emerson in Cincinnati," *The New England Quarterly* (Sept., 1938) XI, 445.

which he manages with a certain poetic grace, and a very impressive delivery."[43] Later it reported significantly: "One thing has particularly struck us, in listening to his addresses, as well as in reading his books, and that is, they are perpetually growing on your admiration."[43]

Emerson the lecturer "grew on" American audiences in spite of reservations. Both the size of the individual audiences, and the scope of his lecture tours increased. Although naturally he spoke most often and most successfully in his native New England, he first lectured in New York in 1840, and in 1842 achieved remarkable success there. For one thing, Horace Greeley's *New York Tribune* publicized his lectures widely and praised them highly. Bryant, an older although less enthusiastic friend, reported most of the lectures fully. Henry James, Senior, came to hear him, was fascinated (although not converted), and later moved to Cambridge, partly to be near him. And in Philadelphia, Baltimore, and Washington Emerson lectured repeatedly with success.

In the new Middle-West, Emerson's lecture tours proved most challenging, both to himself and perhaps to his hearers also. In 1850 he first passed the Alleghanies at the instance of a group of former New Englanders in Cincinnati, where some of his earliest poetry had been published. Here his more realistic lectures proved highly successful, although one reporter added: "We hope he has no idea of *imposing* upon the Western people, by means of his truly singular statements."[44] In 1851, after Emerson's first lectures in Pittsburgh, a *Gazette* reporter enthused that: "no course has been so well attended in this city, nor has ever afforded so much gratification to our citizens. . . . Verily Pittsburgh is becoming a home for all schools of philosophy."[45] For the next twenty years he continued to lecture throughout this new territory, sometimes welcomed with skepticism by Missourian frontiersmen who had to be shown, sometimes celebrated without reservation as an apostle of culture and philosophy.

In St. Louis, for instance, he lectured occasionally from 1851

43. C. J. Glicksberg, "Bryant on Emerson the Lecturer," *The New England Quarterly* (Sept., 1939) XII, 531-532.
44. Louise Hastings, *loc. cit.*
45. W. Thorp, *loc. cit.*

on. But in 1867 he found that the "St. Louis Philosophical Society" had grown to such proportions that it boldly challenged his philosophy on the grounds of Hegelian dialectic."[46] Led by Henry Conrad Brokmeyer, former lieutenant-governor of Missouri, and by William Torrey Harris, later U. S. Commissioner of Education, this remarkable group had earlier invited Bronson Alcott to expound his philosophy before them, only to tear him limb from limb, philosophically speaking. But to Emerson, who spoke the next year, they rendered deference, if not agreement. And on Emerson's return home, he received from Harris articles on Hegel and a subscription to the new *Journal of Speculative Philosophy,* published in St. Louis—the first successful journal of pure philosophy in America, in which John Dewey was to publish his early articles. Later Harris also returned to Concord to help Alcott found the Concord School of Philosophy. So, in this case, the intellectual intercourse between New England and the Middle West proved mutually valuable—not merely the carrying of culture from East to West.

Meanwhile, Emerson had made his second trip to England and in his turn had sought to repay some of his own debt to the culture of Europe—and, of course, to earn money and to visit his old friend Carlyle. Typically he delivered a series of lectures at the un-literary cities of Liverpool and Manchester, and then a succession of single lectures at outlying manufacturing towns, speaking as usual at local Athanaeums and Mechanics Institutes, before he finally was persuaded to give a course in London before a more aristocratic and "guinea-paying" audience. And in England, as well as in America, the size of his audiences increased during the latter lectures of the series. Complaints came, violently at times, from the orthodox Anglicans and Presbyterians whose conservatism he shocked, rather than from the rank and file of the audiences; and some, like Carlyle, objected to his "moonshine" in England as they had in America. But for the most part he convinced the "curious company that came to hear the Massachusetts Indian,"[47] that he was really both civilized and eloquent. And, most important to him, he formed many lasting friendships,

46. H. A. Pochmann, *New England Transcendentalism and St. Louis Hegelianism* (Philadelphia, 1948).
47. From a letter of Emerson's, quoted in Rusk, *op. cit.*, p. 352.

and inspired the lasting enthusiasm of many younger men.

His return from England found him at the height of his influence as a lecturer, and the rising issue of anti-slavery made audiences more tense and enthusiastic than before. His friend Ellery Channing noticed that "it was after his English visit that he became so much happier and more joyous . . . and also assumed a more public life and habit, as he became more and more a lecturer."[48] Early in 1851 he spoke in Rochester to an audience of 1,200, calling "a league of youth to strife for a new America."[49] Later that year he plunged into the anti-slavery campaign with an impassioned oration attacking the Fugitive Slave Law. During the next ten years he often suffered from the heckling which every political orator must meet, but he also achieved his greatest successes during this time. His speech at the Robert Burns festival in 1859 drew the highest praise from Lowell and Holmes, and led Judge Hoar to say that "though he had heard many of the chief orators of his time, he never witnessed such an effect of speech upon men."[50] And when he read his "Boston Hymn" at a mass meeting celebrating the Emancipation Proclamation, the audience rose as a man at the lines:

> Who is the owner? The slave is the owner,
> And ever was. Pay him.

and cheered for several minutes.

After the Civil War he mostly repeated the speeches and revisited the places where he had formerly lectured. In 1872 he traveled to California for the first time and read a few lectures which were well-received, although rambling and anecdotal. Actually he was beginning to lose his powers of concentration, often fumbling with his manuscript and losing his place. And so it was inevitable that when, in 1875, he finally visited the South and spoke at the commencement of the University of Virginia, he should fail to weave his old spell. Actually the festive mood of the students and the poor acoustics of the hall helped to drown out his weakened voice, but the failure of this final excursion was complete.[51] Emerson had ended his working career.

48. Quoted from manuscript notebook by Rusk, *op. cit.*, p. 360.
49. W. Thorp, *loc. cit.*
50. O. W. Holmes, *Emerson*, p. 173-174.
51. H. H. Hoeltje, "Emerson in Virginia," *New England Quarterly* V (October, 1932), 753-68.

But Emerson's comparative failure as a lecturer in his latter years only emphasizes the magnitude of his achievement during most of his life. For a scholarly individualist and writer of mystical essays, his success as a popular lecturer was nothing less than astounding. Partly he forced himself to his task for financial reasons and because he considered it his duty as "American scholar," but chiefly because he genuinely loved eloquence and wholeheartedly enjoyed his relations with his audiences. Lecturing was his profession, and what he called "the reason and the passions of the multitude" were both the subject and the object of his lectures. His greatest successes were as a speaker on controversial subjects whether religious or political, and as a describer and judge of human character, whether that of Napoleon, of Robert Burns, or of his friend Henry Thoreau. In the vocation of lecturing he was able to approximate his own ideal of "the great man who in the midst of the crowd keeps with perfect sweetness the independence of solitude."[52]

### 6. *Loves and Friendships*

Just as the anti-social Emerson who "failed" as a minister and retired from the "proud world" of social institutions contrasts with the successful Emerson who became one of the most popular public lecturers of his time; so in private life, the solitary Emerson who was "born cold" and shrank from personal contacts contrasts with the sociable man whose home became a haven for kindred spirits and who corresponded familiarly with the great of his time. Neither his "Love" nor his "Friendship" was purely Platonic: both found realization in many warm human loves and friendships.

The myth of the bloodless idealist had some foundation in fact, of course. Emerson suffered both from a weak physical constitution and a temperamental New England reserve, although he greatly exaggerated both in his *Journals* and in his *Letters*. Moreover, the personal tragedies which he experienced did leave scars; his second marriage was never so romantic as his first, and his later friendships were never so wholehearted as his love for his brothers and classmates. Finally his ideal of "Love" was Platonic to the extent that it considered all personal love as partial, and all "personality" as a limitation. But if Emerson was born less

52. From "Self-Reliance."

warm-blooded than most, he also realized extraordinarily many loves and friendships. And although his first wife and his best friends died young, he replaced these with other deeply felt attachments. He considered human love to be partial, but he experienced it to the full and celebrated it in his writing.

Emerson's first marriage to Ellen Tucker was as emotionally perfect as was humanly possible. Although Ellen suffered from an hereditary weakness more severe than his own, he loved and idealized her throughout the year and a half of their marriage, and throughout the rest of his life. Moreover, his own admiration was reflected by all who knew her—even his crusty Aunt Mary describing her as [*sic*] "the lovliest Maddona of my imajanation."[53] When the young couple visited his old friend, William Furness in Philadelphia, the host described them "walking with arms around each other up and down their parlor."[54] And in his memoir of Emerson, Furness emphasized that "the nearer the approach to the warmth of home and hearth, the more his coldness thawed. . . . Within the sacred circle of home, his love was unconfined."[55]

But the beloved Ellen died, and Emerson wrote sadly that: "There is one birth, and one baptism, and one first love, and the affections cannot keep their youth any more than men."[56] When, four years later, he met and married Lydia Jackson, he told her of this feeling for Ellen which time had not dissipated. Emerson's second wife therefore neither received nor quite expected from him the love poems and the romantic letters which he had written for Ellen: in their stead came letters quietly affirming his devotion, but excusing himself for an inability to feel or express the youthful enthusiasms of romantic love. His first letter set the tone:

> I am a man and hate and suspect the over-refiners, and do sympathize with the homeliest pleasures and attractions by which our good foster mother, Nature, draws her children together. Yet am I well pleased that between us the most permanent ties should be the first formed and thereon should grow whatever others human nature will.[57]

53. Quoted from manuscript in Rusk, *Life,* p. 144.
54. Quoted from manuscript in Rusk, *Life,* p. 145.
55. *Records of a Lifelong Friendship,* ed. H. H. Furness, p. vi.
56. *Journals,* for February 13, 1831.
57. *Letters,* I, 434.

With his second wife, Emerson lived happily for forty-five years, had four children, and made his home a social center both for neighbors and literary friends. But as late as 1839, he was still copying Ellen's poems, and in the same year his first daughter was named Ellen. In 1849, when he had been absent almost a year on his second trip to Europe, Lidian took to her bed and wrote plaintively, both of his absence and of his reticence, and hoped vainly for what he termed "that unwritten letter always due, it seems, always unwritten."[58]—Although steadily affectionate to his second wife, Emerson knew only one romantic love. And so Lidian, perhaps as a defence, gradually reverted to the comfortable orthodoxy of her fathers and constantly teased him about his individualism. Later visitors to their home have recalled many half-humorous anecdotes of their later life together.[59]

As the death of Ellen stole away a love that could never be wholly replaced, so the death—first of his brother, Charles, and then of his first child, Waldo—left voids. For Charles had grown up with him, had continued to live with him, and always had been his intellectual and spiritual intimate. When Charles died, he exclaimed: "When one has never had but little society—and *all that society* is taken away—what is there worth living for?"[60] Later, after his son, Waldo, died, although the scar remained, other children came to take his place; but after his brother Charles' death,[61] he could only seek new and unfamiliar friends.

New friends he made in plenty, but always, as with his second wife, he had somehow to excuse himself for an inability wholeheartedly to celebrate their friendship. Margaret Fuller especially taxed him with reserve, and he partly agreed but also argued with her.[62] To his friend, Samuel Gray Ward, who was engaged to marry his and Margaret Fuller's mutual friend, Anna Barker, he wrote hopefully:

58. Quoted in Rusk, *Life*, p. 358. (After marriage, Emerson changed the name "Lydia" to "Lidian.")

59. See Mary M. Engel, *I Remember the Emersons* (Los Angeles, 1941).

60. Quoted in Rusk, *Life*, p. 230 and *Letters*, ed. Rusk, vol. II, 19.

61. He also lamented the death of his "ideal friend" in the chapter on "Discipline" in *Nature*.

62. See the interesting series of letters to and from her: *Letters*, II, 336, *passim* (1840).

When I see you again I think I can talk with you. This is a great, perhaps a rash, hope. . . . And yet I must say in some moments your angel has appeared at all the doors [and] melted my reserves and prepared me to say things never before spoken. But if you grow so fast on my love and reverence that I can dare believe that this dear style we are learning to use to each other is to become very fact, then we can drop our words-of-course and can afford the luxury of sincerity.[63]

Although his letters to Ward later filled a small volume,[64] this friendship, like most others, had to be "learned." And so the impression of "reserves" to be "melted" and reticences to be overcome persisted, and finally led Oliver Wendell Holmes to ask: "What man was he who could lay his hand familiarly upon his shoulder and call him Waldo?"[65]

Fortunately Emerson's old boyhood friend, William Furness, could answer Dr. Holmes' question, through his son: "I am very certain that my father would not have hesitated . . . to lay his hand familiarly on his old friend's shoulder."[66]—The difference between Holmes and Furness lay in the fact that Furness, like Emerson's brother, Charles, had grown up with him, so that their friendship did not have to be "learned." To Margaret Fuller, Emerson carefully explained that "the tie of schoolfellow and playmate from the nursery onward is the true clanship and key that cannot be given to another."[67] As with love and marriage Emerson felt that new "friendships" could never become spontaneously perfect after the age of thirty, but must be consciously cultivated.

Naturally most of Emerson's literary friendships were formed after this age. Of these his friendships with Carlyle and with Thoreau affected significantly the course of literary history.[68] Friendships with Alcott and with Margaret Fuller influenced the development of American Transcendentalism. And others, such as with Arthur Hugh Clough, John Sterling, and Herman Grimm, remain significant for different reasons. All these enlarged and

63. Letters, II, 338-9.

64. *Letters from Ralph Waldo Emerson to a Friend,* ed. C. E. Norton (Boston, 1899).

65. Oliver Wendell Holmes, *Ralph Waldo Emerson,* p. 285.

66. *Records of a Lifelong Friendship,* ed. H. H. Furness, p. vii.

67. *Letters,* III, 116.

68. Emerson's friendship with Whitman will be discussed in the final chapter on literary influence.

enriched both his personal experience and the literary life of his time.

Carlyle[69] came first and remained last, in spite of the fact that he was often not very friendly nor very agreeable. As a matter of fact, Carlyle and Emerson disagreed about most things; but they shared and agreed on the fundamental virtue of sincerity or self-reliance, and they had need of each other. Carlyle inspired Emerson, and welcomed him as an equal at the beginning of his career. Emerson gave Carlyle admiration, and (what he needed even more) a kind of faith. From their first visit at Craigenputtock, when Carlyle described Emerson going over the hill "like an angel," until thirty-seven years later, when Carlyle wrote to praise Emerson's last essay for its magnificent "Fiat Lux," Carlyle the pessimist and skeptic valued Emerson for his deeply religious faith, even while criticizing his "moonshiny" optimism. If their friendship was one of opposites, they complemented each other. And if Carlyle's temperament was thorny, the Atlantic Ocean was good insulation.

Their friendship went through several phases. The first was all enthusiasm: Emerson sought out Carlyle in the country which they both loved, when Carlyle was lonely, when he had not yet become a literary lion, and when he had not become embittered by personal or political frustrations. And Emerson, after his unsatisfactory visits to the aging Landor, Wordsworth, and Coleridge to whose declamations he could only listen, found a man with whom he could talk enthusiastically as an equal. Before Emerson's visit Carlyle's *Journal* read: "I am left here the solitariest, stranded, most helpless creature that I have been for many years." But afterwards he wrote: "That man came to see me, I don't know what brought him, and we kept him one night, and he left us. I saw him go up the hill . . . and vanish like an angel."[70] Three years later Mrs. Carlyle referred to the "enchant-

69. See *The Correspondence of Carlyle and Emerson, 1834-1872;* ed. C. E. Norton (Boston, 1888). The story of this friendship has been told brilliantly by Townsend Scudder, *The Lonely Wayfaring Man: Emerson and Some Englishmen* (New York, 1936); also, in briefer outline, by G. H. Hartwig, "An Immortal Friendship," *Hibbert Journal,* XXXVIII, 102-114, (Oct., 1939). For brief studies by F. T. Thompson and others on the literary influence of Carlyle on Emerson, see "Bibliography."

70. Quoted in Hartwig, *op. cit.*

ment"[71] of that visit, and eleven years later still recalled it vividly. And Emerson confided to his *Journal* for September 1st, 1833: "Carlyle is so amiable that I love him."

After this many enthusiastic letters followed. Emerson praised *Sartor Resartus* unreservedly when the book was unpopular. Carlyle even toyed with the thought of migrating to America. Emerson performed the very practical service of arranging the publication of Carlyle's books in America, and of securing due royalties to their author. Meanwhile Carlyle praised Emerson's books, both privately and publicly, and introduced the first series of *Essays* to English readers.

But meanwhile Carlyle found many of Emerson's American friends (properly supplied with personal letters of introduction) insufferable. Alcott was lovable, although ridiculous: "The good Alcott; with his long, lean face and figure, with his gray worn temples and mild radiant eyes; all bent on saving the world by a return to acorns and the golden age."[72] But Alcott's table manners turned Carlyle's stomach. Margaret Fuller was much less prepossessing, and many minor Yankees drove Carlyle to distraction. Moreover, Carlyle found *The Dial* hopelessly transcendental, and began to find fault with Emerson's own writing. When in 1847 Emerson arrived in England to deliver a series of lectures which Alexander Ireland had scheduled for him, and hurried to London to visit the Carlyles, times had changed.

This second visit of the two men began with enthusiasm, and talk flowed for four days; but four days was long enough to grow tired, and the two found many points of disagreement. Finally, when Emerson ventured to criticize Carlyle's hero, Cromwell, Carlyle exclaimed "with a terrible fierceness: 'Then, sir, there is a line of separation between you and me as wide as that, and as deep as the pit.' "[73] And Emerson noted briefly, in his *Journal,* "In Carlyle, a large caprice." Although Carlyle was later instrumental in arranging Emerson's lectures in London, and then accompanied his friend on a holiday excursion to Stonehenge, and although they finally parted with renewed friendship, the old warmth had been dissipated. The two continued to correspond,

71. *Ibid.*
72. *Correspondence of Carlyle and Emerson,* II, 8.
73. Quoted in Scudder, *The Lonely Wayfaring Man,* p. 60.

but Carlyle's complacency over the issue of slavery in the South, and his violent criticisms of Americans in general, widened the gap.

Nevertheless, the spontaneous, deeply-felt friendship which had joined the two in their youth could not be wholly destroyed by disagreements. Emerson still introduced friends to Carlyle, and one of these finally brought back to him Carlyle's gift of a new photograph, inscribed affectionately to his old friend. Then, as a kind of peace-offering, Carlyle bequeathed the books which he had used in writing his *Life of Frederick the Great* to the Harvard Library. Finally, when Emerson visited England for the third time, the two old men met and talked freely, although Emerson had prudently refused Carlyle's offer to stay at his house. Back in Concord, Emerson noted "Thomas Carlyle's 80th birthday" among the last entries in his *Journal.* And during his final illness, he pointed to Carlyle's picture, saying: "That is my man—my man."[74] Thus, his long friendship with Carlyle shared miraculously "the tie of schoolfellow," and "the clanship which cannot be given to another."

Emerson's friendship with Thoreau[75] was that of an older man with a younger, although for a time it shared the magic of equality. As with Carlyle it followed a pattern of early enthusiasm and later criticism; but too much familiarity finally bred too particular criticism, and Thoreau's seeming position of poor relation intensified his aggressive individualism. Toward the end Thoreau "rejected"[76] Emerson, as every pupil finally rejects his master, but with emphasis. But Emerson returned at last to pronounce the funeral oration over his dead friend.

Surprisingly, Emerson almost always took the initiative in this friendship. Emerson naturally had sought out the older Carlyle, and Whitman naturally first addressed his older "master"; but Emerson discovered the younger Thoreau, welcomed him as an equal, helped him to publish, helped him to find jobs, and con-

74. Quoted from ms. in Rusk, *Life,* 507.

75. See André Bruel, *Emerson et Thoreau* (Paris, 1929); C. Cestre, "Thoreau et Emerson," *Revue Anglo-Américaine* VII, 215-30 (Feb., 1930), summarizing the evidence and conclusions of A. Bruel; J. B. Moore, "Thoreau Rejects Emerson," *American Literature,* IV, 241-256 (Nov., 1932); and H. S. Canby, *Thoreau* (Boston, 1939), 88-92, 166-171, 303-306.

76. See Moore, *op. cit.*

tinued to praise his works even after Thoreau had withdrawn from intimacy. In 1836, Thoreau had read Emerson's *Nature,* and Emerson officially helped Thoreau with his Harvard scholarship, but relatives finally introduced the two men personally. Soon Emerson began praising Thoreau's manuscript journals and poems, although—as Professor Canby has pointed out—"No one but Emerson . . . thought that Thoreau was even remarkable in 1838."[77] Without reserve, Emerson welcomed Thoreau both as a friend and as (potentially) a literary equal. If he spoke in his *Journal* of "my young Henry Thoreau" and "my brave Henry," he also spoke of Carlyle as "my" man, meaning to adopt both into what Sainte-Beuve has called his "family of minds." "My" Henry realized for Emerson the "spiced rebellion" of Montaigne, and the simple, sensuous perception of the best nature writers.

From 1838 to 1848 the Journals of both men record the many walks and long talks which they shared, although, as Professor Moore has pointed out,[78] Emerson's *Journals* refer to Thoreau more than twice as often as Thoreau's to Emerson. During this time Thoreau described to his friend both the sensory and the scientific aspects of that Nature which Emerson celebrated more abstractly, and Thoreau progressively realized in his life that ideal of self-reliance which Emerson practiced only with qualifications. Both men first experienced, and then described at this time their ideal of friendship, in words so similar that they reflect frequent mutual discussions of the subject.[79] Meanwhile Emerson was introducing Thoreau to his literary friends, was printing his poems and prose in *The Dial,* was inviting him to work and live at his house, first as handy man, and later (when Emerson was in England) as man of the house, was getting him employment and lodging with his brother William on Staten Island and supplying him with letters of introduction to Horace Greeley and the *Tribune,* was praising and helping him publish *A Week,* and was lending him the land on Walden for his most famous experiment. It was small wonder that Thoreau increasingly felt his indebtedness so that it ultimately caused a revulsion. But if his nature

77. Canby, *Thoreau,* p. 89.

78. J. B. Moore, "Thoreau Rejects Emerson," p. 241.

79. See Emerson's "Friendship" in *Essays, Second Series,* and Thoreau's essay in *A Week,* "Wednesday."

drove Thoreau to assert his complete independence, his letters to Emerson[80] (especially when the latter was in England) described in friendly detail his life in Emerson's family, and struggled sincerely to express his gratitude.

For whatever reasons, the two friends drifted apart after Emerson's return from England in 1848. Perhaps—as some French critics suggest—the psychological strain of a too-intimate family relationship, and of Thoreau's idealization of Lidian Emerson disturbed the friendship. Perhaps Thoreau felt an accumulated resentment against what he called the "alloy of patronage"[81] in Emerson's otherwise "discriminating" praise of his own writing. Perhaps the inevitable differences of temperament and opinion, such as Thoreau's stubbornness, love of paradox, and bitter humor, or Emerson's idealism, lack of practical skill, and willingness to compromise with society, made them drift apart. Perhaps Emerson "took the initiative in slackening the rhythm of the friendship,"[82] or perhaps Thoreau did the rejecting. But the mutual criticisms recorded in the Journals of each man became increasingly severe during the 1850's. When Emerson carried a rifle on his Adirondack vacation in 1858, Thoreau became particularly scornful. And after his return, the two seem to have quarreled, for Emerson became increasingly critical, and Thoreau wrote plaintively in his *Journal.*[83] "I ask myself if it is possible to have friends." Until Thoreau's death and Emerson's funeral oration, that was the end of intimacy.

Of course, there was fault on both sides. Their mutual ideal of absolute sincerity and absolute sympathy was impossibly high. Thoreau's uncompromising individualism repelled friendship, and his increasingly rebellious withdrawal in later life helped to destroy it. Emerson, on his side, never fully understood Thoreau, imputing his withdrawal to a lack of ambition, and his rebellion to perversity. Only a little better than Lowell, he considered the whole Walden experiment a kind of "huckleberry party." But the fact remains that Emerson discovered Thoreau, and that he recognized his greatness long before anyone else, that the two

80. See "The Emerson-Thoreau Correspondence," ed. F. B. Sanborn, in *The Atlantic Monthly* (May and June, 1892).
81. *The Writings of Thoreau* (Boston, 1906), *Journal,* III, 256.
82. See C. Cestre, in *Revue Anglo-Américaine,* VII, 222.
83. For November 3, 1858.

men enjoyed an intimate and nearly-perfect friendship during the most important ten years of their lives, and that Emerson never lost faith in his friend nor allowed bitterness to interfere with his final praise. His essay on Thoreau remains one of the most vivid and human of his character sketches, partly because he valued Thoreau so greatly both as a friend and as a writer.

Emerson's third—and in many ways most important—literary friendship was that with Bronson Alcott.[84] Unlike Carlyle and Thoreau, Alcott sought Emerson out, and unlike them, his friendship with Emerson increased rather than diminished with the years. Lacking Carlyle's genius for literary expression, and lacking Thoreau's power of realizing his ideals, Alcott possessed uniquely a genius for human friendship—even the hostile Carlyle called him "lovable." And so, in spite of his repeated literary failures, and in spite of his practical failures to realize his ideal progressive school or his ideal transcendental community, and even in spite of his failure to provide a living for himself and his own family, Alcott survived all his friends, and enjoyed—as it were vicariously—the praise and appreciation of their disciples in his old age. Where Emerson's friendships with Carlyle and Thoreau had failed of perfection, his friendship with Alcott flourished to the end.

From the beginning, Emerson valued Alcott as a source of inspiration, but from the beginning recognized his practical faults. Alcott first visited him in 1835, and left the manuscript of "Psyche" for his criticism: either his writing or his conversation or both may have suggested to Emerson the extreme transcendental ideas ascribed to "a certain poet" in the concluding section of *Nature.* But just as these extreme ideas have puzzled and repelled readers from that time to this, so Alcott's absolute idealism and humorless self-importance bothered Emerson from the beginning. Before publishing *Nature,* Emerson had criticized his new friend because "he cannot delight in Shakspear," and had noted drily that: "He made here some majestic utterances, but so inspired me that even I forgot the words often."[85] Through the years he

84. See H. H. Hoeltje, *Sheltering Tree: A Story of the Friendship of Emerson and Alcott* (Durham, N.C., 1943).

85. *Journals,* June 22, 1836.

repeatedly characterized his friend as "a tedious archangel,"[86] and "a pail without a bottom." Yet in the end he remembered this friendship above all others, and wrote: "I see that I cannot exaggerate its importance among the resources of inspiration."[87]

Meanwhile Alcott failed repeatedly, and Emerson repeatedly sought to help him. Emerson praised Alcott's *Record of a School,* and defended his *Conversations with Children on the Gospels* from charges of indecency, obscenity, and absurdity.[88] Emerson helped finance Alcott's trip to England, but warned his English friends not to trust Alcott's practical judgment. When Alcott brought Lane and Wright to America and founded Fruitlands, Emerson remained skeptical, and Alcott was hurt. When Fruitlands failed, Emerson again helped financially, but Alcott was prostrated. During all these years Alcott often criticized Emerson for his lack of faith. But it is clear that Emerson never wavered either in his friendly sympathy or in his practical aid: if Alcott believed that Emerson was failing him, it was because, as Professor Hoeltje remarks, "Alcott was simply unaware that Emerson, who was endeavoring so ineffectually to understand and to assist his friend, had his own difficulties."[89] And so, after many failures and wanderings, Alcott finally returned to Concord and to Emerson, and outlived his master. But if Emerson had outlived his friend, he had intended to write a biography to justify Alcott, and had kept a manuscript book of notes for that purpose.[90]

The relation of Emerson and Alcott shows Emerson at his best, and illustrates the strength both of his character and of his thought.[91] For Emerson did not misunderstand Alcott's purpose (as he did Thoreau's), nor did his optimistic convictions interfere with his sympathy (as perhaps with Carlyle). Alcott embodied Emerson's own transcendental ideals, but lacked both Emerson's Yankee realism and his courageous self-reliance. Yet

86. *Journals,* November 21, 1841.

87. *Journals,* May, 1868.

88. See Odell Shepard, *Pedlar's Progress* (Boston, 1937) 193-4.

89. *Sheltering Tree,* p. 35.

90. H. Hoeltje, *Sheltering Tree,* p. 57. (The notebook is preserved in the Houghton Library.)

91. See F. I. Carpenter, "Bronson Alcott: Genteel Transcendentalist" in *The New England Quarterly,* XIII, 34-48 (March, 1940). See also Part III, "The Genteel Tradition."

Alcott, for all his aberrations, seemed to make "the Platonic world . . . as solid as Massachusetts"[92] to Emerson, and encouraged and inspired him to the end.

Like Alcott, Margaret Fuller sought Emerson out and won his friendship, but with more difficulty.[93] He himself described their first meeting (arranged by his wife): "Her extreme plainness,—a trick of incessantly opening and shutting her eyelids,—the nasal tone of her voice,—all repelled; and I said to myself, we shall never get far."[94] But he also emphasized her physical and intellectual power: "She had a face and frame that would indicate fulness and tenacity of life. . . . She had large experiences.[95]

The instinctive repulsion first aroused by Margaret gradually disappeared, and the appreciation of the "largeness" of her character progressively increased in Emerson. Partly this was due to her unremitting efforts to win the friendship of the man whom she most admired. The series of visits at his house, and the series of letters and books which she sent to him, and her personal services in teaching him to pronounce German and to read Goethe and to translate Dante, and to appreciate the great paintings of the world, all contributed to their friendship. Gradually he "learned"; and when Alcott and Margaret Fuller visited him casually on an evening in October, 1839, he noted characteristically in his *Journals:* "Cold as I am, they are almost dear." Later their mutual labors in editing the ill-fated *Dial* cemented the friendship.

But more important, Emerson's appreciation of Margaret Fuller grew with the growth of her own personality. At first she had sought him out as a disciple, hanging on his every word, asking what he could not give. But as their relationship progressed, she became more independent. She noted: "We had an excellent talk: we agreed that my God was love, his truth."[96] And in 1843 he enthusiastically noted in his Journals: "I have never known any

92. Emerson's *Journals* for July, 1852.

93. See H. R. Warfel, "Margaret Fuller and R. W. Emerson," *PMLA*, L, 576-594 (June, 1935). The extraordinary series of letters exchanged between the two in 1840-41 has already been mentioned.

94. R. W. Emerson, W. H. Channing, and J. F. Clarke, *Memoirs of Margaret Fuller Ossoli* (Boston, 1859), I, 202.

95. *Ibid.*, I, 202, 204.

96. Quoted by Warfel, *op. cit.*, p. 593.

example of such steady progress from stage to stage of thought and of character."[97] As she left for New York to write for Horace Greeley's *Tribune,* as she published successively her books on *Woman in the Nineteenth Century,* on the West, and *Papers on Literature and Art;* and as she traveled to Euorpe, worked for and wrote of the Italian Revolution, married, and had her child, and finally died by shipwreck off the coast of America, Emerson watched her with growing admiration. He sent Thoreau to the scene of her death, and later helped to write her *Memoir,* with understanding and with sympathy.

The friendship of Emerson and Margaret Fuller is important for more than personal reasons, because she embodied perfectly one aspect of Emerson's transcendental ideal: "she had large experiences." For the same reason that Hawthorne violently condemned Margaret, and caricatured her as Zenobia in *The Blithedale Romance,* Emerson was attracted to her, and praised her. Margaret Fuller seemed to him "to rise before me at times into heroical and godlike regions . . . and . . . I thought of Ceres, Minerva, Proserpine."[98] For Margaret Fuller had gradually developed from a genteel Boston bluestocking to a successful literary critic, a writer for woman's rights, and an active worker for the Italian Revolution, till at last she fell in love, and in the face of social disapproval, married—happily for her own heart, but tragically, for social conventions. In Emerson's terms, she "gave all to love." In Hawthorne's terms, she "fell, as the weakest of her sisters might."[99] Her dilemma, like Hester's in *The Scarlet Letter,* was essentially tragic, and her life illustrates the tragic implications of the transcendental ideal. It is to Emerson's credit that he learned to appreciate her significance and to value her friendship so highly.

Carlyle, Thoreau, Alcott, Margaret Fuller (and later, Whitman) were Emerson's closest and most important literary friends. Others, like John Sterling,[100] the young English admirer whom

97. *Journals,* VI, 364 (March 23, 1843).
98. *Journals,* VI, 365.
99. *The Heart of Hawthorne's Journals,* ed. N. Arvin, p. 272.
100. *A Correspondence Between John Sterling and R. W. Emerson,* ed. E. W. Emerson (Boston, 1897); and T. Scudder, *The Lonely Wayfaring Man,* pp. 61-64.

Emerson never met, and the famous Herman Grimm,[101] who first began correspondence with Emerson in 1856, were pleasant to him and helped widen his personal and literary horizons. But his friendship with Arthur Hugh Clough was in every way extraordinary.[102]

In the life and writing of Arthur Hugh Clough, the conflict between Emerson's pioneer optimism and Carlyle's old-world pessimism took dramatic form. After meeting Clough during his second visit to England, Emerson corresponded with him, praising his lively poetry, and urging him (as he had Carlyle) to come to America. Clough came, visited Emerson, and settled in Cambridge where he tutored students, and wrote. Emerson rejoiced in their friendship, and predicted a bright future for his friend. But Carlyle in his turn wrote to Clough, offering him a secure living as a clerk in the Education Department in London; and Clough suddenly returned to England, abandoning his adventurous plans, and resigning himself to a life of routine. Emerson was deeply disappointed, but continued to correspond warmly, and secured the publication of Clough's new poem in *The Atlantic*. But this poem reflected Clough's world-weariness and disillusion, and the author died soon afterwards at the age of forty-one. Later, Clough's friend Arnold was to praise Emerson as friend and aider of those who would live in the spirit. But for Clough this friendship and aid did not suffice.

Meanwhile, in America, Emerson attracted many lesser friends. Henry James the elder met and corresponded with him frequently for thirty years, 1842-72.[103] The two men stimulated each other: James' Swedenborgian ideas appealed to Emerson, and Emerson inspired both the father and his two famous sons to write their different interpretations and appreciations of him.[104] More in-

101. *Correspondence Between R. W. Emerson and Herman Grimm*, ed. F. W. Holls (Boston, 1903).

102. *Emerson-Clough Letters*, ed. H. F. Lowry and R. L. Rusk (Cleveland, 1934); and T. Scudder, "Incredible Recoil," in *The Lonely Wayfaring Man*, 154-167. (First published in *The American Scholar* (Winter, 1936).

103. The story of their friendship has been told by R. B. Perry, *The Thought and Character of William James* (Boston, 1935), I, chapters 3-5; by Austin Warren, *The Elder Henry James* (New York, 1934); and by Hansell Baugh, "Emerson and the Elder Henry James," in *Bookman* (Nov., 1928) LXVIII, 320-22.

104. See final chapter on Emerson's Fame and Influence.

tensely, for a brief space of two years (1838-40) Emerson became the friend of the mystical Jones Very, and helped him publish a volume of poems and essays.[105] Charles King Newcomb and William Ellery Channing, the younger, also shared his friendship and encouragement. But these many lesser friends repeated the patterns of his major friendships.

It is true that Emerson's friendships failed of ideal perfection, and sometimes failed even to overcome differences of temperament and of philosophy. But they were many and deep, and they included a wide variety of nationality, profession, ability, and faith. On the literary level, they were extraordinary and significant. The factual record of these human relationships does much to qualify both the platonic idealism of his essays, and the harshness of his own self criticism.

### 7. *Reform and Slavery*

The conflict between the ideal and the actual, which took so many forms throughout Emerson's life, appeared most clearly toward its end in the field of public affairs. The transcendentalist who stood aside and observed the human struggle gradually gave way to the Yankee who participated almost to the point of enthusiasm: the growth of the abolition movement specifically impelled him to abandon his "scholar's" objectivity, and to enter partisan politics. Typically, this has been described by some as a surrender of principles, and by others as courageous action according to principles. But in either case, it has seemed inconsistent with his earlier role of "man thinking."

Perhaps the history of Boston and of Concord, Massachusetts, will suggest a solution. Emerson's first published address celebrated the history of the town of Concord, and his first (and greatest) occasional poem was the "Concord Hymn." The

> "Spirit that made those heroes dare
> "To die, and leave their children free,"

was the subject of both works. In 1835 he believed that this spirit of freedom had been realized. But as the years advanced, he came increasingly to believe that the existence of slavery in the

105. See C. Baker, "Emerson and Jones Very," *New England Quarterly* (March, 1934), VII, 90-99. For criticism see Yvor Winters, *In Defense of Reason* (New York, 1947), 262-283.

South actually interfered with the freedom of Americans, even in New England; until finally, in his "Boston Hymn" which celebrated the Emancipation Proclamation, he proclaimed:

"To-day unbind the captive,
"So only are ye unbound"

The change in Emerson from ideal scholar and celebrator of the spirit of freedom, to active participant in the struggle for the abolition of slavery, was typical of his role as leading citizen of Concord, Massachusetts, in the middle third of the nineteenth century.

When Emerson said good-bye to the proud world, he went home to Concord and immediately accepted not only the duties of citizen, but also a position of leadership in town affairs. His Concord Address and Hymn were contemporaneous with his Address on the American Scholar: his historic Concord became a symbol of all American liberalism, while his ideal Scholar also remained historically American and local. But by temperament and vocation he was primarily the scholar: the next year, when a Concord mass meeting condemned the government's treatment of the Cherokee Indians, and he wrote the letter of protest to President Van Buren,[106] he described the duty as "like dead cats around one's neck."—"I hate myself when I go out of my sphere," he wrote to a friend, "but a man must have bowels sometimes."[107] Thus Emerson recognized the conflict between observer and participant, and knew his own position in it; but he also recognized his duty to his fellow men. That duty prevailed over his inclination only when he felt that the rights or liberties of his fellow men were endangered.[108]

Otherwise, Emerson distrusted the reformers of his day, although he always sympathized with them.[109] But characteristically, he emphasized the sympathy more than the distrust, and characteristically he often blamed himself for not joining the reformers actively. Thus, on October 17, 1840, he described in

106. *Works,* XI, 87-96.
107. Quoted from manuscript by Rusk, *Life,* p. 267.
108. John C. Gerber, in his excellent dissertation on *Emerson's Economics* (University of Chicago, 1941) makes this distinction clearly.
109. See Van Wyck Brooks, *Emerson and Others.*

his Journals the early planning of Brook Farm (at his house), and his own reactions to it:

Yesterday George and Sophia Ripley, Margaret Fuller and Alcott discussed here the Social Plans. I wished to be convinced, to be thawed, to be made nobly mad by the kindlings before my eye of a new dawn of human piety. But this scheme was arithmetic and comfort. . . . Not once could I be inflamed, but sat aloof and thoughtless; my voice faltered and fell. . . . I do not wish to remove from my present prison to a prison a little larger. I wish to break all prisons. I have not yet conquered my own house. It irks and repents me. Shall I raise the siege of this hen-coop, and march baffled away to a pretended siege of Babylon?

But if the ideal communities of Brook Farm and Fruitlands always had his personal sympathy, they never had his intellectual support. He often visited Brook Farm, and with Margaret Fuller he did take part in a woodland picnic such as Hawthorne described in *The Blithedale Romance;* but he never lived there, and his later description of it as "a perpetual picnic, . . . an Age of Reason in a patty-pan"[110] differed from Hawthorne's only in its kindliness. Any connection between Emerson and Hawthorne's fictional reformer, Hollingsworth, existed only in Hawthorne's imagination, for Emerson generalized on the selfishness and falseness of philanthropic reformers in much the same terms as Hawthorne: "It is the worst of community that it must inevitably transform into charlatans the leaders. . . ."[111] Finally, when the earlier, liberal Brook Farm became a formal, Fourieristic "phalanx," Emerson condemned it enthusiastically.

In Fruitlands Emerson believed even less than in Brook Farm, although he participated more, because of his friendship for Alcott. When Wright and Lane returned from England with Alcott to found their ideal community, Emerson, as trustee, accepted the title to the land at Harvard, Massachusetts, but remained the aloof observer. On July 8, 1843, he visited them, but noted drily in his Journals:

The sun and the evening sky do not look calmer than Alcott and his family at Fruitlands. . . .

110. *Works,* X, 364; "Historic Notes of Life and Letters in New England."
111. *Works,* X, 354. See also the essay, "New England Reformers."

I will not prejudge them successful. They look well in July. We will see them in December.

The next year Emerson, as trustee, helped liquidate Fruitlands.

In other reforms also, Emerson sometimes participated because of his friendships, although half-heartedly. His correspondence with Margaret Fuller had included a discussion of woman's rights, and he had helped publish her early essay on the subject in *The Dial.* Characteristically, he believed that when women were denied equal rights, they suffered injustice; but he disliked the militant suffragettes, and believed conservatively that women were at their best in the feminine sphere of the home. After Margaret Fuller's death, he twice refused to speak at Woman's Rights Conventions, but finally read his lecture on "Woman" in Boston in 1855.[112]

Earlier, in 1838, he had read a lecture on "War" to the American Peace Society,[113] but had qualified his remarks heavily. And about 1842, when he allowed himself to be persuaded to lecture on "Temperance," he spoke only in the most general terms, and wisely withheld the manuscript from publication.[114]

But if Emerson distrusted the communities, and praised peace and temperance with qualifications, and urged woman's rights only to rectify social injustices, he did progressively become an enthusiastic abolitionist.[115] His attitudes toward slavery and its abolition fall into three fairly distinct periods.

In Emerson's youth, he accepted some of the prevailing, conservative interpretations of the subject. In 1822 he noted in his Journals that "Nature has plainly assigned different degrees of intellect to these different races, and the barriers between are insurmountable.[116] But at the same time he added that slavery is "the worst institution on earth."

As he began to observe and think for himself, however, he became an abolitionist by conviction, although for a quarter century he remained non-militant. On his trip South in 1827 he attended a meeting of the Bible Society in St. Augustine, which

112. See *Works,* XI. 403-426; and "Notes" by E. W. Emerson.

113. *Works,* XI, 149-176, and "Notes."

114. The manuscript is still preserved in Houghton Library.

115. See M. M. Moody, "The Evolution of Emerson as an Abolitionist," *American Literature,* XVII, 1-21 (March, 1945).

116. *Journals,* I, 181.

was held next door to a slave auction. "Almost without changing our position we might aid in sending the Scriptures into Africa, or bid for 'four children without the mother' who had been kidnapped therefrom."[117] Clearly, this experience helped to inspire his distrust of "official goodness," as well as his hatred of slavery.

In 1831, when abolition was still unpopular and the first issue of William Lloyd Garrison's *Liberator* had just appeared, Emerson lent his pulpit to an anti-slavery speaker. In 1837, he himself gave his first public address on slavery,[118] although he emphasized the need of free discussion rather than the evils of slavery. Then in 1844, again to his fellow citizens of Concord, he gave an address celebrating "Emancipation in the British West Indies."[119] Typically, he recanted his youthful errors, saying: "Not the least affecting part of this history of abolition is the annihilation of the old indecent nonsense about the nature of the negro."[120] But later in the address he suggested the causes of his future militancy, when he severely condemned the interference by Southerners with Northern negroes traveling in the South, and with Northern agitators urging abolition.

Emerson suddenly shifted from theoretical interest to active participation in the abolition movement in 1850, following Daniel Webster's famous speech and support of the Fugitive Slave Law. Emerson referred to Webster in his *Journal* more often than to any living man,[121] mostly to condemn his apostasy from the cause of freedom. And his exclamation against the Fugitive Slave Law has become famous: "I will not obey it, by God."[122] But the reason for Emerson's sudden shift from calm observer to excited participant in the abolition movement has only recently been emphasized by Miss Moody: the Fugitive Slave Law not only sought to compromise an ideal issue (Emerson might well have accepted this), but it also sought to compel citizens of Massachusetts to act against their own consciences, and thus infringed upon the sacred freedom of the individual.[123] This active denial

117. *Journals*, II, 177.
118. Cabot, *Memoir*, II, 425-6.
119. *Works*, XI, 97-148.
120. *Works*, XI, 140.
121. See M. M. Moody, *op. cit.*, p. 12.
122. *Journals*, VIII, 236.
123. M. M. Moody, *op. cit.*, 13, 15.

of his own freedom as a citizen infuriated Emerson, and led to the climax of his Boston Hymn: "So only are ye unbound."

But even in the heat of struggle, Emerson felt himself torn. After his earlier address on "Emancipation in the British West Indies," he had explained to Carlyle: "though I sometimes accept a popular call . . . I am sure to feel . . . what an intrusion it is into another sphere, and so much loss of virtue in my own."[124] And in his "Ode" inscribed to Channing he generalized the problem: "Every one to his chosen work."[125] Finally, even after the passage of the Fugitive Slave Law, he still complained to his Journals: "I have quite other slaves to free than those negroes, to wit, imprisoned spirits, imprisoned thoughts, far back in the brain of man. . . ."[126] As the delegated scholar, he still (in 1852) mistrusted himself in the role of reformer.

As the tension began to mount, however, he progressively subordinated his scruples to his duty. Speaking in New York in 1854, he prefaced his remarks: "I do not often speak on public questions . . . it seems like meddling or leaving your work." But he ended by hoping that "we have reached the end of our unbelief, have come to a belief that there is a divine Providence in the world which will not save us but through our own cooperation."[127]

There followed the attack upon his friend, Senator Charles Sumner, in 1856, which deeply aroused Emerson. And in the years following he helped arrange John Brown's speeches in Concord, and to finance his activities in Kansas. After the raid on Harper's Ferry he spoke twice in praise of "the Saint whose martyrdom . . . will make the gallows as glorious as the cross"; and thus shocked the conservatism of Hawthorne—and many others—"unutterably."[128] When the news of Fort Sumter came, he was one of the first to celebrate the new, war-sentiment "mightier than logic, wide as light, strong as gravity."[129] Soon he was chafing at Lincoln's delay in proclaiming emancipation. But after this proclamation finally came, he celebrated it wholeheartedly, both in

124. *Correspondence of Carlyle and Emerson,* II, 85.
125. *Works,* IX, 79.
126. *Journals,* VIII, 316.
127. *Works,* XI, 217, 244.
128. Quoted in Rusk, *Life,* p. 402.
129. Cabot, *Memoir,* II, 600.

public address and in poetry. For him this event marked the victory of the ideal of liberty—he felt his duty accomplished.

The reasons for Emerson's progressive emotional involvement in the civil struggle were realistic: first, the infringement upon his own liberties as citizen; next, the actual violence done to friends whose integrity and idealism were unquestioned; and finally the identification of this struggle for liberty with the historic struggle symbolized by the old monument "by the rude bridge that arched the flood." But this emotional involvement also had its unfortunate effects: it made him abandon the perspective and impartiality of his earlier writing; it led him to the excess of nationalistic patriotism which colored not only his wartime speeches, but also his later addresses, such as "The Fortune of the Republic"; and, after the victory of the Civil War, it confirmed and expanded his already extreme optimism.

Today, we may sympathize with, and even praise Emerson's involvement in the patriotic struggle of a war for freedom; even while we may find his optimism alien to our times, and condemn it. But both sprang from the same source: Emerson's life shared, and his writings made articulate the ideal aspirations and the actual struggles of his age and of his country.

## The Chief Biographies

The most important biography of Emerson is also the most recent: *The Life of Ralph Waldo Emerson* by Ralph L. Rusk (1949). This nearly fulfils the specifications for a "definitive" biography: it is the most realistic, the most complete, the most scholarly, and the most impartial. Its interpretations are always well documented, and fully reasonable. But these interpretations are seldom made fully explicit: as criticism, it suffers from the author's primary concern with fact and event, and (possibly) from his too-scrupulous objectivity. The briefer biographies and studies still interpret more clearly and explicitly Emerson's life in its relation to his writings and ideas.

Professor Rusk's *Life* realizes for the first time "the tangible density of Emerson's career," as Professor Perry Miller has pointed out.[130] The impressive body of detail here collected and

130. In *The New York Times*, Book Section, May 22, 1949.

organized portrays Emerson in all his daily relationships as a human being more intimately than the sketchy outlines of any of the other, older biographies. Emerson the man rather than Emerson the bloodless idealist comes to life in these pages.

This realism is a triumph of scholarship rather than of narrative technique. It results from Professor Rusk's rich accumulation of significant detail, quoted usually at first hand. Drawing heavily upon Emerson's *Letters* (which he had edited), and upon the published biographies and reminiscences of those who knew Emerson personally, Professor Rusk has also studied all the manuscript material by and about Emerson. His biography becomes therefore not only the most realistic, but also the most complete and scholarly. The eighty-four double-column pages of Notes and Bibliography at the end furnish the best guide to Emerson's life and to the biographical sources for it now existing.

Finally, Professor Rusk's *Life* attempts and almost achieves impartiality. Emerson reveals himself, and his contemporaries reveal him, both by quoting his own words and by commenting upon and criticizing him. But those quoted were his contemporaries, and usually admired him: later critics and biographers are not considered. The result is a portrait whose realism sacrifices some of the perspectives of time and of considered criticism. The problems of psychological and philosophical interpretation are left implicit in this biography.

The second most complete and authoritative biography is one of the earliest: *A Memoir of Ralph Waldo Emerson,* by Emerson's friend and literary executor, James Elliot Cabot (1887). Until the publication of Professor Rusk's *Life,* this was the only comprehensive biography, and it still remains a source-book for all biographers. But it lacks, not only the critical perspective and philosophical analysis (which its successor also lacks), but also the intimate and realistic detail which, in Professor Rusk's biography, makes Emerson seem to live before the reader's eyes.

As a friend of Emerson and of his family, Cabot had access to the vast mass of Journals and Letters, then unpublished, and he selected from these with skill and taste, quoting in detail most of the important passages which later biographers have also emphasized. But with the publication of most of these materials, his *Memoir* became less valuable. Moreover, as a friend of the family who shared much of Emerson's own New England reserve, Cabot refrained from quoting many of the intimate details which modern readers have found essential to a true understanding of the man. And so his book has always seemed a factual record and source book—truly a "memoir," rather than a complete biography.

This *Memoir,* however, still remains valuable for its rich accumulation of facts and first-hand reminiscences about Emerson, and for its appendices, listing Emerson's contributions to *The Dial,* and listing and summarizing his unpublished Lectures and Addresses. If these Lectures are finally published, as were the Journals and Letters, the *Memoir* will still remain a source book to students of Emerson's biography.

Among the many briefer, critical biographies, three may be singled out for special mention. The most critically incisive is still that published by George Edward Woodberry in 1907. Written before the publication of Emerson's *Journals,* this interprets his life largely in terms of the essays and poems, failing fully to realize, for instance, the tensions and struggles of Emerson's early life. It assumes that his self-reliance sprang Minerva-like from his brain, without the attendant birth-pangs of human suffering. But on the level of ideas, it recognizes both Emerson's greatness and his limitations. Although admitting to "little intellectual sympathy with him in any way," Woodberry characterized Emerson's as "the only great mind that America has produced in literature."[131] If his lack of sympathy combined with his lack of intimate knowledge to prevent him from writing the ideal brief biography, it set him free to describe Emerson's ideas clearly and to criticize them effectively.

After the publication of Emerson's *Journals,* O. W. Firkins wrote an authorized biography in 1915. With greater sympathy and fuller biographical knowledge than Woodberry's, Firkins described Emerson's literary personality, instead of criticizing his intellectual idealism. Moreover, Firkins' own style was more colorful than logical, and resulted in literary description and aesthetic judgment, rather than philosophical analysis. In some chapters he achieved brilliance, in others merely impressionism. His individual descriptions and critical analyses of Emerson's separate

131. G. E. Woodberry, *Emerson,* p. 176.

essays and works, in "The Harvest," remain useful to all students. His topical description of Emerson's literary characteristics, both as "Prose-Writer" and as "Poet," and his atomic analysis of Emerson's philosophic ideas remain highly original and suggestive. But for the average student, Firkins' biography is less successful intellectually than Woodberry's, and less successful as personal interpretation than Professor Perry's.

Strictly speaking, Professor Bliss Perry's study, *Emerson Today,* is not a biography; and it contains only 136 pages of text. But its author is the dean of all teachers and scholars of Emerson, and in this study he has succeeded in evoking the literary personality of the man, and in outlining his ideas, while at the same time sketching in the facts of his life and summarizing the critical discussions of him. Sympathetic where Woodberry was antagonistic, his final chapter, "Revaluations," answers effectively many of the criticisms of Emerson. As a brief general introduction to Emerson's life and writings, Professor Perry's book is unsurpassed.

The other biographies of Emerson are briefly characterized and criticized in the following Bibliography. Four are notable, however, for particular reasons: Oliver Wendell Holmes, in 1884, besides including much reminiscence, described Emerson vividly in relation to his ancestral and social background. Edward W. Emerson, in *Emerson in Concord* (1889), described his father in his daily life, and, like Cabot, his "Memoir" remains valuable as a source book. (Edward Emerson's plentiful "Notes" to the Centenary Edition of Emerson's *Works* remain similarly valuable.) Marie Dugard's biography in French (1907) remains probably the best by a European. And Mr. Van Wyck Brooks' *Life* (1932), using Emerson's own words as far as possible, described the man with unusual insight, and inspired several other scholars of Emerson (e.g. Hoeltje and Foster) to employ the same method.

## SELECTED BIBLIOGRAPHY

The following Bibliography is selective and critical. It includes only items concerning Emerson Bibliography, and Biography. For items concerning the text of Emerson's Prose and Poetry, his Ideas, and his Reading and Reputation, see Bibliographies at the end of Parts II, III, and IV.

## BIBLIOGRAPHIES

Cooke, George Willis. *A Bibliography of Ralph Waldo Emerson.* Boston: Houghton Mifflin and Co., 1908. 340 pp. (This is the standard bibliography, and is complete to the time of its publication. No modern, complete bibliography exists.)

Booth, Robert A. and Roland Stromberg. "A Bibliography of Ralph Waldo Emerson, 1908-1920." *Bulletin of Bibliography*, XIX, 180-183 (Dec., 1948).

*The Cambridge History of American Literature.* New York: 1917. Vol. I, 551-556. (For material up to 1917.)

*Articles on American Literature Appearing in Current Periodicals: 1920-1945.* Ed. by Lewis Leary. Durham, N. C., Duke University Press, 1947. Pp. 48-57. (This includes all recent articles, but omits books.)

"Doctoral Dissertations in American Literature," Compiled by E. E. Leisy and J. B. Hubbell, in *American Literature,* IV, 427-429 (Jan., 1933). A similar compilation, 1933-1948, by Lewis Leary, appeared in *American Literature,* XX, 178-180 (May, 1948).

*Literary History of the United States.* Ed. R. E. Spiller, W. Thorp, T. H. Johnson, H. S. Canby. New York, Macmillan Co., 1948. Vol. III, 492-501. (This is the most recent and the most inclusive selected bibliography. Arranged topically.)

Since 1945, "Articles on American Literature Appearing in Current Periodicals" have been listed quarterly in *American Literature,* Durham, N. C. Books and important articles are listed annually in the "American Bibliography" of *PMLA.*

The present bibliography emphasizes material since 1917.

## BIOGRAPHIES[132]

Albee, John. *Remembrances of Emerson.* New York: 1901 and 1903. 203 pp. ("A narrative of Emerson's influence upon the thoughtful young men of his time." Good first-hand reminiscence.)

Alcott, Amos B. *Ralph Waldo Emerson: Philosopher and Seer.* Boston: 1882. 81 pp. (Alcott the rhapsodist. Very little biography, or even reminiscence.)

Brigance, William N., Editor. *A History and Criticism of American Public Address.* New York, 1943, 2 vols. Chapter on Emerson by H. A. Wichelns, II, 501 ff. Also, see Index for further material on Emerson, and on the Lyceum movement.

Brooks, Van Wyck. *Emerson and Others.* New York, 1927. 250 pp.

132. For critical discussion of the more important biographies, see above. All biographies of any significance are included in the following list.

(Contains "Six Episodes" of Emerson's life in Concord, pp. 3-107.)

——. *The Life of Emerson*. New York, 1932. 315 pp. (A sympathetic biography, "written largely in Emerson's own words." This technique, developed by Mr. Brooks, has inspired many imitators. Here it has resulted in an informal, readable biography, full of psychological insights, but lacking sharp criticism or discussion of ideas.)

Bruel, André. *Emerson et Thoreau*. Paris, 1929. 217 pp. (A detailed study of the relations of the two men, told chronologically. Originally a doctoral dissertation.)

Cabot, James Elliot. *A Memoir of Ralph Waldo Emerson*. Boston, 1887. 2 vols. 809 pp. (By Emerson's friend and literary executor. This was the standard and most complete biography, until the publication of Rusk's *Life;* and still remains uniquely important both as source book and contemporary account. Omits criticism and interpretation.)

Cary, Elizabeth Luther. *Emerson, Poet and Thinker*. New York, 1904. 284 pp. (A thoughtful discussion, partly biographical. Reproduces many pictures.)

*The Centenary of the Birth of Ralph Waldo Emerson*. Concord, Mass., 1903. 137 pp. (Fifteen addresses by various speakers, including C. E. Norton, T. W. Higginson, William James, and Hugo Münsterberg, including some reminiscence.)

Conway, Moncure Daniel. *Emerson at Home and Abroad*. Boston, 1882. 383 pp. (An imaginative, but discursive biography by a friend and disciple, containing much original material.)

Cooke, George Willis. *Ralph Waldo Emerson: His Life, Writings, and Philosophy*. Boston, 1881. 390 pp. (An able but uninspired study, half biographical, by the Unitarian clergyman who later compiled the Bibliography of Emerson.)

Crothers, Samuel McCord. *Ralph Waldo Emerson: How to Know Him*. Indianapolis, 1921. (A well-written, thoughtful interpretation, not primarily biographical.)

Dillaway, Newton. *Prophet of America: Emerson and the Problems of Today*. Boston, 1936. 423 pp. (An interesting popular interpretation of Emerson.)

Dugard, Marie. *Ralph Waldo Emerson, sa Vie et son Oeuvre*. Paris, 1907. (Enthusiastic, and sometimes illuminating. Probably still the best biography by a European.)

Emerson, B. K. *The Ipswich Emersons*. Boston, 1900. (Genealogical. Minor.)

Emerson, Edward Waldo. *Emerson in Concord: A Memoir*. Boston, 1889. 266 pp. (An informal biographical study by Emerson's son, containing much original material. After Cabot's *Memoir*, the most valuable source book.)

Engel, Mary M. *I Remember the Emersons.* Los Angeles, 1941. 185 pp. (Reminiscences of the later years.)

Firkins, Oscar W. *Ralph Waldo Emerson.* Boston, 1915. 379 pp. (A readable and thoroughly original interpretative study, half biographical. The emphasis is on Emerson's literary personality. One of the best shorter biographies.)

Garnett, Richard. *Life of Ralph Waldo Emerson.* London, 1888. "Great Writers" series. 207 pp. (Unsympathetic, and often external, though ably written.)

Gay, Robert M. *Emerson: A Study of the Poet as Seer.* New York, 1928. Murray Hill Biographies. 250 pp. (A thoughtful study.)

*The Genius and Character of Emerson.* Ed. by F. B. Sanborn. Boston, 1885. 447 pp. (Sixteen essays by various writers, including A. B. Alcott, Julian Hawthorne, Elizabeth Peabody, Julia Ward Howe, and W. T. Harris. Much valuable reminiscence, and some excellent criticism.)

Guernsey, Alfred H. *Ralph Waldo Emerson: Philosopher and Poet.* New York, 1881. 327 pp. (Early. Minor.)

Haskins, David Greene. *Emerson's Maternal Ancestors.* Boston, 1887. 151 pp. (Includes reminiscences. Minor.)

Hill, J. A. *Emerson and His Philosophy.* London, 1919. 116 pp. (Emphasizes the "spiritual." Minor.)

Hoeltje, Hubert H. *Sheltering Tree: A Story of the Friendship of Ralph Waldo Emerson and Amos Bronson Alcott.* Durham, N. C., 1943. 209 pp. (A scholarly but somewhat idyllic account of the friendship, using Mr. Brooks' technique of allowing the two men to tell their own story.)

Holmes, Oliver Wendell. *Ralph Waldo Emerson.* Boston, 1884. "American Men of Letters" Series. 441 pp. (A readable biography, containing much original material, and emphasizing Emerson's social relationships. Good as biography, especially of the later years, but often poor as criticism.)

Ireland, Alexander. *Ralph Waldo Emerson: His Life, Genius, and Writings.* London, 1882. 338 pp. (By an English journalist and friend, containing some personal reminiscences.)

James, Henry, Jr. "Emerson" in *Partial Portraits.* London, 1888, pp. 1-33. (A thoughtful blend of reminiscence and criticism.)

Lowell, James Russell. "Emerson the Lecturer," in *My Study Windows.* Boston, 1871, pp. 375-384. (Important reminiscence and characterization.)

McGiffert, Arthur C., Jr. *Young Emerson Speaks.* Boston, 1938. XL, 276 pp. (A selection of twenty-five sermons, edited with an important introduction, which summarizes much new information about Emerson's life as a young minister.)

McQuiston, Raymer. *The Relation of Ralph Waldo Emerson to Public*

*Affairs*. Lawrence, Kansas, 1923. Humanistic Studies, Vol. III, No. 1. 63 pp. (An able but brief study, partly biographical.)

Michaud, Régis. *Emerson: The Enraptured Yankee*. Tr. by George Boas. New York, 1930. 444 pp. ("I have merely dramatized . . . the spiritual adventures of Emerson." A popular biography by a scholar, somewhat rhapsodic in style.)

Perry, Bliss. *Emerson Today*. Princeton, N. J., 1931. 141 pp. (Brilliant characterization and criticism, not primarily biographical.)

Pochmann, Henry A. *New England Transcendentalism and St. Louis Hegelianism*. Philadelphia, 1948. 144 pp. (Tells of Emerson's and Alcott's visits to St. Louis, and of their consequences.)

Rusk, Ralph L. *The Life of Ralph Waldo Emerson*. New York, 1949. 592 pp. (The most complete, realistic, and scholarly biography yet written; based upon an exhaustive study of all the manuscript sources by and about Emerson; full of new material, well-selected and well-written. Mostly omits criticism.)

Russell, Phillips. *Emerson: The Wisest American*. New York, 1929. 320 pp. (A popular biography, emphasizing the Yankee wisdom of the man, but omitting discussion of his ideas.)

Sanborn, Franklin B. *The Personality of Emerson*. Boston, 1903. 133 pp. (Reminiscences of Emerson, from 1853 on, by a personal friend, including original letters, and table talk.)

——. *Ralph Waldo Emerson*. Beacon Biographies. Boston, 1901. 140 pp. (Brief, minor.)

Scudder, Townsend, III. *The Lonely Wayfaring Man: Emerson and Some Englishmen*. New York, 1936. 228 pp. (A brilliantly-written story of Emerson's visits to England—especially that of 1847-8—and of his friendships with Carlyle, Clough, and others. Based on original, scholarly research.)

Searle, January [George Searle Phillips]. *Emerson: His Life and Writings*. London, 1855. 48 pp. (The first volume upon Emerson. Brief.)

Snider, Denton J. *The Life of Emerson*. St. Louis, 1921. 384 pp. (Thoughtful, but awkwardly-written, by one of the "St. Louis Hegelians.")

Thayer, James B. A *Western Journey with Mr. Emerson*. Boston, 1884. 141 pp. (An account of Emerson's trip to California in 1871.)

Woodberry, George E. *Ralph Waldo Emerson*. New York, 1907. "English Men of Letters" Series. 205 pp. (Perhaps the best short biography, although written before the publication of the *Journals*, and admittedly unsympathetic. Excellent criticism of ideas.)

Woodbury, Charles J. *Talks with Ralph Waldo Emerson*. New York, 1890. 177 pp. (Reminiscences by a student at Williams College who "Boswellized" Emerson, often uniquely interesting.)

## BIOGRAPHICAL ARTICLES AND STUDIES[133]

Baker, Carlos. "Emerson and Jones Very." *New England Quarterly,* VII, 90-99 (March, 1934).

Baugh, Hansell. "Emerson and the Elder Henry James." *Bookman,* LXVIII, 320-322 (Nov., 1928).

Boynton, Percy H. "Emerson in his Period." *International Journal of Ethics,* XXXIX, 177-189 (January, 1929).

Cestre, Charles. "Thoreau et Emerson." *Revue Anglo-Américaine,* VII, 215-230 (Feb., 1930). (A good summary of the book by A. Bruel.)

Curtis, George W. "Emerson Lecturing," reprinted in *From the Easy Chair* (New York, 1891), 21-26. (For other reminiscences of Emerson, see Cooke, *Bibliography,* p. 252.)

Fields, Annie. "Mr. Emerson in the Lecture Room." *Atlantic Monthly,* LI, 818-832 (June, 1883). (Reporting Emerson's lectures at Harvard.)

Glicksberg, Charles I. "Bryant on Emerson the Lecturer." *New England Quarterly,* XII, 530-534 (Sept., 1939).

Hartwig, G. H. "An Immortal Friendship [Carlyle and Emerson]." *Hibbert Journal,* XXXVIII, 102-114 (Oct., 1939).

Hastings, Louise. "Emerson in Cincinnati." *New England Quarterly,* XI, 443-469 (Sept., 1938).

Hoeltje, Hubert H. "Emerson, Citizen of Concord." *American Literature,* XI, 367-378 (Jan., 1940).

——. "Emerson in Virginia." *New England Quarterly,* V, 753-768 (Oct., 1932).

——. "Ralph Waldo Emerson in Iowa." *Iowa Journal of History and Politics,* XXV, 236-276 (April, 1927).

Hotson, Clarence P. "Emerson and the Swedenborgians." *Studies in Philology,* XXVII, 517-545 (July, 1930). (For twenty other studies on the same general subject, see *Articles on American Literature,* 1920-1945, pp. 52-53.)

Marchand, Ernest. "Emerson and the Frontier." *American Literature,* III, 149-174 (May, 1931).

McNulty, John B. "Emerson's Friends and the Essay on Friendship." *New England Quarterly,* XIX, 390-394 (Sept., 1946).

Moody, Marjory M. "The Evolution of Emerson as an Abolitionist." *American Literature,* XVII, 1-21 (March, 1945).

Moore, John B. "Thoreau Rejects Emerson." *American Literature,* IV, 241-256 (Nov., 1932).

Nye, R. B. "Emerson in Michigan and the Northwest." *Michigan Historical Magazine,* XXVI, 159-172 (Spring, 1942).

133. The following list is selective. For complete lists, see Cooke's *Bibliography,* and *Articles on American Literature . . ., 1920-45,* ed. by Lewis Leary.

Richmond, Mrs. H. L. "Ralph Waldo Emerson in Florida." *Florida Historical Quarterly,* 75-93 (Oct., 1939).

Scott, Eleanor B. "Emerson Wins the Nine Hundred Dollars." *American Literature,* XVII, 78-85 (March, 1945). (Emerson's western lecture tour of 1856.)

Scudder, Townsend, III. "A Chronological List of Emerson's Lectures on his British Lecture Tour of 1847-1848." *PMLA,* LI, 243-248 (March, 1936).

——. "Emerson in London and the London Lectures." *American Literature,* VIII, 22-36 (March, 1936).

——. "Emerson's British Lecture Tour, 1847-1848." *American Literature,* VII, 15-36 and 166-180 (March and May, 1935).

Smith, Henry N. "Emerson's Problem of Vocation: A Note on 'The American Scholar.'" *New England Quarterly,* XII, 52-67 (March, 1939).

Stewart, Randall. "The Concord Group." *Sewanee Review,* XLIV, 434-446 (Oct.-Dec., 1936).

Thompson, F. T. "Emerson and Carlyle." *Studies in Philology,* XXIV, 438-453 (July, 1927).

Thorp, Willard. "Emerson on Tour." *Quarterly Journal of Speech,* XVI, 19-34 (Feb., 1930).

Warfel, Harry R. "Margaret Fuller and Ralph Waldo Emerson." *PMLA,* L, 576-594 (June, 1935).

Wasung, C. J., "Emerson Comes to Detroit." *Michigan Historical Magazine,* XXIX, 59-72 (Jan., 1945).

## PART II

# EMERSON'S PROSE AND POETRY[1]

### The Prose Works

Some of the volumes which Emerson published during his lifetime were clearly planned as wholes, such as *Representative Men* and *English Traits.* Others, such as the First and Second Series of *Essays,* were written during one period and from one point of view, but were not clearly unified. Other volumes, especially those collected after his death, were frankly *Miscellanies.* The Centenary Edition, edited by his son Edward in 1903, has been accepted as definitive: although it does not always follow chronology strictly, we shall consider Emerson's prose writings in the order in which they appear in it.

*Nature, Addresses and Lectures* includes Emerson's first book, published in 1836, and nine other essays written between 1836 and 1845. As the title implies, it is a miscellany. Besides *Nature* it includes his two most famous addresses, "The American Scholar" and "The Divinity School Address." After these nothing is of major importance. However, "Man the Reformer," "The Conservative," "The Transcendentalist," and "The Young American" have each been anthologized more than once.

*Nature* was Emerson's first book and has remained one of the most interesting, although never the most popular, of his writings. Its influence upon men of letters—and through them upon the history of literature—has proved out of proportion to its popular

1. Part II is intended primarily for the student of Emerson rather than for the general reader, although the sections on "Method and Style" and "Poetic Theory" are of general interest. It discusses Emerson's individual works separately, rather than his personality, or thought, or fame as a whole. It supplements the general discussion of "Emerson's Ideas" (Part III) with specific summaries of particular idea-essays, such as "Self-Reliance." For more factual information concerning the individual works, the reader will consult Edward W. Emerson's "Notes" at the end of each volume of the "Centenary Edition" of *The Complete Works.* For vivid but rather impressionistic criticisms of the individual essays, O. W. Firkins' Chapter IV, "The Harvest," in his study of *Emerson,* is valuable.

acceptance. Published anonymously in 1836 in a small edition of 500 copies, it was not reprinted until 1849, yet even in those thirteen years its fame spread far and wide. It was recognized as a kind of manifesto of American Transcendentalism, as well as the challenging first utterance of a new and important writer.

The facts of the writing and publication of *Nature* are well described in the "Notes" of the Centenary Edition. The book took form in Emerson's mind during the three years of ferment which followed his break with the ministry and his first trip to Europe in 1832-33. In it he tried to express a new philosophy of life all at once, and it is not surprising that he failed. But he suggested or outlined all his major ideas, and he wrote in a poetic but concentrated style which challenged attention even if it evaded definition. The criticisms of his friends and contemporaries are indicative.

Carlyle wrote from England: "Your little azure-colored *Nature* gave me true satisfaction . . . You say it is the first chapter of something greater. I call it rather the Foundation and Groundplan on which you may build whatsoever of great and true has been given you to build. It is the true Apocalypse." Oliver Wendell Holmes described it as "a reflective prose-poem. Beginning simply enough, it took on more and more the character of a rhapsody. . . ." The *Christian Examiner,* official organ of the Unitarians, also called it "a poetical rhapsody containing much beautiful writing and not devoid of sound philosophy," but added: "producing the impression of a disordered dream."

Later critics have expressed a similarly mixed appreciation. G. E. Woodberry wrote that "it has the bloom of the mind upon it," and analyzed it well in his chapter on "*Nature* and its Corollaries."[2] O. W. Firkins described it as possessing "the elation of spiritual discovery." Modern editors and anthologists have praised and reprinted it frequently. But increasingly the modern temper of pessimism and "disenchantment" has tended to prejudice readers and students against this book of optimism and youthful enthusiasm.—For *Nature* expressed not only Emerson's own "elation," but that characteristic of the American nineteenth century

2. See also the excellent analysis by W. T. Harris, "Emerson's Philosophy of Nature," in *The Genius and Character of Emerson,* ed. F. B. Sanborn (Boston, 1885).

as well. Therefore, its popularity has tended to decline much more than the popularity of his less rhapsodic essays, such as "Self-Reliance."

There is also a clear logical flaw in Nature which Emerson himself recognized specifically. He planned it as two "essays" and as late as June 28, 1836 noted in his *Journals* his "design to follow *Nature* with another essay, *Spirit*, and the two shall make a decent volume." And on August 8 he noted: "The book of Nature still lies on the table; there is, as always, one crack in it, not easy to be soldered or welded." The "crack" occurred between the chapter on "Discipline" and that on "Idealism." This flaw was nothing less than Emerson's failure to solve the [so far] insoluble philosophic problem of mind and matter. After describing nature in its material aspects Emerson merely jumped to the conclusion that nature might better be described as ideal. Yet he always recognized the dualism of mind and matter—of "law for man" and "law for thing."

Yet the flaw in *Nature* was not so much caused by Emerson's failure to solve this insoluble problem, as by the impression given that he somehow had solved it. This first book derives some of its "elation" and excessive optimism from its overemphasis on the "correspondence" of "law for man" with "law for thing," and from its underemphasis on their difference and the difficulty involved in reconciling these two laws. In the section entitled "Language" Emerson had written that "The laws of moral nature answer to those of matter as face to face in a glass. 'The visible world and the relation of its parts, is the dial-plate of the invisible.' The axioms of physics translate the laws of ethics."—This idea of "Correspondence" and the sentence quoted above, Emerson had borrowed from Swedenborg.[3] Later, of course, he was to qualify the idea radically—especially at the end of his essay on "Experience," where he admitted that "the world I converse with in the city and in the farms, is not the world I *think*." But *Nature* emphasized "the analogy that marries matter and mind" and oversimplified this fundamental problem of philosophy and of religion.

Nevertheless, by emphasizing the ways in which human "language" translates "the symbolism of nature" and the way in

3. See Clarence Hotson, "Emerson and the Doctrine of Correspondence," *The New-Church Review,* XXXVI (January, 1929).

which nature "disciplines" the human mind through experience with such unpleasant realities as "Debt" and "Property," Emerson also prepared the way for the later philosophy of Pragmatism.[4] Although *Nature* made many extreme and exaggerated statements it also suggested many unique and seminal ideas. Moreover its style was so fresh and challenging that it appealed aesthetically to many men of letters who cared comparatively little for formal philosophy.

The first edition of *Nature* has become an important and valuable collector's item, partly because of its rarity and its literary and historical interest and partly because of the differences between the first and the later editions. Recently the first edition has been reprinted in facsimile and edited with an introduction and scholarly notes by Kenneth W. Cameron;[5] and the student will find much valuable information there. Of general interest, however, is the change made by Emerson from the motto of the first edition to the second—a change indicative of the development of his thought as a whole.

The first edition of *Nature* was prefaced by a motto quoted from the Neoplatonic philosopher, Plotinus, which suggested the old, idealistic, and mystical theory of "emanation."[6] But the second edition was prefaced by some original verses of Emerson's, ending:

> And, striving to be man, the worm
> Mounts through all the spires of form.

These clearly implied the modern theory of evolution, with its scientific and materialistic assumptions.[7] Between 1836 and 1849 Emerson's thought and writing became progressively less transcendental and progressively more realistic. But *Nature*, especially in the first edition, was a purely transcendental book, with both the faults and the virtues of Transcendentalism.

"The American Scholar" was, as Bliss Perry has called it, "Emerson's Most Famous Speech."[8] Together with "Self-Reliance" it

4. See Part III.
5. Scholars' Facsimiles and Reprints, 100 West 31st Street, New York, 1940.
6. See "The Over-Soul."
7. See Part III, "Experience and Nature."
8. Bliss Perry, *The Praise of Folly and Other Papers* (Boston, 1923), pp. 81-113.

has proved Emerson's most popular prose writing. It has become one of the most famous essays in American literature; considered historically its influence has been greater than that of any single modern literary work of comparable scope. Although "Self-Reliance" has proved more popular in modern times, "The American Scholar" has become a historic literary landmark.

The reasons for this are various but are all suggested by the phrase of Oliver Wendell Holmes who called it "our intellectual Declaration of Independence." James Russell Lowell later elaborated this same idea:

> The Puritan revolt had made us ecclesiastically, and the Revolution politically independent, but we were still socially and intellectually moored to English thought, till Emerson cut the cable and gave us a chance at the dangers and the glories of blue water. . . . His oration before the Phi Beta Kappa Society at Cambridge, some thirty years ago, was an event without any former parallel in our literary annals, a scene always to be treasured in the memory for its picturesqueness and its inspiration. What crowded and breathless aisles, what windows clustering with eager heads, what enthusiasm of approval, what grim silence of foregone dissent.

The key phrase of "The American Scholar" is: "We have listened too long to the courtly muses of Europe." But lest modern Americans think of this as merely literary nationalism Carlyle's letter of praise should also be quoted:

> My friend! You know not what you have done for me there. . . . Lo, out of the West comes a clear utterance, clearly recognizable as a man's voice, and I have a kinsman and a brother; God be thanked for it, I could have wept to read that speech; the clear, high melody of it went tingling through my heart.

And in modern times John Erskine[9] emphasized the positive modernism of this address: Emerson did not attack European literature and culture negatively, but rather declared the new opportunity for independent, creative writing and thinking which a new America offered. "The American Scholar" was not a declaration of American chauvinism but of American independence.

More specifically, however, "The American Scholar" was addressed to intellectuals and has inspired American scholars for over a century. Professor Erskine's essay on "The American

9. John Erskine, *The American Scholar*, I (Winter, 1932), 5-15.

Scholar" in 1932 specifically celebrated the launching of a new magazine by the Phi Beta Kappa Society of America which bore the title of Emerson's address of ninety-five years before—a magazine which has followed Emerson's principles and has flourished from that time to this. And frequently in the last century Emerson's title has been borrowed by scholars and thinkers to describe the ideas which he has inspired. In 1936, for instance, Professor William Allen Neilson proclaimed to the American Association for the Advancement of Science that "the day Emerson foresaw has arrived, and American scholarship now stands on its own feet.[10] Then he went on to celebrate Emerson's attempt to destroy the barrier between science and the humanities and to renew Emerson's liberalism.

But Emerson's address advocated much more than "scholarship"—it was also his formulation of his own intellectual ideal.[11] When he defined the "Scholar" as "Man Thinking" he was defining his own goal in life. Neither a minister nor a professor nor a popular writer, he wished to be much more than these. He wished to be "man converting experience into wisdom."[12]

In his essay on "Emerson's Most Famous Speech"[13] Professor Perry has emphasized that the theme of Emerson's address was not new but timeworn and familiar—previous "scholars" had frequently called for a new "National Literature" and had urged an independence of European models. Emerson's eloquence was merely the catalytic agent. It inspired its hearers then, as it has inspired its readers since. And it antagonized the conservative among its hearers then, as it has antagonized conservative readers since. James Russell Lowell described "the grim silence of foregone dissent." Emerson enunciated the American ideal of intellectual independence in language that was both polemic and classic.

"The Divinity School Address," delivered in Cambridge one year later, developed many of the ideas of "The American Scholar" but applied them specifically to religion. Attacking the

10. W. A. Neilson, "The American Scholar Today," *The American Scholar*, V (Spring, 1936), 149-63.

11. See H. N. Smith, "Emerson's Problem of Vocation: A Note on 'The American Scholar,'" *New England Quarterly*, XII (March, 1939), 52-67.

12. O. W. Firkins, *R. W. Emerson*, p. 160.

13. Bliss Perry, *op. cit.*

abuses of "historical Christianity" rather than of "historical scholarship" and advocating perfect freedom of conscience rather than of intellect, Emerson aroused immediate and violent controversy. After stirring up the hornet's nest he then retired to Concord and let his friends defend his ideas as they wished. When his former associate, the Reverend Henry Ware, Jr., wrote to protest and to argue, Emerson replied deprecatingly on October 8, 1838 that "I could not give an account of myself, if challenged."[14] When he was so challenged by Andrews Norton, a former professor of divinity and leader of the conservative Unitarians, his position was defended by George Ripley (later leader of Brook Farm) and by the young Theodore Parker. Norton in turn was supported by orthodox professors at Princeton while other Transcendentalists wrote to support Ripley and Parker.[15] The controversy finally established Emerson's fame as a brilliant liberal but also made him notorious as a dangerous heretic.

The logical and psychological implications of "The Divinity School Address" have been developed by Professor Stephen Whicher,[16] under the title: *The Lapse of Uriel.*—Emerson's later poem "Uriel" told the fable of the demi-god who dared to challenge the heavenly host by proclaiming the heresy of the relativity of evil, but who was made to suffer for it:

> A sad self-knowledge, withering, fell
> Upon the beauty of Uriel.

Professor Whicher's thesis is that Emerson, like Uriel, became disillusioned by the reception of "The Divinity School Address" and that he lost the conviction earlier expressed in *Nature* that "all things are possible"; and that as a result he abandoned the belief of the prophet that his own eloquence might actually bring about a new order, and retired to the belief of the poet, that his true function was merely to describe the beauty of the world.

Actually the influence of the "Divinity School Address" on its immediate hearers was slight; Dr. Trueblood[17] has shown that the

14. *Letters,* II, 167.
15. The important documents in this famous controversy have been selected and edited by Perry Miller, *The Transcendentalists,* pp. 192-247.
16. In an unpublished doctoral thesis (Harvard, 1942).
17. D. E. Trueblood, "The Influence of Emerson's 'Divinity School Address,'" *Harvard Theological Review,* XXXII (Jan., 1939), 41-56.

graduating members of the School did not distinguish themselves. But, like "The American Scholar," it crystallized many ideas which were "in the air" at the time. And, especially through its influence on Theodore Parker, it inspired the whole "modernist" interpretation of religion.[18] The "Divinity School Address" challenged "fundamentalism" in every form. And, just as "The American Scholar" had attacked the petrifaction of historical scholarship and philosophy, this attacked the petrifaction of historical Christianity and religion.[19]

*Essays, First Series* includes many of Emerson's most famous essays. "Self-Reliance" is probably his greatest and has proven his most popular. "Compensation" and "The Over-Soul" have been frequently reprinted. "History" and "Spiritual Laws" express highly original ideas and have replaced the old favorites "Love" and "Friendship" in popular and critical esteem in modern times. —As a whole these essays continue the challenge and freshness of the earlier "Addresses," but formulate and develop the ideas more carefully. As Emerson himself wrote, he was trying "to spin some single cord out of my thousand and one strands of every color and texture."[20] But he did not succeed too well in achieving unity.

"History" began this "First Series" of essays—not "Self-Reliance." The significance of this fact has only recently been emphasized by Dr. Caponigri, who has shown how Emerson's interpetation of "History" as psychological and relative, rather than objective and absolute, underlay all his philosphy.[21] The idea of "Self-Reliance," that the individual conscience should have the final authority, follows from this premise. Emerson had previously given a series of lectures on "The Philosophy of His-

18. See Clarence Gohdes, "Some Remarks on Emerson's 'Divinity School Address,'" *American Literature,* I (March, 1929), 27-31; and H. S. Commager, "Tempest in a Boston Tea Cup," *New England Quarterly,* VI (Dec., 1933), 651-75.

19. See G. H. Hartwig, "Emerson on Historical Christianity," *Hibbert Journal,* XXXVII (April, 1939), 405-12. For a detailed analysis of the ideas involved, see G. E. Woodberry, *Emerson,* pp. 55 ff.

20. *Works,* II, 373.

21. A. R. Caponigri, "Brownson and Emerson: Nature and History," *New England Quarterly,* XVIII (Sept., 1945), 368-90. See also Hedi Hildebrand, *Die Amerikanische Stellung zur Geschichte und zu Europa in Emerson's Gedankensystem* (Bonn, 1936) for a more detailed study of Emerson's philosophy of history.

tory" and here condensed them into one essay. This idea of the relativity of time and space has also been fundamental to all philosophies of mysticism.[22]

"Self-Reliance" is Emerson's greatest essay, partly because of the brilliance of its language and partly because of the universal applicability of its ideas. It appeals to every individual who struggles to achieve maturity and to cast off dependence on his elders. One key sentence is: "There is a time in every man's education when he arrives at the conviction that . . . he must take himself for better for worse as his portion." Its appeal has always been to the young in spirit. But, as modern psychologists[23] emphasize, most men never achieve true maturity. Therefore, Emerson's true appeal is not only to the young but to men of all ages that they may achieve maturity of mind as well as of body.

"Self-Reliance" is brilliant and challenging, however, partly because it overstates its case. Only at the end does the essay qualify its radicalism and define its terms: "Nothing can bring you peace but yourself. Nothing can bring you peace but the triumph of principles." That is, the "self" to be relied on is the higher "self" which is governed by principles rather than by circumstances. So Emerson stated even more clearly in a later essay: "Self-reliance, the height and perfection of man, is reliance on God."[24] The "Self" of the essay is the "soul" or conscience, which communicates directly with the "Over-Soul" or God. "Self-Reliance," therefore, assumes that the individual has been "educated" by a civilization which has formulated some "Moral Laws" which the individual is now to interpret and to act upon, according to his own best conscience.[25]

"Compensation," which follows "Self-Reliance," is one of Emerson's most characteristic and original essays. As his *Journals* show he had been developing the idea since early college days, and his reading in the science of his time contributed to it. Indeed, by applying the scientific law of "polarity" to the realm of morals he was developing the idea of "correspondence" which he had announced in *Nature*.

22. See "Mysticism," Part III.

23. See H. A. Overstreet, *The Mature Mind* (New York, 1949); and Walter Lippmann, *A Preface to Morals*.

24. *Works*, XI, 236.

25. See section on "The Moral Law," Part III.

Emerson's statement that "crime and punishment grow out of one stem" was to be illustrated later in Dostoevski's novel *Crime and Punishment.* The murderer is punished by his own conscience or by the deterioration of his own character, whether he is punished physically or not. But the criticism has often been made that the law of compensation does not apply to the person murdered. To this modern psychology has suggested that some persons are "accident-prone" and subconsciously wish to become victims. More mystically, Emerson's poem "Brahma" suggests that from the point of view of God both the slayer and the slain may be valuable and necessary to the evolution of the life process as a whole.

Philosophically this idea of "Compensation" has been attacked as mere moral equivalence or ambivalence.—If nothing is really better than anything else why try to be moral? Kenneth Burke has answered this in his essay on "Acceptance and Rejection"[26] (later incorporated in his book, *Attitudes toward History).* The doctrine of equivalence is not—and cannot be—final. Emerson specifically qualified "Compensation" toward the end of his essay: "The soul is not a compensation, but a life. The soul *is* . . . Calamities arise, and by compensation, they force us to turn them into benefits lest we perish." The individual, because he is human—because of the very nature of his "self"—is compelled to choose and to act according to his best judgment or conscience.

"Spiritual Laws" then describes in rather mystical language the moral laws of the conscience, or "spirit." It attacks the old Puritan emphasis on the conscious will and on systematized morality, emphasizing rather that subconscious "inclination" which Jonathan Edwards had long ago emphasized and which modern non-rational psychology also emphasizes. This essay also attacks the self-righteousness of reformers, as does "New England Reformers," in *Essays: Second Series.*

"Love" is essentially Platonic and should be compared with Emerson's poem "Initial, Daemonic and Celestial Love." "Friendship" is closely related to Emerson's biography.[27]

26. K. Burke, "Acceptance and Rejection," *Southern Review,* II (Winter, 1937), 600-32.

27. See Part I, "Loves and Friendships," and J. B. McNulty, "Emerson's Friends and His Essay on 'Friendship,'" *New England Quarterly,* XIX (1946).

"The Over-Soul" gives classic expression to Emerson's mysticism; therefore, it has been praised by those who appreciate mysticism and attacked by those who dislike it. Both in subject matter and in style it contrasts with "Self-Reliance" and complements that essay. Holmes made fun of it, and Carlyle wrote (in his Preface to the English edition of the *Essays*), "I do not advise the British public to trouble itself much with all that." In modern times critics have tended usually to accept Carlyle's advice. Nevertheless, the essay is excellent of its own kind and describes well the psychological idea behind both Emerson's mysticism and William James' more specific *Varieties of Religious Experience.*

The metaphor suggested by "The Over-Soul" is derived from the idea of "emanation" which the Neoplatonic philosopher, Plotinus,[28] developed in ancient Alexandria. The Over-Soul is conceived as a kind of "ocean of light" or reservoir of spiritual power from which beams of light "emanate" or streams of power flow down to the individual "souls" or physical selves, when (and if) the individuals open themselves to this influx of power and rely on this Over-Soul rather than upon material laws and circumstances. The metaphor is essentially literary, yet implies the philosophy of intuition which Emerson shared with many mystical and transcendental philosophers.

*Essays, Second Series,* published in 1844, is less challenging but more realistic than the *First Series,* both in subject matter and in style. Instead of the idealistic "Self-Reliance" and "The Over-Soul" the more practical "Experience" and "Politics" dominate. Besides these two, "The Poet," "Manners" and "New England Reformer" have often been praised and reprinted.

"The Poet" introduces this *Second Series;* but since it embodies Emerson's fundamental ideas on aesthetics and the theory of poetry we shall consider it later in that connection. The structure of this essay has been analyzed well by Professors Blair and Faust.[29] Here Emerson's thought moves from ideal statement and definition to particular illustration; whereas in "Experience" (the next essay) the reverse is true. Professor Stephen Whicher

28. See F. I. Carpenter, *Emerson and Asia* (Cambridge, 1930), pp. 75-78.
29. Walter Blair and Clarence Faust, "Emerson's Literary Method," *Modern Philology,* XLII (Nov. 1944), 79-95.

has suggested that "The Poet" is indicative of Emerson's shift from his early mood of prophetic exhortation to his later, more sober, mood of literary description and pure expression.

"Experience" is one of the most brilliant of all the Essays and has been the favorite of many critics, although its general popularity has never approached that of "The American Scholar" and "Self-Reliance." "Experience," as O. W. Firkins wrote, "seems one of the boldest essays in literature, though its boldness has almost a casual air, as if a man should blow up a minister by way of correction of the monotony of an evening walk." It was never given as a lecture but seems to have been written all at once in a mood of reaction against his earlier idealism, caused by the death of his son. His apparently heartless reference to this tragedy near the beginning of the essay was the expression of a passing mood which his enduring grief in later life disproved.

Although "Experience" seems to have been written spontaneously and at white heat its structure is carefully planned and its development clear and logical. It has been analyzed twice in detail[30] and, if studied carefully, suggests the whole scope of Emerson's thought. Beginning with a description of the transitory moods and apparent illusions of individual experience, it ends by suggesting how truth can be discovered by piecing together these partial experiences and by seeing life as a whole. "The party-colored wheel must revolve very fast to appear white."

Although "Politics" deals with a subject distasteful to Emerson it remains one of his best-balanced essays. (For a discussion of the ideas involved see Part III, "Politics and Economics.") "New England Reformers" deals with the problem of political action in more concrete terms and defines well Emerson's position midway between the idealistic reformers and the political realists. (For vividly concrete *descriptions* of certain New England Reformers, see Emerson's essays on "The Chardon Street Convention" and "Historic Notes on Life and Letters in New England," both in *Lectures and Biographical Sketches.)*

*Representative Men* (1850) is one of Emerson's most unified books although not his best. It represents a selection and rewrit-

30. W. T. Harris, "Ralph Waldo Emerson," *The Atlantic Monthly,* L (August, 1882), pp. 238-52; and F. I. Carpenter, *R. W. Emerson* (New York, 1934), pp. 446-47.

ing of the best of the series of biographical lectures which he had been giving at different times since 1835. It also marks his most sustained attempt to apply his general ideas and to illustrate them by individual characterizations and judgments. His earlier essays on "Heroism" and "Character" had described these general ideas. "The Poet" had set forth his conception of the "representative" quality of great men and makes perhaps the best introduction to this volume. The present introductory essay on "The Uses of Great Men" is probably less valuable than any of these three.

Emerson's basic idea for *Representative Men* is original and important. The volume has often been compared to Carlyle's *Heroes and Hero-Worship,* yet its thesis is the opposite of Carlyle's. Emerson's emphasizes the "representative" quality of great men, in contrast to Carlyle's emphasis on the "uniqueness" of heroes. Throughout, Emerson's conception is democratic, Carlyle's authoritarian. For Emerson the function of great men is to teach and inspire others to greatness; for Carlyle heroes are "guides to the dull host, which follows." Emerson's great men are less god-like, less tyrannical and are never to be worshiped or followed as disciples. It has even been suggested[31] that Emerson wrote *Representative Men* as an answer to Carlyle's *Heroes.* . . .

For Emerson great men were "representative" in two ways. First, they were representative of their own fellowmen in their own places and times—like democratic representatives in an American Congress. Second, they were also representative of the ideal and timeless potentialities of all mankind in their different "vocations" of "Poet," "Scholar," "Philosopher" and the like. This idea of Emerson's is specifically related to Swedenborg's doctrine of the "correspondence"[32] between the ideal and the real: the great man is a kind of demi-god who relates man to God by realizing some of the god-like potentialities inherent in all men.

Dr. Kenneth Kurtz has studied *The Sources and Development of "Representative Men"* in an excellent doctoral dissertation with especial reference to Emerson's reading and earlier lectures. The

31. By the German critic, Van Wiecki, quoted in Kenneth Kurtz's unpublished dissertation, *The Sources and Development of "Representative Men"* (Yale, 1947), p. 54.

32. *Works,* IV, 8. See above, *Nature;* and later discussion of "Swedenborg."

six "Representative Men" were Emerson's favorites throughout life, except that Jesus and Plutarch might well have been added. Emerson's reasons for omitting Jesus were obvious—although his interpretation of Jesus as the greatest of men, rather than as a God, agreed perfectly with the basic idea of his *Representative Men.* And Plutarch was both a life-long favorite and a model of Emerson's because of his combination of interest in individual characters as "Lives," and in "Morals" in general. Like Plutarch's, the basis of Emerson's judgment of character was always moral.

"Plato; or, the Philosopher" was Emerson's own favorite and incorporated his earliest college essay on "The Character of Socrates." The essay on "Plato" was repeatedly revised and lacks artistic unity, partly because it tries to say too much. Regarding Plato as both "Philosopher" and "Poet" Emerson ranked him second only to Jesus in greatness. He also imputed to Plato some ideas which, historically, derived rather from the later Neo-Platonists and even from the ancient Orient.[33] Many readers, like Carlyle, have preferred Emerson's more concrete characterizations of "Montaigne" and "Napoleon."

"Swedenborg; or, the Mystic" has never been popular. The essay is interesting, partly because of Emerson's unusual interest in this comparatively unpopular figure and partly because of Emerson's unusual definition of the "mystic," as the antithesis of the "poet." His criticism of Swedenborg is essentially that he was an allegorist who tried to define the meaning of each poetic symbol too narrowly; yet, of course, this is not a fair criticism of a true "mystic," and is not what Emerson himself usually meant by "mystic." Emerson's interpretation of Swedenborg has also been attacked as false by Swedenborgian scholars.[34]

"Montaigne; or, the Skeptic" has proved a popular essay because it is both thoughtful and racy. Emerson's enthusiasm for Montaigne is typical of the realistic, anti-transcendental half of his nature.[35]

"Shakespeare; or, the Poet" does not follow out the logic of Emerson's essay on "The Poet" but rather contrasts the "poet"

33. See Part IV.
34. See Part IV.
35. See Part IV. *Emerson's Montaigne* has been studied in detail by C. L. Young (New York, 1941).

as verbal technician with the "mystic" as moral idealist: therefore its moralistic conclusion condemning Shakespeare as merely "master of the revels of mankind" has never seemed just. Nevertheless, the essay has proved popular and was delivered as a lecture oftener than any other of the series. Shakespeare, like Plato, was a genuine, life-long favorite of Emerson's, and the essay communicates his enthusiasm for the subject in spite of its conclusion.

"Napoleon; or, the Man of the World" has always been the most popular essay of this series and illustrates Emerson's realistic appreciation of pure power and human vitality. His *Journals* show that until 1827 he considered Napoleon as the embodiment of pure evil—like many others of his time. Then, influenced by his reading of Goethe, he gradually achieved the more objective point of view described in this essay.

"Goethe: or, the Writer" has never been popular. It is interesting as evidencing the catholicity of Emerson, compared with most of his American contemporaries; but it also shows his moralistic limitations.[36]

*English Traits* (1856) resembles *Representative Men* in being the best unified and most concrete of Emerson's books. It is a mixture of personal experience and philosophical judgment. It begins concretely with an account of Emerson's "First Visit to England" and ends concretely with a brief account and summary of his "Speech at Manchester" ending his second visit. The book was frequently given in lecture form during the seven years between the second voyage and its publication.

Professor Scudder has described the historical and biographical background of *English Traits* in *The Lonely Wayfaring Man: Emerson and Some Englishmen,* and has shown how Emerson adapted and often altered the factual *Journals* of his two English trips in writing this book. For instance, Emerson's first chapter, which describes vividly his first visits to Carlyle, Coleridge, and Wordsworth, actually describes a composite of his two visits, separated by fifteen years, and imputes the humorously detached perspective of his second visit to his first. But as a whole *English Traits* accurately describes his judgment of Englishmen. As he

36. See Part IV. See F. W. Wahr, *Emerson and Goethe* (Ann Arbor, Mich., 1915).

wrote to Margaret Fuller: "I leave England with an increased respect for the Englishman . . . My respect is the more generous that I have no sympathy with him, only an admiration."[37]

The two most interesting chapters of *English Traits* are "First Visit to England" and "Character." Those on "Race," "Ability," "Truth," and "Wealth" have been praised and reprinted more than once. As a whole, the book has often been compared to Hawthorne's *Our Old Home*—with honors about even.

*The Conduct of Life* (1860) was Emerson's last major book. It is farthest removed from his challenging, transcendental essays and addresses of the 1830's but is more mature and—as the title implies—pragmatic. It contains some of his best writing and appealed strongly to his contemporaries. But, in modern times, critics have objected to its calmness and have preferred the earlier, more exciting essays.

After reading *The Conduct of Life* Carlyle wrote:

> You have grown older, more pungent, piercing:—I never read from you before such lightning-gleams of meaning as are to be found here. The finale of all, that of "Illusions" falling on us like snow-showers, but again of "the gods sitting steadfast on their thrones" all the while,—what a *Fiat Lux* is there, into the deeps of a philosophy, which the vulgar has not, which hardly three men living *have*, yet dreamt of! *Well done*, I say; and so let the matter rest.

The two best and most famous essays, on "Fate" and "Illusions," which begin and end the volume, deal with ideas originally oriental but domesticate them by means of illustrations and metaphors from the modern world. These essays, more than any others, give "that feeling of eternity" in his thought, which Woodberry calls "the sign-royal of greatness." In contrast to the earlier "addresses," which were essentially timely, these essays are timeless —with both the faults and the virtues which that adjective implies.

"Fate" is a well-developed essay, suggesting successive definitions of the idea which make it vivid to the modern reader. It also contains passages remarkable for their recognition of the natural evil and cruelty of life. Then, half-way through, Emerson makes his counter-statement: "But Fate has its lord; limitation its limits . . . Fate is immense, so is Power." Therefore "Fate" really describes the whole range of Emerson's thought on the

37. Quoted in *Works*, V, 323.

subject and does not need the following essay on "Power" for completeness. Emerson's emphasis on "Power" in all its forms, which here finds final expression, made his writings appeal to so alien a writer as Neitzsche.[38]

After "Power" the essays on "Culture" and "Beauty" have been praised and reprinted. "Considerations by the Way" is remarkable for its sudden diatribe against "the masses."

"Illusions" is the most eloquent essay of this volume and the most often reprinted. Its final paragraph, which Carlyle praised, marks the climax of Emerson's writing. The oriental ideas and sources which underlie the essay have been studied in detail.[39] The basic idea—that disconnected experiences are "illusions"—had been described in his earlier essay "Experience." But here Emerson reverses the oriental condemnation of these illusory experiences and describes them rather as "beneficient illusions" and as the only means by which wisdom and truth can ever be achieved. In a later essay on "Works and Days" he developed this same idea in more concrete and simple—but more pedestrian—language. "Illusions" is rather a poetic description of the psychological experience of illumination.

*Society and Solitude* (1870) is the last volume which Emerson personally prepared for publication. *Letters and Social Aims* (1875) was prepared for him after he had suffered loss of memory in his old age. Neither volume contains anything of great importance, and neither amounts to more than a collection of late essays. In *Society and Solitude* "Civilization" contains the famous quotation "Hitch your wagon to a star," which means not merely "aim high" but "see your chores done by the gods themselves." "Farming" and "Works and Days" are vivid and concrete. In *Letters and Social Aims* the first essay on "Poetry and Imagination" contains many brilliant if disconnected ideas on the subject, as do also "The Comic" and "Quotation and Originality." Both volumes sold well but rather because of Emerson's fame than their own value.

The last three volumes of Emerson's prose, published posthumously, are less pretentious but much more valuable than the two preceding. *Lectures and Biographical Sketches* reveals Emer-

38. See Part IV.
39. See F. I. Carpenter, *Emerson and Asia*, pp. 63-65.

son's genuine and surprising talent for personal observation and characterization. His essay on "Thoreau" is the best of these and one of the best on the subject. If Emerson frankly reveals his own bias toward his friend, he also describes vividly the living man against their common background of shared experience; and if his criticism is partial, it is consistent and clear. "Thoreau" has been praised and reprinted more often than any written after *Essays: Second Series.* His essay on "Carlyle" is good but less vivid and less well balanced. The two sketches of his relatives "Ezra Ripley" and "Mary Moody Emerson" are both brilliant and combine genuine affection with detached humor and objective understanding; if neither subject is very important, each is colorful and characteristic of that Puritan New England which produced not only Emerson but the "American Renaissance" as a whole. "Historic Notes of Life and Letters in New England" contains several brief sketches and critiques of characters and institutions of the Transcendental era—especially one of Brook Farm. "The Chardon Street Convention" gives a beautifully comic thumb-nail sketch of this "Convention of Friends of Universal Reform."—Among the *Lectures* that on "Education" has proved both influential and of enduring value.

*Miscellanies* collects essays and speeches—mostly occasional—given over the whole course of his career. Many of these are important, for different reasons. The first, on "The Lord's Supper,"[40] was Emerson's farewell sermon, occasioned by his resignation from the ministry. Besides giving his personal reasons for this step it is remarkable for its skillful marshaling of arguments and its disciplined logical organization. Here Emerson demonstrated brilliantly that he could use the conventional logical techniques of theology and philosophy when he wished and that his preference for intuition, rhetoric, and poetry did not spring from any inability of his own. "The Lord's Supper" is the only sermon included in the *Complete* Works. Two important occasional addresses are "The Fugitive Slave Law" (given at Concord in 1851) and "John Brown" (given at Boston in 1859). The final essay on "American Civilization" (1862) has been both praised and

40. See M. C. Turpie, "A Quaker Source for Emerson's Sermon on The Lord's Supper," *New England Quarterly,* XVII (March, 1944), 95-101.

damned for its mood of optimistic and patriotic enthusiasm following the Union victory in the Civil War.

The final volume, *Natural History of Intellect,* is interesting for its title essay, which includes Emerson's notes for the lectures on philosophy which he gave at Harvard University in 1870, now edited for publication by J. E. Cabot. The title is significant, and the essay, although disconnected, outlines many new ideas which the great Pragmatists,[41] William James and C. S. Peirce, were later to develop. Indeed, these notes, composed in Emerson's declining years, are extraordinary for their originality and for their clarification of ideas which had been vague, although implicit, in Emerson's earlier writing. Besides the title essay, "Milton," "Art and Criticism," and "The Tragic" are notable. An excellent "General Index" to the twelve volumes of "The Centenary Edition" concludes this volume.

A volume of Emerson's *Uncollected Writings*[42] was published in 1912, containing much miscellaneous prose: some essays, one sermon, several addresses, many "Papers from *The Dial,*" more "Book Reviews from *The Dial*" and some important letters, together with a few poems. But only Emerson's introduction of *The Dial:* "The Editors to the Reader"[43] achieves real excellence.

*The Journals of Ralph Waldo Emerson* were selected and edited in ten volumes in 1909 by E. W. Emerson and W. E. Forbes. An excellent one-volume selection of *The Heart of Emerson's Journals* was edited by Bliss Perry in 1926. In some respects these *Journals* make better reading than the formal *Essays:* they relate Emerson's ideas to the biographical experiences and to the historic occasions which suggested them, and they express separate thoughts and insights without attempting to argue them logically or to relate them to any philosophic system. Since Emerson was both an informal person and an informal writer the informal style of the *Journals* suited him perfectly.

Particularly the *Journals* reveal the surprising richness and variety of Emerson's character. They are full of an unexpected

41. See Part III, "Pragmatism."
42. Edited by C. C. Bigelow (New York: The Lamb Publishing Co., 1912).
43. See Part III, "Transcendentalism."

humor largely lacking in the *Essays*. There are many flashes of characterization: "Alcott is a tedious archangel." There are gems of informal definition: "Transcendentalism means . . . *a little beyond.*" There are bits of perfectly phrased criticism: "American geniuses . . . all lack nerve and dagger." There are brief, accurate prophecies: "Brook Farm will show a few noble victims. . . ."—And there are many passages of perfect self-knowledge: "After this generation one would say mysticism should go out of fashion for a long time."

Beyond this rich and various—but atomic and occasional—literary brilliance the *Journals* were—as Emerson himself called them—"my Savings Bank." Bliss Perry has so described them and has pointed to the many passages of apprentice writing which they contain—passages later rewritten into formal essays and poems.[44] There are many other passages suggested by other writers—part summary, part criticism—often to be used or transformed later. And there are some literary "deposits" of value, made by his own personal friends and relatives: "Lidian says that the only sin which people never forgive in each other is a difference of opinion."

But, of course, the *Journals* suffer the faults of these virtues. Professor G. R. Elliott,[45] in his study of "Emerson as Diarist," has emphasized that the dualism of Emerson's thought escapes notice when the *Journals* are read separately from the *Essays*. The parodox of Emerson's transcendental belief in "perfect freedom" and "self-reliance," contrasting with his orthodox belief in "divine grace" and a "moral law" which determines the "freedom" of the "self," simply disappears in the atomic brilliance (and disorganization) of the *Journals*. But many readers who are neither theologians nor philosophers find in the *Journals* the "heart" of Emerson's writing.

*The Letters of Ralph Waldo Emerson* were collected and edited in six large volumes in 1939 by Ralph L. Rusk. These collected *Letters* complement seven books or series of letters to individuals collected and published at earlier dates: to Carlyle, Thoreau,

44. B. Perry, "Emerson's Savings Bank," *The Praise of Folly and Other Papers*, pp. 114-29.

45. G. R. Elliott, "Emerson as Diarist," *University of Toronto Quarterly*, VI (April, 1937), 299-308.

John Sterling, S. G. Ward, Herman Grimm, H. H. Furness, and Arthur Hugh Clough: these individual series of letters are listed in a "calendar" incorporated in the collected *Letters*. In so far as the *Letters* illustrate Emerson's biography and personality they have been described in Part I of this Handbook: "Loves and Friendships."

In general, Professor Rusk has well summarized the characteristics of Emerson's *Letters* in his "Introduction." Like the *Journals* the *Letters* show us the informal side of Emerson and let us follow the gradual development of his personality, philosophy, and literary style. Like the *Journals* they reveal his informal humor, his self-criticism, and the depth of his inner struggles, which belie any cliché about easy optimism. And they reveal the variety of his experience, the catholicity of his reading, and the scope of his interests.

Yet, as Granville Hicks has said, "Emerson was not a great, nor even most of the time a very good, letter writer."[46] According to Henry James, he "has only one style and he had it for everything." As an individualist and a philosopher, he lacked the ability to enter wholeheartedly into the interests of others. His *Journals* were much better adapted than his *Letters* for the expression of his essentially introspective mind. His *Letters* were best when discussing literary matters with intellectual equals, such as Carlyle or Margaret Fuller.

Only one of Emerson's Sermons was included in the Centenary Edition of his *Works* and that ("The Lord's Supper") was certainly his best. The twenty-five sermons which Dr. A. C. McGiffert, Jr. selected and published in 1938 bear the title: *Young Emerson Speaks*. And their interest is chiefly biographical and religious. They show how the young minister gradually developed from a fairly conventional Unitarian preacher to an independent radical thinker. And they show how the early liberalism of the Unitarians gradually evolved into the later radicalism of the Community Church and of Comparative Religion. But the purely literary interest of the sermons is slight.

The same is true of Emerson's lectures. Of course, the difference between his "Lectures" and "Essays" was never of kind but

46. Granville Hicks, in a feature review of the *Letters*, in *Virginia Quarterly Review*, (1939), p. 643.

of degree; the "Essays" were usually merely rewritten "Lectures." Many of the better "Lectures" were published as such in the Centenary Edition. Professor Gohdes edited summaries of seven *Uncollected Lectures*[47] in 1932. But for the most part all the "Lectures" are merely early, or occasional, or unsuccessful "Essays," whose interest is chiefly biographical or historical.

Indeed, only Emerson's *Journals* add significantly to the literary stature established by his *Essays* and *Poems:* most of his *Letters,* Sermons, and Lectures are of minor literary value.

### The Unpublished Manuscripts

Emerson published nine volumes of essays and two of poems during his life, and left many thousand manuscript pages of journals, letters, sermons, and lectures at his death. More than twenty-three volumes of these have since been published, but much remains.

Between 1938 and 1942 the Ralph Waldo Emerson Memorial Association presented its collections of Emerson manuscripts to the Houghton Library of Harvard University. These collections are now available for study by accredited graduate students and scholars. Many of them may be consulted only by special permission. Photostats are usually not permitted. And, of course, the Ralph Waldo Emerson Memorial Association reserves the right to publication.

The bulk of this manuscript material consists of the complete journals. When *Emerson's Journals* were edited and published in ten volumes in 1909, much was rejected. Roughly one-quarter of the journals of the earlier years of Emerson's life, and roughly one-half of those of his later years were considered either repetitious or of minor interest. Since then almost all of these have been copied and are available for study in typescript. Besides the day-to-day journals from which the published volumes were selected, many topical journal-books remain, entitled (for example): "Naturalist," "Orientalist," "Gulistan," and "Journal in the West." This last, which records in detail Emerson's first trip to the Mississippi Valley, has been studied in detail.[48] In general,

47. C. Gohdes, ed., *Uncollected Lectures by Ralph Waldo Emerson* (New York, 1932).

48. By Louise Hastings in an unpublished doctoral dissertation (Indiana, 1942).

Professor Pochmann[49] has pointed out probable errors in dating Emerson's published *Journals* (especially those used in preparing his first book on *Nature*), and has suggested the need of re-editing some of the old, and of publishing some of the new manuscripts.

Besides Emerson's own journals, these collections include many unpublished letters and journals by Emerson's relatives and friends, such as his brothers Edward and Charles, his Aunt Mary, and Margaret Fuller and Henry Thoreau. There are manuscript poems by his first wife, Ellen; letters and account books of his father, William Emerson; and many miscellaneous ledgers and memoranda. Much of this material has been used effectively by Professor Rusk in his *Life,* but much of genuine interest remains unpublished.

The manuscripts of Emerson's sermons and of his public lectures are also preserved here. Professor McGiffert[50] published only twenty-five out of about one hundred and seventy sermons, in 1938. And the lectures remain largely unpublished, although both Cabot and Rusk have summarized them effectively. Since these lectures were often experimental or preliminary formulations of the later essays, their importance is obvious. Selections of these will undoubtedly be published in the future. Especially interesting are those on "Natural History" dating from as early as 1833.

Finally, the collection in the Houghton Library includes the greater part of Emerson's letters. Although almost all of these have been published,[51] many important manuscripts, such as those of the famous Emerson-Carlyle correspondence, and many letters written to Emerson by various friends and relatives, remain unpublished.

Yet, however rich a variety of Emerson's manuscripts remains unpublished and of interest to the special student, the published writings have been well selected and they, only, concern the general reader.

49. H. A. Pochmann, "The Emerson Canon," *University of Toronto Quarterly,* XII (July 1943), 478-84.

50. A. C. McGiffert, Jr., *Young Emerson Speaks.*

51. See especially *The Letters of R. W. Emerson,* edited in six volumes by R. L. Rusk (New York, 1939).

## Method and Style

The problem of form in Emerson's writing is even more difficult than the problem of idea. Just as Emerson began with the conventional logic of theology and philosophy but soon "transcended" it for intuitive thought, so he began with the conventional method of composing sermons and addresses but soon transcended it for "spontaneous" or "organic" expression. Or so it seems. Many critics believe that Emerson abandoned all method and form in his mature essays. But others believe that "Emerson's Literary Method"[52] can be defined sharply. Still others (including the present writer) believe that Emerson had different literary methods which he used in different essays according to need.

As usual, Emerson was his own severest critic, and constantly condemned his own writing for its formlessness, describing each sentence as an "infinitely repellent particle." He toyed with the title of "Forest Essays," each essay and each idea seeming a separate tree. Carlyle repeated the criticism by comparing his friend's essays to canvas bags of buck-shot—each sentence carefully rounded and weighty, but each atomically separate. And certainly Emerson's philosophy of individualism and intuition logically justified this atomic literary method. If the isolated flash of insight is all-important, "conscious" form is unimportant. Or, if the best art is organic, each separate idea should naturally grow into its own individual form, without the conscious shaping of the author.

On the other hand, Emerson's early sermons, addresses, and essays are often methodically organized: Parts I, II, III; Sections 1, 2, 3, 4, etc. *Nature,* his earliest book, is most consciously patterned. Even "Self-Reliance" still lists some arguments by number. And "Experience" in the *Second Series* can be briefed with assurance,[54] even though the numerical guideposts have been omitted. Clearly, Emerson often intended a definite pattern; and often a natural pattern clearly persisted, even if unconsciously.

In general, Emerson's least friendly critics have found the least literary method in his essays, though most have found some. F. O.

52. Walter Blair and Clarence Faust, "Emerson's Literary Method," *Modern Philology,* XLII (Nov., 1944), 79-95.

54. See above.

Matthiessen defined the bare minimum: "Since his chief preoccupation was to demonstrate identity beneath all manner of variety, his formula for an essay was an abstraction instanced by an indefinite number of embodiments."[55] And all agree that Emerson's method was, in its simplest form, to define an idea (or a set of ideas) and then to illustrate it in various ways.

But this "method" is too simple and too obvious, being inevitable to any discussion of ideas. Emerson's literary method can be defined with more significance—and still with assurance—as that of describing and illustrating an idea (or set of ideas) from two or more points of view—from the idealistic and from the realistic, *sub specie aeternitatis* and *sub specie temporis*. Being both a transcendental idealist and a Yankee realist, Emerson considered every idea both from the point of view of God (eternity) and of man (time). Although the idealist usually dominated, the realist usually spoke up for the loyal opposition. Therefore, Emerson's essays seldom remain static expositions of an abstract idea, followed by concrete illustrations; but achieve the vitality of polemic statement and counterstatement.

In its most complex form, "Emerson's Literary Method" has been analyzed and illustrated by Walter Blair and Clarence Faust,[56] and has been fathered upon Plato and his theory of "the twice-bisected line." As everyone knows, Plato sharply distinguished between the ideal and the real, especially in his parable of the cave: men see only the shadows or appearances of objects, and often mistake the shadows for realities. But Plato again divided between men's thinking about these shadows of things (which give fallible "opinions"), and their thinking about the realities behind these shadows (which give "truth"). The visible, or physical, world is divided into shadows and realities; the invisible, or intelligible, world is again "bisected" into opinions and truths. Emerson noted this theory in his reading of Plato: Professors Blair and Faust argue that Emerson adopted this theory as a method and used it constantly in the organization of his own thinking and writing.

Take, for instance, Emerson's essay on "The Poet." The first nine paragraphs describe the ideal poet, or "sayer" of truth, in

55. F. O. Matthiessen, *American Renaissance*, p. 66.
56. Blair and Faust, *loc. cit.*

contrast to the versifier of fantasies. Paragraphs ten to thirty-five then describe the materials of poetry, contrasting nature as significant language, with nature as insignificant facts: "What would be base, or even obscene, to the obscene, becomes illustrious, spoken in a new connection of thought." Finally, the last five paragraphs criticize existing poetry for its failure to suggest the true meaning of those "facts" which seem "obscene" or ugly (i.e. "the factory village" and its machinery); and for its false emphasis upon merely pretty facts and upon merely metrical verse. Thus the essay first contrasts ideal truth with fanciful opinion; then contrasts facts seen by the true poet (as if from the point of view of God) with the "pretty" facts that appeal to the fancy of man; and finally applies this division concretely to the problem of contemporary poetry.

Often, of course, Emerson reverses this "method" and considers the "commodity" of "nature" and the "illusions" of human "experience" first, before describing the ideal aspects of Nature and of the human Spirit. The poem "Each and All" follows the same pattern as the essay on "The Poet," but in reverse order. And the early *Nature* does the same. The essay on "Experience," which follows "The Poet," also reverses the order. But whether Emerson's essays move from actual to ideal, or from ideal to actual, they always describe their subjects from two (or more) points of view. Like a stereopticon picture, they give the impression of three-dimensional reality even to the most abstract subjects by examining them from different angles.

Many years ago, John J. Chapman described this psychological method in simpler language: "Emerson's method is, not to give a generalization and trust to our making the allowance, but to give two conflicting statements and leave the balance of truth to be struck in our own minds by the facts."[57] If we add that Emerson usually illustrated each "conflicting" generalization by reference to concrete experience and that he usually advocated one "generalization" (e.g. self-reliance) over its opposite, we have a fair statement of his usual method.

Sometimes, however, Emerson's method was less purposeful. Sometimes he developed an idea by expanding it in more and more general terms. This method has been related to his essay,

57. Quoted by O. W. Firkins, *Emerson*, p. 251.

"Circles," which describes each larger circle including more and more territory. Sometimes he treated his ideas almost entirely "*sub specie aeternitatis,* and therefore not subject to the time element."[58]

And sometimes Emerson's method was almost entirely psychological, rather than logical. W. T. Harris described this as "unfolding a subject according to its natural growth in experience,"[59] rather than logic. However, this usually approximated the "logical" method of beginning with specific experiences in time and progressing to a generalized statement of truth, or "idea." *Nature* followed this method, purposefully.

But whatever Emerson's methods, one must admit that the essays do lack "art," in the sense of aesthetic (rather than philosophic, or polemic) form. W. C. Brownell called it "the style of a writer who is artistic but not an artist."[60] And this lack of art may be related to Emerson's basic training and purpose: he was primarily a man of religion, a philosopher, or a moralist, before being an artist; and his purpose was to argue persuasively and to express clearly what he conceived to be the truth, rather than to present it beautifully. Moreover, his actual method of composition—from personal journals through informal lectures to final essays—encouraged the accumulation, the rewriting, and the ordering of successive, separate ideas and sentences, rather than the aesthetic formulation of perfect works of prose art.

Emerson's style, like his method, was highly personal, as well as informal. Henry James complained (as we have seen) that he had "only one style"; and many critics have decried the excessive use of the "first person singular." Emerson both practiced and preached the theory that "what is true in your own heart is true for all men": he both saw and described the world as "saturated with his own humors." His style was an extension of his own theory; it is also an integral part of the universal theory of the personal essay, as opposed to drama and to fiction. Like other masters of the essay—Bacon, Montaigne, Charles Lamb—Emerson

58. See W. T. Harris, "Ralph Waldo Emerson," *Atlantic Monthly,* L (Aug., 1882), 238-52.

59. W. T. Harris, "The Dialectic Unity of Emerson's Prose," in *Journal of Speculative Philosophy,* XVIII (April, 1884), 195-202.

60. W. C. Brownell, *American Prose Masters,* p. 184.

used one personal style because the prose essay as a literary form has always been essentially personal, and not dramatic or narrative.

Perhaps the greatest virtue of his style is that it was not merely personal, but also—in a special sense—"colloquial." As Brownell said: "What he wrote has the vitality of the spoken word. Every sentence is addressed to the mind directly."[61]—Not "colloquial" in the sense of slangy, but of "spoken" rather than written, this quality resulted naturally from his training and practice as preacher and lecturer. Two of his greatest essays were actually "addresses." If he used the words and discussed the subjects of religion and philosophy, he spoke with the idiom and emphasis of the common man, directly. Therefore, just as his literary method reproduced the dynamic tension of the speaker, so did his style.

Of course, this "spoken" style has the faults of its virtues. There are many passages of pure, unadulterated rhetoric. And even his most eloquent sentences often follow the patterns of conventional oratory: "Not so, brothers and friends—please God, ours shall not be so." Worse still to the modern taste, he often remembers the phrases of the preacher—as in the sentence just quoted. Rhetoric, oratory, preaching, all contributed their conventions to the formation of his style.

But besides avoiding these conventional patterns by means of his feeling for the natural rhythms and emphases of common speech, his style also evidenced his feeling for the natural meaning of individual words. "No writer," said Brownell, "ever possessed a more distinguished verbal instinct, or indulged it with more delight."[62] "Words" became actual "things" in his style, as well as in his philosophy. From his earliest discussion of "Nature as Language" to his latest essay on "Farming" he used words—not like an artist perhaps—but like a pragmatic artificer, remembering their material and instrumental value.

Therefore, in spite of its individual singularity, its formal oratory, and its occasional colloquialism, his style at best achieves an intensity of feeling and a concentration of meaning which makes it sometimes proverbial, sometimes epigrammatic. "Emer-

61. Brownell, *op. cit.*, p. 181.
62. Brownell, *op. cit.*, p. 182.

son aspired toward two traits or qualities of style, the intense and the organic. To multiply significance, to charge words with the quality of things—this was the aim."[63] Like the buckshot to which Carlyle compared them, his words often have terrific impact. His style, at best, achieved "the intense."—As to "the organic"—that quality belongs rather to his philosophy of art, or poetics.[64]

## The Poetry

First and last Emerson was a poet. His first recorded literary composition was a poem, "Fortus,"[65] written at the age of ten. Often he "spouted" poetry at Boston Latin School. At Harvard he was chosen class poet, and a "Freshman Poem" of his has recently been published.[66] Besides many poems in magazines, he published two complete volumes of poetry in his lifetime: *Poems,* in 1847; and *May Day and Other Pieces,* in 1867. Most of his essays were prefaced with poetic mottoes, and he translated many poems from foreign languages. In his old age he edited an anthology of poems, entitled *Parnassus* (1874). And his own poem, "Terminus," celebrated symbolically the end of his creative literary life.

As to the excellence and permanent value of his poetry, however, there has always been greater disagreement than of his prose. Some critics have judged him a greater poet than prose writer. Others have judged his poetry inferior. His best poems have been more highly praised and his worst poems more completely damned than any of his essays. But there has always been a significant agreement as to the characteristic virtues and faults of his poetry, and which of his poems are best.

G. E. Woodberry summarized it neatly: "The *Poems* are a more brief and condensed form of the *Essays,* in many respects a far finer form, and for that reason they appeal less broadly to men. The thought gains in brilliancy and external beauty by being given under the forms of imagination"[67]—rather than of

63. O. W. Firkins, *op. cit.,* p. 268.
64. See Part II, Section on "Poetic Theory."
65. Published in H. H. Furness, ed., *Records of a Lifelong Friendship* (Boston, 1910).
66. Tremaine McDowell, "A Freshman Poem by Emerson," *PMLA,* XLV (March, 1930), 326-29.
67. G. E. Woodberry, *Emerson,* p. 159.

logic. Being more condensed than his prose, the poems express the quintessence of his thought, without that tedium of continuity and slow development at which he was never especially skillful anyway. Being frankly imaginative and symbolic, rather than logical, they excel at those very characteristics at which he himself excelled. In general, critics who value imagination above logic have preferred the poetry, but those who value logical thought above symbolic suggestion have judged the poetry inferior.[68]

Emerson's short poems have proved more popular than the long with many readers for the same reasons that the poems have often seemed better than the essays. The brief poems which describe a single symbol, or illustrate a single idea, or tell a single parable, or narrate a single experience, have sometimes achieved perfection of form, as well as of phrase. And to a greater degree than the prose, single lines or stanzas of the poems have seemed memorable and easily separable from the text. Some of the short poems and some of the verses or stanzas of the long poems are perfect by themselves because poetry may deal with single images and symbols, whereas prose is by nature more diffuse and discursive.

Five short poems of Emerson may be said to have achieved perfection, each of its own kind: "Brahma," "Days," "The Rhodora," "The Snow-Storm," and "Concord Hymn." And curiously each represents a different kind of poetry and each kind is typical of Emerson. These are: the philosophical, the personal, nature generalized, nature described, and the patriotic or occasional. These five poems have been anthologized most often, and the first two have been praised and analyzed most often by modern critics (excepting perhaps two of his longer poems).

To discover the critical popularity of Emerson's poems, the present writer collated thirteen typical anthologies (either of "American Literature" or of "Modern Poetry") all published in the twentieth century. "Brahma" was reprinted most often (12); then "Days," "Rhodora," and "The Snow-Storm" (11); "Concord Hymn," "Each and All," "The Problem," "The Humble-Bee" and "Ode [to Channing]" (10); "Terminus" (9); "Uriel," "Woodnotes I," "Give All to Love," "Apology," "Two Rivers" and "Hamatreya"

68. See O. W. Firkins, *Emerson*, p. 274.

(7); "The Sphinx," "Forbearance" and "Fable" (6). But these are all relatively short poems, chosen perhaps with an eye to space. Dr. R. E. Amacher,[69] studying "Emerson's Literary Reputation," listed ten poems "roughly in order of esteem by the critics": "Threnody," "Woodnotes," "Days," "Concord Hymn," "Brahma," "Rhodora," "The Snow-Storm," "The Humble-Bee," "Each and All," and "The Problem." The first two longer poems, "Threnody" and "Woodnotes," obviously have been praised and discussed by critics more than they have been read by the public. —Otherwise the order is the same.

Considered according to subject Emerson's poems fall into four groups: nature, personal experience, philosophical (or moral), and political (or occasional). His prosody and general poetics will be discussed in a later section.

*The Individual Poems:* Emerson's first volume of *Poems* (1847) began with "The Sphinx," but Edward Emerson deferred to popular opinion and began the Centenary Edition (volume IX) of the collected *Poems* with "Good-Bye." Since the latter was the first, chronologically, that Emerson wrote and published, the choice has seemed fitting. From 1839, when "Good-Bye" and three others were published in *The Western Messenger,* through the four years of *The Dial,* many of these poems had appeared in various magazines.

"Good-Bye," written at the age of twenty, expressed an exaggerated, youthful rebellion which has often been misunderstood and which caused Emerson to withhold it later from his *Selected Poems* (1876). But, of course, the "proud world" is only another name for that "society" which he attacked in "Self-Reliance." As poetry, the diction is often conventional and trite.

"Each and All" is a skillfully constructed philosophical poem, illustrating concretely one of Emerson's favorite ideas, of "unity in variety," borrowed originally from Plato. Analysis reveals a clear pattern:[70] the first lines (1-12) describe the relation of "each to each"; the middle lines (13-36) describe the relation of "each to all" (each thing is beautiful, if seen in its proper place

69. In an unpublished doctoral dissertation, *The Literary Reputation of R. W. Emerson,* 1882-1945 (Pittsburgh, 1945).

70. W. Blair and C. Faust, "Emerson's Literary Method," *Modern Philology,* XLII (Nov., 1944), 79-95.

in the whole); while the final lines (37-51) suggest the beauty of the whole. Beginning with the individual's point of view, it progresses (typically) toward the point of view of God—of "the perfect whole."

"The Problem" is one of Emerson's most successful philosophical poems describing "the problem" of artistic creation, as contrasted with clerical, routine formalism—"the poet" is contrasted with "the priest." Together with Emerson's essay on "The Poet," this expresses vividly his "organic" philosophy of art, which he first found in Coleridge. The poem contains many memorable lines: Edward Emerson called it "better known and more often quoted than any other which Mr. Emerson wrote."[71] But many of the best lines were the product of continuous revision. (Dr. Strauch[72] has shown how Emerson steadily improved the poem through four or more rewritings.) Irving Babbitt, critical leader of the new humanists, often quoted the couplet:

These temples grew as grows the grass;
Art might obey, but not surpass.

to illustrate the *reductio ad absurdum* of the romantic, or "organic" philosophy of art.

"Uriel" describes, in the form of a parable, two things: the philosophy of the relativity of good and evil, which Emerson had announced in his "Divinity School Address," and his own personal experience of "sad self-knowledge," or disillusion, which followed his proclamation of this heresy, or "infidelity."[73] W. T. Harris has analyzed the philosophy of the poem, relating it to "Emerson's Orientalism"[74] and to "Brahma."

"The Sphinx," Emerson's own favorite, and the subject of endless conjecture and criticism in his own lifetime, seems less popular and less interesting now. "Each and All" and "Brahma" deal with the same general idea more clearly and effectively.[75]

71. See *Works,* IX, 405.

72. Carl F. Strauch, *A Critical and Variorum Edition of the Poems of Emerson* (unpublished dissertation; Yale, 1946).

73. See above, and the unpublished thesis of Stephen E. Whicher, *The Lapse of Uriel.*

74. In *The Genius and Character of Emerson,* ed. F. B. Sanborn, pp. 381-84.

75. See also R. L. Rusk, *Life of Emerson,* pp. 312-14.

"Hamatreya" was inspired by a passage from the *Vishnu Purana.*[76] Its metrical variety is striking and suggests the sharp contrast between oriental mysticism and Yankee realism, which the poem describes explicitly. Its first lines have seemed prophetic of the modern, Yankee poetry of Robert Frost.

"The Rhodora" was written in 1834 and represents the traditional aspect of Emerson's writings, both by its eighteenth century techniques of diction, metre, and rhyme and by its explicit moral idealism.[77] Nevertheless, it achieves a kind of personal simplicity and directness. It has often been criticized by those who admire the modernism of some of Emerson's other, later poems, yet its honest traditionalism has kept it a favorite with popular readers.

"The Humble-Bee," written after 1837 (when a *Journal* entry described the experience and outlined the idea behind the poem), makes a perfect contrast to "The Rhodora."[78] Where "The Rhodora" was traditional, simple, and explicit in its idealism, "The Humble-Bee" is modern and symbolic, and suggests its idea only by implication. Indeed, "The Humble-Bee" implies much by its very title, which is unusual enough. The honey-bee becomes symbolic of the poet, who gathers and distils the sweetness of nature for man, yet does so almost by instinct, "humbly," without the pride of conscious intellect. (This idea of instinctive creation is also described in "Spiritual Laws" and "The Problem.") The diction and metre and rhyme of the poem are irregular and complex, in absolute contrast to "The Rhodora:"

> Zigzag steerer, desert cheerer,
> Let me chase thy waving lines.

But, if the complex symbolic modernism of "The Humble-Bee" has made it interesting and suggestive to modern critics, the popular reader still prefers the simple traditionalism of "The Rhodora."

"The Snow-Storm," which has proved one of Emerson's most successful poems, stands midway between the traditional and the modern in its poetic practice. Like "The Rhodora" it is traditional in metre and simple in its description of nature. But like "The

76. See F. I. Carpenter, *Emerson and Asia*, pp. 121 ff.
77. See F. O. Matthiessen, *American Renaissance*, pp. 48-49.
78. See Thomas G. Henney, *The Craft of Genius* (unpublished thesis; Princeton, 1946), for a detailed analysis.

Humble-Bee" it implies its complex idea (especially in the second part) without ever descending to explicit philosophizing. It achieves perfection in that most difficult of forms, the blank-verse lyric. (See also, "Days.") Yet it changes and syncopates its pentameter:

> Built in an age, the mad wind's night-work,

to suggest the changes of the storm, and the changes of idea from the eternal ("an age") to the temporal ("night-work"). The poem directly inspired Whittier's "Snow-Bound," for which it supplied the poetic motto. A comparison of these two poems does much to suggest the difference between the concentrated, suggestive power of a major poet like Emerson, and the discursive, homely popularity of a minor poet like Whittier. But, partly because of its very concentration and multiple meaning, "The Snow-Storm" has never been as widely popular as "Snow-Bound."

"Woodnotes," together with "Threnody," has proved Emerson's most successful long poem. Professor Cestre has called it "le chef d'oeuvre d'Emerson."[79] It suggests, or describes poetically, his philosophy of nature. Joseph Warren Beach[80] has praised it as "Emerson's great comprehensive nature poem" and has analyzed it in detail. Like his first book on *Nature,* this poem includes all aspects of his literary and philosophical thought: Emerson's observation and study of nature, the beauty of nature, its wholesome, sanative influence on human life, and its universality or idealism. And, like *Nature,* the poem is divided sharply into two parts—the first concrete and real, the second philosophical and ideal. "Woodnotes I" describes external nature concretely and draws the portrait of "a forest seer" which has usually been identified with Thoreau, although the portrait is obviously not fully individualized. Because of its vivid poetic imagery and concrete characterization this first part has proved more popular and successful poetically than "Woodnotes, II" which describes the typically Emersonian idea that only by reference of the part

79. Charles Cestre, "Emerson Poète," *Études Anglaises,* IV (Jan., 1940), 9.

80. J. W. Beach, *The Concept of Nature in Nineteenth Century Poetry,* Chapter XII. See also Part III of this *Handbook,* "Experience and Nature." Its less philosophic aspects have been discussed by Van Wyck Brooks in *The Flowering of New England.*

(man) to the whole of nature can man realize her beauty and his own share in it.[81]

"Ode (Inscribed to W. H. Channing)" is typical of many of Emerson's poems: it is excellent in parts and brilliantly epigrammatic, but imperfect as a whole. Its greatness lies chiefly in the famous lines which contrast "Law for man and law for thing." As a whole, it restates Emerson's *apologia* for refusing to become a "New England Reformer" or to enter into politics: "Everyone to his chosen work."

"Give All to Love" is perhaps Emerson's best statement of his philosophy of love, which is fundamentally Platonic. It may be read and compared with his longer poem, "Initial, Daemonic, and Celestial Love," and with his essay on "Love." His idea, suggested by the title of the second poem, is that there are three levels of human love: the physical ("Initial"), the romantic ("Daemonic"), and the ideal, or suprapersonal ("Celestial"). The title, "Give All to Love," is used ironically to suggest the romantic ideal of love which Emerson described as partial and as a dangerous "half-god." The concluding lines of his poem on "Daemonic Love" were quoted by the modern poet, Robinson Jeffers, as a motto for his early *Californians:*

> And ever the Daemonic Love
> Is the ancestor of wars
> And the parent of remorse.

"Bacchus" is a poem which has appealed greatly to a few excellent critics but which has obvious flaws and has never been popular. G. E. Woodberry[82] called it "Emerson's most original poem" and praised it for vividly expressing that dionysiac joy and power which attracted Nietzsche (see Part IV) and which later attracted Jeffers (see preceding paragraph). In "Bacchus," as in "The Humble-Bee," Emerson's method is wholly symbolic and allusive:[83] "wine" becomes the symbol of all creative inspiration and of its illuminating energy, while the imagery suggests metaphorically a fusion of physical and of mystical "illumination:"

81. See J. W. Beach, *op. cit.*, p. 352.
82. See G. E. Woodberry, *Emerson*, p. 167.
83. T. G. Henney, in his unpublished thesis *The Craft of Genius*, analyzes these two poems to explain Emerson's mature technique and to show his kinship to modern, symbolic poetry.

Wine that is shed
Like the torrents of the sun
Up the horizon walls.

"Saadi," like "Merlin," describes both Emerson's ideal poet and his poetic ideal. The Persian poet "Saadi" actually influenced him deeply, and he edited a translation of "The Gulistan, or Rose Garden" by Saadi (also spelled "Seyd"). But his "Saadi," like "Merlin," is more mystical and imagined than historical and real.[84]

"Threnody" has been praised by some critics as Emerson's best poem and is consistently good throughout its length, without ever achieving the heights of poetry. Moreover, it is one of his most skillfully planned and developed poems. Describing his grief over his son's death, it was written over many years and expresses both the mood of immediate grief, of recovery from that mood, and of philosophical consolation. It has been analyzed in detail.[85] The first half of the poem describes the feeling of loss and isolation which grief brings: Stanzas 1-2, the separation of the boy from nature; stanzas 3-4, his separation from other men; stanza 5, the resultant feeling of alienation of other men from nature; stanza 6, the feeling of the poet-father that he has lost part of himself. The second half of the poem (beginning: "The deep Heart answered, 'Weepest thou?'") describes the poet's recovery from grief through remembrance of his relation to the whole: to the "deep Heart" of nature, and of God. The movement of thought is much the same as in the poem "Each and All," but the feeling is more personal. The genuineness of this feeling of grief contrasts with the mood of revulsion described in the essay, "Experience."

*May-Day and Other Pieces* (1867) merely collects the best poems which Emerson wrote between 1847 and 1867. The quality and technique of the later poetry shows less change, perhaps, than that of the later essays.

"Brahma" is extraordinary in almost every way. It is the most often anthologized and also the most often parodied of Emerson's poems. In perfectly regular stanzas it develops an oriental idea almost entirely alien to American—and even to Western—literature and thought. Most of the lines of the poem are borrowed or re-

84. See N. F. Adkins, "Emerson and the Bardic Tradition," *PMLA* LXIII (1948), 662-677.

85. W. Blair and C. Faust, "Emerson's Literary Method," *loc. cit.*

phrased from passages in various Hindu scriptures which Emerson read at various times, yet they move with a regular poetic rhythm and logic through a regularly constructed poem. No more perfect example exists of that "Meeting of East and West" which is perhaps the most significant phenomenon of modern history.

The central idea of "Brahma" is to be found in the greatest of the Oriental scriptures, *The Bhagavad Gita.* One of the best English poetic translations of this book[86] merely borrows one of Emerson's stanzas in its original form to render a passage. Four scholarly studies have traced three other Hindu sources of the poem, have related the different lines of the poem to Hindu philosophy, and have traced the development of the poem in Emerson's *Journals.*[87]

The general idea of "Brahma" is the oriental counterpart of the Platonic idea of Unity in Variety, and is common to all mystical speculation. But the uniqueness of the poem lies in its adoption of the point of view of God—and of God conceived as the impersonal creative energy of the universe, paradoxically personified as unconcerned with the life or death of man has proved congenial the "I" of "Brahma." This concept of an impersonal God of energy to the spirit of modern science, and several great atomic scientists have been students of the *Bhagavad Gita* and of "Brahma."

The "Ode (Sung in Concord, 1857)" and the "Boston Hymn" (1863) were highly successful occasional poems, now remembered chiefly for a few perfect, but isolated, lines and stanzas—in contrast to the famous "Concord Hymn" which achieved perfection as a whole. Bliss Perry[88] tells of the tremendous emotional effect which Emerson's reading of the "Boston Hymn" had upon

86. *The Bhagavad Gita,* translated by Arthur Ryder (Chicago, 1929).

87. Carl F. Strauch, in his *Critical and Variorum Edition of the Poems of Emerson* (unpublished doctoral dissertation; Yale, 1946), has collected and collated these studies: (1) W. S. Kennedy, "Emerson's Brahma," *Boston Evening Transcript,* Aug. 6, 1886; (2) W. T. Harris, "Emerson's Brahma," *Poet Lore,* I (June 1889), 253-59; (3) D. L. Maulsby, *Emerson's Contribution to Literature* (Tufts College, 1911), pp. 123-25; (4) F. I. Carpenter, *Emerson and Asia* (Cambridge, 1930), pp. 110-22. Harris and Carpenter both analyze the ideas of the poem in detail.

88. B. Perry, *Emerson Today,* p. 88. See also C. F. Strauch, "The Background of Emerson's 'Boston Hymn,'" *American Literature,* XIV (March, 1942), 36-47.

its audience, who were gathered to celebrate Lincoln's signing of the Emancipation Proclamation.

"Days," together with "Brahma," is perhaps Emerson's most perfect poem, and with "Brahma" has most often aroused the interest and admiration of scholars and critics, especially in modern times. Like "Brahma" the poem developed gradually from suggestions and tentative fragments of prose and verse jotted down in the *Journals*, and finally crystallized itself all at once in his mind,[89] in 1851. In his *Journals* he noted with wonder: "I have written within a twelvemonth verses ("Days") which I do not remember the composition or correction of, and could not write the like today, and have only, for proof of their being mine, various external evidences, as the ms. in which I find them."

The idea of "Days," however, is much more typical of Emerson than the idea of "Brahma." Where the latter expresses the purely ideal or mystical half of Emerson's thought, "Days" suggests its duality of ideal and real. Where "Brahma" was written from the point of view of God, "Days" was written from the point of view of man—specifically of the Yankee Emerson. But, typically, "Days" suggests both points of view and structurally is divided into two parts: the first six lines personify the "Days" as demigods who offer the gifts of life to mortals; then the last five lines describe Emerson's dual consciousness—first his actual failure to realize the value of these gifts, and then his ideal recognition of this mortal failure.

Thus "Days" becomes a kind of poetic parable of the tragic mortality of man and appeals particularly to those who see life in terms of human tragedy,[90] rather than of divine comedy. In "Days" Emerson the Yankee farmer—who happened also to be a poet—suggested his own frequent feelings of failure. In his later essay, "Works and Days," he developed the same parable and the same idea in realistic prose. But—because he was a transcendental poet and idealist before being a Yankee farmer—"Days," like the

89. Egbert S. Oliver, "Emerson's 'Days,'" *New England Quarterly*, XIX (Dec., 1946), 518-24, traces the gradual development of the poem through the *Journals* and *Letters*.

90. F. O. Matthiessen, in *American Renaissance*, pp. 58-64, analyzes "Days" effectively and praises it highly in contrast to what he describes as a "pseudo-mysticism."

final essay "Illusions," achieves greatness by emphasizing the god-like potentialities of man, who in moments of illumination can see beyond his human illusions and achieve the point of view of God.

"Terminus," Emerson's final poem,[91] also achieves excellence by suggesting this typical dualism of experience and thought. The poem first personifies "The god of bounds" and speaks from his point of view; and then, at the end, affirms the mortal poet's obedience to this immortal "voice."

"Poems of Youth and Early Manhood" and other poems are included as appendices to the complete *Poems* (volume IX) of the Centenary Edition. Two early poems are especially remarkable for their expression of a traditional idealism which Emerson accepted in youth, but which he later repudiated. "Thought," written in 1823, expressed an anti-pragmatic enthusiasm for the pure intellect which he contradicted in 1837 in "The American Scholar," and frequently afterwards.

"Grace," written between 1831 and 1833, is a more interesting and important poem. It expresses a traditional praise of that "grace" of God which protects man from his own sinfulness, which Emerson's later philosophy of "Self-Reliance" was to qualify if not contradict.[92] It may have been suggested by his reading of a Swedenborgian article on "External Restraint," or by his reading of Milton, or both. But "Grace" uses both an imagery and an idea of external "defences" which protect "me against myself," which is entirely opposite to the imagery and idea of "Self-Reliance." Professor Elliott therefore declares that in youth "Emerson saw that his self-reliance was due to his ancestors"[93] and to their Puritan tradition. It might be more accurate to say that in youth "Emerson saw that his self-reliance was partly due to his ances-

91. Carl F. Strauch, "The Date of Emerson's 'Terminus,'" *PMLA*, (June, 1950), 360-70, proves that the poem, like many others, was not written all at once, but was rather the product of long preparation, unconscious thought, and conscious revision.

92. See G. R. Elliott, "On Emerson's 'Grace' and 'Self-Reliance,'" *New England Quarterly*, II (Jan., 1929), 92-105. See also C. P. Hotson, "A Background for Emerson's Poem 'Grace,'" *New England Quarterly*, I (April, 1928), 124-32.

93. G. R. Elliott, *op. cit.*, p. 97.

tors;" but that later he saw further, that any man who hides behind the "defences" of his ancestors and their tradition, forfeits his manhood.

### Aesthetic and Poetic Theory

Emerson's prosody, or practice of poetry, was closely related to his poetics, or theory of poetry; and this, in turn, to his aesthetics or theory of art. But where his theory of poetry was almost identical with his theory of art (his "poet" being the prototype of all artists) his practice of poetry was often at odds with his theory of poetry. That is—he preached fairly consistently, but he often failed to practice what he preached.

Until recently when the manuscript versions of his poems were made available to scholars, Emerson's method of composing verse, and the variant forms of his poems were little studied. Critics sometimes accepted at face value his statements that he composed spontaneously and sometimes overlooked his revisions, in spite of the fact that his published *Journals* often included many variants of poems and that the earlier magazine forms often differed considerably from the later forms published in his collected *Poems.* Recently Dr. Carl F. Strauch has completed a critical and variorum edition of his poetry[94] which establishes several important facts.

"Few poets have kept such an astonishing mass of manuscripts, and few have exposed so completely in rough drafts the secrets of their poetic art. . . . A good half of Emerson's manuscripts reveal crude work and painful improvement."[95] Even the best poems often started poorly. For instance, "The Problem" was continuously improved by revision. The couplet which now reads:

> The hand that rounded Peter's dome
> And groined the aisles of Christian Rome

originally read:

> The hand that curved St. Peter's dome
> And the dread piles of Christian Rome

94. C. F. Strauch, *A Critical and Variorum Edition of the Poems of Emerson* (Yale, 1946). This doctoral dissertation, as yet unpublished, contains much valuable material, both as to detail and as to theory (see next two paragraphs).

95. Strauch, *op. cit.*, p. 132.

—Not only did the final version discard "the dread piles" which had been "curved"; but it substituted a new and powerful motor image—almost sexual in its suggestion of the process of artistic creation. And many other lines of "The Problem" and of other poems improved equally.

Not only did Emerson's best poems often develop thus "painfully," but sometimes their first drafts were, as Dr. Strauch says, "incredibly bad." Thus, an early version of "Terminus" (which certainly could not be excused as apprentice workmanship) originally concluded:

> And hide my age amidst my thrifty pears,
> Each fault of mine masked by a growth of theirs.

After due critical consideration, of course, Emerson excised this and composed a new conclusion in its stead.

In other words, Emerson's poetic inspiration was sometimes poor, sometimes brilliant; and usually he produced his best poems by a process of trial and error. Fortunately his critical judgment of his own poetry was good, so that the revisions almost always did produce improvement. But of course he sometimes kept poems and passages of longer poems which were mediocre or worse; and this partly accounts for the "frequent badness"[96] of his poems and for the poetic "defects so patent that schoolmasters deal with them swiftly."[97] As O. W. Holmes wrote: Emerson's poetry often resembles "the robe of a monarch, patched by a New England housewife."

Of course, Emerson clearly recognized the faults of his own poetry, as he had recognized the faults of his own character and of his own prose style. In a letter to his second wife just before their marriage he wrote: "I am born a poet; of a low class without doubt, yet a poet. . . . My singing to be sure, is very husky, and is for the most part prose. Still I am a poet."[98]

Granted the frequent faults, as well as the frequent virtues of his poetry, what is the nature of it? In the century that has passed since the publication of his first *Poems* critics have essayed many answers. And the question is still broadly significant because Em-

96. O. W. Firkins, *Emerson.*
97. Bliss Perry, *Emerson Today.*
98. J. E. Cabot, *Memoir,* I, 236.

erson's poetry stands midway between the traditional and the modern, with some of the virtues and some of the faults of each. To analyze the nature of these virtues and faults is to suggest the nature of modern poetry itself. Let us begin with the forms.

The verse forms which Emerson's poetry used were mostly traditional. The octosyllabic couplet is most common—or rather the four-stress couplet[99] for Emerson seldom observed exact regularity of metre. This form tended to produce monotony in the longer poems but had the virtue of suggesting at times the short, nervous rhythms of actual speech[100] and also of suggesting the sharp dualism of Emerson's thought, by its counterpoint of rhyme in short couplets.[101] The conventional ballad stanza appears frequently, especially in the patriotic and occasional poems. And blank verse is common although paradoxically more often used in the short lyrics and descriptive poems than in the longer, reflective poems. The heroic couplet appears particularly in the early poetry, such as "The Rhodora." But for the most part Emerson's verse forms are less significant than the liberties which he took with them.

The same is true of his metres which he treated with scant respect. Sometimes his metrical irregularity produced brilliant lines, but sometimes it produced mere confusion. Often, according to his friend Sanborn, "he purposely roughened his verse . . . as a kind of protest against the smoothness and jingle of what he called 'poetry to put round frosted cake.' "[102] Sometimes (one may infer from reading his discarded manuscripts) he wrote poor metres because he had a poor musical ear. But it is safe to say that the irregularity of his metre, whether successful or not, was usually intentional and that his metrical failures were usually the results of a metrical experimentation imperfectly controlled and judged.

Finally, Emerson's rhymes,[103] like his metres, were often irregular. His poems abound in imperfect rhymes of all varieties. "Frequently, though not consistently, irregularities in rhyme and

99. See G. W. Allen, *American Prosody*, pp. 91-127.

100. Josephine Miles, *The Primary Language of Poetry in the 1740's and 1840's*, University of California Publications in English (Berkeley: University of California Press, 1950), p. 304.

101. Allen, *loc. cit.*

102. Allen, *op. cit.*, p. 92.

103. See Kathryn A. McEuen, "Emerson's Rhymes," *American Literature*, XX (March, 1948), 30-42.

metre occur together."[104] Sometimes the irregular rhymes suggest a parallel strangeness of the thought, as in the couplet:

And mount to paradise
By the stairway of surprise.

But often, like the irregular metres, they merely confuse. And like the irregular metres the strangest rhymes were often intentional. The "rhymes" of "noon" with "Napoleon," of "arms" with "psalms," of "Nature" with "favor" are too strange to be merely careless.

Emerson often used traditional verse forms, metres and rhymes with intentional roughness, it is clear, because he considered them of secondary importance. That is—his attitude toward conventional verse, metre and rhyme was essentially negative. He stated this negation emphatically in his poem, "Merlin," where his imaginary bard described his ideal poet:

He shall not his brain encumber
With the coil of rhythm and number;
But leaving rule and pale forethought,
He shall aye climb
For his rhyme.

. . . . . . .

No jingling serenader's art,
Nor tinkle of piano strings,
Can make the wild blood start
In its mystic springs.

Abandoning traditional "rule" and "rhythm" and "rhyme" his ideal poet shall sing out:

Free, peremptory, clear.

"Free." Emerson's poetic theory, like his social theory, demanded self-reliant freedom. Free verse was its logical end-result. But just as his social practice qualified his "self-reliance" by deference to "the moral law," so his poetic practice qualified his "free" verse by deference to the poetic tradition of the past. Even "Merlin," his ideal poet, was clearly inspired by "the bardic tradition"[105] of Celtic and Anglo-Saxon poetry, which ignored the

104. *Ibid.*, p. 41.
105. N. F. Adkins, "Emerson and the Bardic Tradition," *PMLA*, LXIII (1948), 662-77.

verse forms, rhythms, and rhymes of later English poetry. Although Emerson prophesied free-verse, his poetry never practiced it.

In practice, indeed, most of Emerson's best poems remained fundamentally traditional and regular. "Brahma" is as regular as clockwork, as also the "Concord Hymn." "Days" is perfect blank verse, though subtly modulated; and "The Snow-Storm" has only slight variations. Only the less popular poems, like "The Humble-Bee" and "Bacchus," practiced consistently the symbolic suggestion and the metrical "roughness" which Emerson's theory preached.

Emerson's poetic theory, and its relation to his practice, has been studied frequently. Although there is much disagreement two facts have become clear. His poetic practice was never as liberal, or as consistently modern, as his poetic theory. But his poetic theory was consistently modern and did contrast sharply with traditional poetic theory—especially that of the eighteenth century.

In *The Craft of Genius: A Study of Emerson's Poetic Development, 1823-1846*[106] Dr. Henney has partly explained the inconsistency of Emerson's poetic practice by the fact that many of his poems were written in his youth before he had formulated his mature theory in *Nature* or had proclaimed his revolt from tradition in "The American Scholar." "Good-Bye," "The Rhodora," and "The Concord Hymn," for instance, all use conventional eighteenth century diction, metre, and rhyme without any suggestion of his later theory or practice. And many of his later poems, such as "Hamatreya," "The Humble-Bee," "Merlin," and "Bacchus," practice some of the new freedom, the symbolism and metrical irregularity which his theory proclaimed. Certainly there was a marked change in Emerson's poetic practice after 1836, corresponding to the formulation of his new theory. But his practice never achieved the poetic freedom which his theory proclaimed and which Whitman, the symbolists, and the imagists were later to achieve.

But there is general agreement that Emerson's poetic theory was original and in many ways prophetically modern. Indeed his

106. By Thomas G. Henney (unpublished doctoral dissertation; Princeton, 1946).

whole thought, beginning with the chapters on "Beauty" and "Language" in *Nature,* pointed toward a new poetics and aesthetics. His essay on "The Poet" described this most clearly and complemented his address on "The American Scholar." Where the early address had described the ideal "American Scholar" or philosopher, the later essay described the "ideal American poet" or artist; and both clarified his theory by contrast with the traditional.

Negatively, Emerson's poetic theory had attacked traditional verse-forms, metres, and rhymes for not being the essential, constituent elements of poetry. Positively he now advocated rather: ideas, symbols, and imaginative words.

> It is not metres, but a metre-making argument that makes a poem,—a thought so passionate and alive that like the spirit of a plant or an animal, it has an architecture of its own, and adorns nature with a new thing.

—The poet's "argument" or "thought" or (as he later emphasized) "experience" should dictate the form of the poem, rather than traditional techniques. The poet should express this "thought" by means of "symbols." "Things admit of being used as symbols, because nature is a symbol." And the poet should use words for their pictorial or imaginative meaning because "Nature offers all her creatures to him as a picture-language." Positively Emerson's "Poet" proclaimed that organized experience, symbolic suggestion, and imaginative language are the essentials of true poetry.

If Emerson never clearly formulated his poetic theory in logical language it was partly because he always preferred intuitive suggestion to logic, and partly because he was "too young yet by some ages to compile a code." But just as his poetic theory has been clarified by contrast with the formal theory of the eighteenth century it may also be clarified by comparison with the symbolic theory of the twentieth century.

The transition figure is Whitman. Not only did Emerson's poetic theory prophesy Whitman's "free verse"; it also prophesied his language, his feeling, and his subject-matter. Specifically, the "vocabulary" of Emerson's "Poet": "would embrace words and images excluded from polite conversation. What would be base, or ever obscene, to the obscene, becomes illustrious spoken in a new connection of thought. . . . Bare lists of words are found suggestive to an imaginative and excited mind." And Emerson went on to celebrate "the factory village and the railway"[107] as fit subjects for the new poet, prophesying that "America is a poem in our eyes . . . and it will not wait long for metres." The words, the feelings, and the subject matter of Emerson's ideal poet all were to be American, industrial, and modern.

Gradually modern criticism has groped toward the formulation of Emerson's modern poetic theory. Confusion, however, has resulted from the fact that two schools of criticism have interpreted it.[108] The traditional school, headed by Matthew Arnold and Henry James, has always praised Emerson's traditional poetry but has attacked much of his irregular poetry—and much other typically American poetry—as "illegitimate." On the other hand, many modern critics have described Emerson as the precursor of *The American Way in Poetry.*[109] Even the traditional Englishman, Richard Garnett, declared Emerson's "greatest glory as a poet to have been the harbinger of a distinctly American poetry in America."[110] Alfred Noyes praised "the subtlety" of Emerson's "music," his "subtly displaced accent" and his "anticipation of modern methods."[111] And Stuart Sherman compared Emerson to "the Chicago School of Poetry." On the other hand, Norman Foerster and the new humanists have continued the traditional criticism and interpretation.[112]

Without attempting to formulate Emerson's poetic and aesthetic theory exactly—an attempt which Emerson never made and at which many modern critics and scholars have failed—one may say that Emerson's theory emphasized two major ideas: first, the fundamentally symbolic nature of all artistic expression; and second, the organic quality all great works of art have.

Emerson's early chapter on "Language" in *Nature* had em-

107. Régis Michaud, *L'Esthétique d'Emerson,* emphasizes this modernism: "He forecast modern industrial development and the triumph of mechanical arts in the United States. He outlines an aesthetic of the machine," pp. 21-22.

108. T. G. Henney, *op. cit.,* has done much to clarify this confusion.

109. H. W. Wells, *The American Way in Poetry.*

110. R. Garnett, *Emerson* (London, 1888), p. 135.

111. Alfred Noyes, *Some Aspects of Modern Poetry* (1924), p. 65.

112. Norman Foerster, *American Criticism* (Boston, 1928), pp. 52-111.

phasized the symbolic nature of language and the pictorial or imagistic origin of all words: "*Right* means *straight; wrong* means *twisted*. . . . Every long-civilized nation," he continued, tends to abstract words from their original sensuous origins; "but wise men pierce this rotten diction and fasten words again to visible things." "The Poet," then, is merely the wisest man, who carries this process to its conclusion. Poetry is essentially "picture language." From this theory to that of Amy Lowell and the "Imagists" is a short step.

But Emerson also emphasized the partial and incomplete nature of mere imagism: " 'Things more excellent than every image,' says Jamblichus, 'can be expressed through images.' " That is, the poetic "image" should become the meaningful "symbol" and suggest the "thought" or "argument" which lies behind and goes beyond all pictorial imagery. Yet this "argument" must never become logical, explicit, and "discursive" but must remain symbolic, implicit, and "presentational." The symbol implies and suggests the "thought," which, however, is apprehended intuitively and can never be fully explained by mere logic.

This theory of the symbolic nature of language and of poetry has been developed and clarified by a modern school of philosophers and has been brilliantly summarized by Suzanne Langer in *Philosophy in a New Key*.[113] This school describes symbolism as the primary language of mankind—a language embraced first in primitive myth and poetry and continuing in various forms throughout human history, contrasting, however, with the secondary language of scientific and logical abstraction which mankind has increasingly developed for practical purposes. In modern times the development of this rational and abstract language has tended to obscure the primary importance of the original symbolic and pictorial language. Moreover, "discursive" logic and scientific definition have tended to obscure the value of that intuitive insight which works indirectly through symbols, rather than directly through rational argument. Emphasizing the dual nature of all language, *Philosophy in a New Key* unlocks many dark problems of philosophy, such as non-rational psychology and religious myth and also many problems of Emerson's poetic

113. Cambridge, Mass., 1942; New York: Penguin Books, 1948). Dr. Thomas G. Henney, *op. cit.*, develops this symbolic theory effectively.

theory. Emerson's practical rejection of conventional logic and discursive argument, for instance, becomes wholly consistent with and even necessary to his theory of the symbolic nature of poetry. In the language of modern philosophy,[114] Emerson used and valued the "presentational" or symbolic forms of art above the "discursive" or abstractive forms of logic because these forms were primary, both in history and in human psychology.

In the language of classical philosophy, this symbolic theory of poetry and art was related to the Aristotelian idea that tragic poetry is "more philosophical and highly-serious (ϛρουδαιότερον) than history"—an idea which Plato occasionally rejected but which the Neoplatonists (from whom Emerson probably developed it) enthusiastically expounded. Poetry, which communicates through symbols, is "universal"; but history and science, which describe and define explicitly, are "particular."

Emerson's transcendental philosophy, exaggerating the value of intuitive thought and symbolic language, treated history and science as branches of religion and psychology and often minimized one-half of human experience. But Emerson's poetic theory, describing symbolism as the essential language of poetry and art, reasserted a neglected truth and righted the balance which neo-classical formalism and rationalism had all but destroyed.

Even more important and prophetically modern than this symbolic theory, however, was Emerson's organic theory of art. If art is largely intuitive, working through symbols rather than reason, the work of art will develop organically in the mind of its creator, expressing the idea which potentially preexists in the symbol. So Emerson's "Poet" had described "a thought so passionate and alive that like the spirit of a plant or an animal, it has an architecture of its own." Not only poetry, but modern architecture and the plastic arts have developed this organic theory. And with good reason, because it is not merely "romantic" (as it has often been called) but derives from the fundamental Platonic concept of preexistent, archetypal ideas. Moreover, it merges with the scientific concept of natural law and natural

114. See S. Langer, *Philosophy in a New Key,* Chapter IV, "Discursive and Presentational Forms."

forms; as Emerson suggested in the motto of the second edition of *Nature:*

And, striving to be man, the worm
Mounts through all the spires of form.

This organic theory of art, however, because it is so universal, has often seemed vague and indefinite. An excellent study of Emerson's aesthetic theory[115] has recently sought to define its component ideas.

First, the organic theory holds that a work of art should imitate projects and patterns in nature. So Emerson's poem, "The Snow-Storm," described "The frolic architecture of the snow." More obviously art should imitate the purely organic forms of nature: modern architecture, for instance, has often sought to design houses on the organic analogy of trees. Clearly the classic theory of the "imitation of nature" has always implied this idea. But modern theory has developed it in extreme forms.

More moderately, Emerson's organic theory of art praised "the development of details in a work according to one controlling purpose."[116] It attacked the prevailing neo-classic theory of ornamentation, with its accompanying emphasis on rhyme in poetry and on decoration in architecture. Emerson declared flatly that "outside embellishment is deformity . . . Our taste in building . . . refuses pilasters and columns that support nothing, and allows the real supporters of the house honestly to show themselves."[117] If the gingerbread architecture of the late nineteenth century ignored Emerson's theory of organic art, modern architecture has progressively realized it. And the aesthetic theory of John Dewey has developed it philosophically.

More significantly this organic theory of art has contributed to the modern idea of functionalism. Positively a "controlling purpose" will create "an architecture of its own." If this pragmatic idea of functional form has sometimes contradicted the other "organic" idea of the imitation of natural forms, the two have often been associated in practice. Of the two, the theory that

115. Vivian C. Hopkins, *Spires of Form* (Cambridge, Mass., 1951), pp. 64-77.
116. *Ibid.*, p. 67.
117. *Works,* VI, 290-91, essay on "Beauty."

form should be dictated by inner purpose is the more important both to Emerson and to modern aesthetic theory.

Beyond poetry Emerson's "organic" theory has thus contributed significantly to the development of the modern arts in America, particularly architecture.[118] As we have seen, Emerson used many examples from architecture to describe his theory of "Beauty." His artist friend, Horatio Greenough,[119] helped to inspire many of his aesthetic ideas. The great leaders of modern American architecture, Louis H. Sullivan and Frank Lloyd Wright,[120] have avowed their debt to him through his disciple Whitman. Although in practice Emerson was sometimes insensitive and sometimes blind to certain aspects of the fine arts,[121] his aesthetic theory was extraordinarily progressive and modern.

Finally, Emerson's aesthetic theory was integrally related to the whole of his thought. It emphasized that aesthetic form was not separate from life: form is not determined by the classic "unities," nor by the neo-classic rules of art, but rather is created by the imaginative insight of the artist and is intended pragmatically to stimulate in the observer a similar imaginative experience. Actually, Emerson's aesthetic theory minimized the importance of conscious form—"organic" form is often not self-conscious. Rather he emphasized the fundamental importance of the subjective aesthetic experience, both for the artist and the audience.[122]

Although Emerson's theory of organic form in art has influenced modern thought, actually he had most to say about the primary phase of aesthetic theory—that of creation by the artist. "Inspiration," "Imagination," and "Expression" were his themes—and

118. See Vivian C. Hopkins, *op. cit.*, Chapter II, "Organic Form in the Fine Arts."

119. F. O. Matthiessen, *American Renaissance*, "The Organic Principle," pp. 133-78.

120. See Part IV.

121. See Donald MacRae, "Emerson and the Fine Arts," *Art Bulletin*, XX (March 1938), 93.

122. The distinction of the three phases of aesthetic theory in Emerson's work has been excellently described by Vivian C. Hopkins in *Spires of Form* under the titles: "The Creative Process," "The Work of Art," and "The Aesthetic Experience." The same three phases have been distinguished and illustrated for the whole field of literary criticism in the recent anthology: *Criticism: The Foundations of Modern Literary Judgment*, ed. Mark Schorer, Josephine Miles, Gordon McKenzie (New York, 1948).

often his titles—in writing about "Beauty" or "Art." To him "Inspiration" was the source, not merely of artistic creation, but of all psychological and physical activity—the source of that influx of "Power" which is distinctly human. And "Imagination" he described as "symbolic sight"—the means by which man understands and interprets the "Language" of *Nature.* Finally, he valued "Expression" highly—perhaps too highly—because of its subjective importance. So Ludwig Lewisohn's *Expression in America* quotes Emerson's extreme statement: "Expression is all we need—not knowledge, but vent." Yet seen in perspective Emerson's description of the subjective processes by which the artist creates applies also to the processes by which the observer appreciates the work of art.

In the final phase of the aesthetic process Emerson compares the observer of the art-form to the artist himself: the reader of a poem or the audience of a tragedy is moved and inspired by the experience of the art-form in much the same way that the poet or artist was first inspired by the beautiful forms of nature. Indeed the audience may experience the same "ecstasy" that the artist himself experienced—Emerson's lyrical description of his and Margaret Fuller's response to the ballet of Fanny Ellsler is only an extreme example. Emerson, therefore, often described the aesthetic experience psychologically, much as William James later described the *Varieties of Religious Experience.* Through a kind of empathic identification with the artist and/or his creation, the observer achieves ideally an almost mystical aesthetic experience.

Thus Emerson's aesthetic theory, like his whole philosophy, was based upon a kind of mysticism.[123] The significance of art lies in the fact that the art-form is an embodiment of the aesthetic experience of its author, which (ideally) will move its audience to similar experience. At best, this aesthetic experience will approximate the religious, or mystical, experience: it will produce a kind of ecstasy which will raise the participant above the moods and "illusions" of daily life and allow him to see life as a whole. Art, therefore, may be defined as man's translation of the symbolic language of Nature into organic forms which he can intuitively apprehend.

123. See Part III, "Mysticism."

At the climax of his essay on "The Poet" Emerson specifically compared poetry with mysticism: "Here is the difference betwixt the poet and the mystic, that the last nails a symbol to one sense. . . ."—The poet, that is, suggests all the manifold symbolism of nature, whereas the mystic (in Emerson's rather special use of the word) attempts rather to allegorize and to moralize. Emerson's aesthetic theory thus freed itself from the moralism of his Puritan ancestry, yet allied itself to that mystical piety which was the core of the old religion.[124] Emerson's God, like the deity of Jonathan Edwards, became a kind of supreme artist creating the world with a mystical appreciation of its beauty.

Emerson's ideal poet, or artist, therefore, was the mystic who possessed both the power of appreciating the whole beauty of nature and of translating that beauty into symbolic language. The traditional mystic could appreciate but not adequately translate the beauty. The traditional poet could describe separate aspects of the beauty but (like Emerson's "Shakespeare") could not envision the whole. No wonder that Emerson looked "in vain for the poet whom I describe." He was—in the words of Irving Babbitt—"a golden impossibility."[125] But Emerson's ideal poet was truly "golden"—the ideal embodiment of a valid and consistent aesthetic theory.

## Selected Bibliography: Part II

The following Bibliography includes only items concerning the text of Emerson's Prose and Poetry, and his Poetic Theory. For items concerning his Biography, his Ideas, and his Reading and Reputation, see Bibliographies at ends of Parts I, III and IV.

### Text

For chronological lists of Emerson's separate works and early editions of his collected works see: G. W. Cooke, *A Bibliography of R. W. Emerson* (Boston, 1908). For lists of later editions, selections and collections see: Spiller, Thorp, Johnson, and Canby,

124. See Vivian C. Hopkins, *Spires of Form*, pp. 12, 19. A comparison of the strangely similar combinations of Puritanism and mysticism in the aesthetic theories of Jonathan Edwards and of Emerson has often been suggested but never developed in detail.

125. Irving Babbitt, *Masters of Modern French Criticism* (Boston, 1912), p. 392.

*Literary History of the United States* (New York, 1948), Bibliography (vol. III, pp. 492-94).

The following Bibliography is selective, including only the standard editions.

*The Complete Works of Ralph Waldo Emerson* (Boston: Houghton, Mifflin and Co., 1903-04). Centenary Edition. 12 vols. (This is the standard edition of Emerson's Works. Detailed "Notes" at the end of every volume by Emerson's son, Edward Waldo Emerson, and an Index at the end of the last volume, add to the value of this collection.)

*Uncollected Writings: Essays, Addresses, Poems, Reviews and Letters by Ralph Waldo Emerson* (New York, 1912). Ed. by Charles C. Bigelow. 208 pp. (Contains many essays and reviews reprinted from the *Dial,* and miscellaneous other material.)

*The Journals of Ralph Waldo Emerson,* ed. by Edward Waldo Emerson and Waldo Emerson Forbes (Boston: 1909-1914). 10 vols. (This is the standard edition of the *Journals* in the same format as the Centenary Edition of the *Works.* Many of Emerson's manuscript journals were not included—see "A Note on the Unpublished Manuscripts," pp. 72-74.)

*The Letters of Ralph Waldo Emerson,* ed. by Ralph L. Rusk (New York, 1939). 6 vols. (This includes a complete calendar of all the letters known to exist. It refers to seven major collections of letters to individual correspondents, previously published: those to Thomas Carlyle, Henry D. Thoreau, John Sterling, A Friend [Samuel Gray Ward], Herman Grimm, William Henry Furness, and Arthur Hugh Clough. It prints corrected versions of several hundred letters previously published in whole or in part; and it publishes more than 2,000 letters for the first time. The Index is exceptionally complete and the Introduction excellent. Various new letters continue to be discovered and published from time to time: see current Bibliographies in *American Literature.*)

*Young Emerson Speaks,* ed. by Arthur Cushman McGiffert, Jr. (Boston, 1938). 276 pp. (This publishes twenty-five representative sermons by Emerson for the first time and includes a checklist of all known manuscript sermons. Two other sermons had previously been published in earlier volumes.)

Emerson's lectures are largely unpublished. Two small published collections are: *Uncollected Lectures by Ralph Waldo Emerson,* ed. by Clarence Gohdes (New York, 1938). 60 pp.; *and* "Three Unpublished Lectures of Ralph Waldo Emerson," ed. by Jeanne Kronman, *New England Quarterly,* XIX (1946), 98-110.

## TEXTUAL CRITICISM AND AESTHETIC THEORY[126]

Adkins, Nelson F. "Emerson and the Bardic Tradition," *PMLA*, LXIII (1948), 662-77.

Allen, Gay W. *American Prosody* (New York, 1935). "Emerson," pp. 91-127.

Benton, Joel E. *Emerson as a Poet* (New York, 1883). (An enthusiastic but thoughtful critical study.)

Blair, Walter and Clarence Faust. "Emerson's Literary Method," *Modern Philology*, XLII (Nov., 1944), 79-95. (An excellent study of Emerson's method of organizing his ideas, with analyses of typical essays and poems.)

Brownell, William C. *American Prose Masters* (New York, 1909). ("Emerson," pp. 131-204, criticizes Emerson's style and literary characteristics.)

Burke, Kenneth. "Acceptance and Rejection," *Southern Review*, II (Winter, 1937), 600-32. (Emerson's method of statement and counterstatement with special reference to "Compensation.")

Cameron, Kenneth W. *Emerson the Essayist* (Raleigh, N.C., 1945). 2 vols. (An exhaustive study of the sources of Emerson's thought —see Part IV.)

——, ed. *Emerson's "Nature"* (Scholars' Facsimiles and Reprints, 100 West 31st Street, New York, 1940). (A reproduction and textual study of the first edition of *Nature.*)

Caponigri, A. R. "Bronson and Emerson: Nature and History," *New England Quarterly*, XVIII (Sept., 1945), 368-90. (The essay on "History" and its implications.)

Cestre, Charles. "Emerson Poète," *Études Anglaises*, IV (Jan., March 1940), 1-14.

Commager, Henry S. "Tempest in a Boston Teacup," *New England Quarterly*, VI (Dec. 1933), 651-75. (The effects of the "Divinity School Address," especially on Theodore Parker.)

Elliott, G. R. "Emerson Diarist," *University of Toronto Quarterly*, VI (April 1937), 299-308. (Emerson's *Journals* and their pleasant inconsistency.)

——. "On Emerson's 'Grace' and 'Self-Reliance,'" *New England Quarterly*, II (Jan. 1929), 93-104. (The conflict of ideas between the early poem and the mature essay.)

Erskine, John. "The American Scholar," *American Scholar*, I (Winter 1932), 5-15. (Inaugurating the new magazine.)

Flanagan, J. T. "Emerson as a Critic of Fiction," *Philological Quarterly*, XV (Jan., 1936), 30-45.

Foerster, Norman. *American Criticism* (Boston, 1928). (The chapter on Emerson, pp. 52-111, analyzes Emerson's critical theory from the neo-humanist point of view.)

126. See also chapters in various biographical and critical studies of Emerson, particularly those by Firkins and by Woodberry.

——. "Emerson on the Organic Principle in Art," *PMLA,* XLI (March, 1926), 193-208.

Foster, C. H. *Emerson's Theory of Poetry* (Iowa City, Iowa, 1939). (A study of Emerson's Aesthetics, largely in Emerson's own words, after the method of Van Wyck Brooks.)

Gohdes, Clarence. "Some Remarks on Emerson's 'Divinity School Address,'" *American Literature,* I (March, 1929), 27-31.

Gorely, Jean. "Emerson's Theory of Poetry," *Poetry Review,* XXII (July-Aug., 1931), 263-73.

Harris, W. T. "Emerson's Philosophy of Nature," and "Emerson's Orientalism," *in* F. B. Sanborn, ed., *The Genius and Character of Emerson* (Boston, 1885). (Detailed analyses of *Nature* and of "Brahma." Excellent.)

——. "The Dialectical Unity in Emerson's Prose," *Journal of Speculative Philosophy,* XVIII (April, 1884), 195-202. (An excellent study of Emerson's literary-philosophical method. See also, Blair and Faust.)

Hartwig, G. H. "Emerson on Historical Christianity," *Hibbert Journal,* XXXVII (April, 1939), 405-12. (With special reference to the "Divinity School Address.")

Henney, Thomas G. *The Craft of Genius: A Study of Emerson's Poetic Development* (Princeton, 1946). (An unpublished doctoral dissertation; but far better than many published studies of Emerson's Poetics.)

Hicks, Grenville. "Emerson as Letter Writer," review of Rusk, ed., *Emerson's Letters, Virginia Quarterly Review,* 1939, p. 643.

Hopkins, Vivian C. *Spires of Form: A Study of Emerson's Aesthetic Theory* (Cambridge, Mass., 1951). 276 pp. (An original and thoughtful study.)

Hotson, C. P. "A Background for Emerson's Poem 'Grace,'" *New England Quarterly,* I (April, 1928), 124-32.

——. [Many articles on "Swedenborg."] For bibliographical references see: L. Leary, ed. *Articles on American Literature* (Durham, N. C., 1947), p. 52.

Hubbell, G. S. *A Concordance to the Poems of Ralph Waldo Emerson* (New York, 1932). 478 pp.

Jordan, Leah E. *The Fundamentals of Emerson's Literary Criticism* (Philadelphia, 1945), 37 pp. (Summary of a doctoral dissertation; Pennsylvania, 1945).

Kreymborg, Alfred. "The Intoxicated Emerson," *in Our Singing Strength* (New York, 1929), pp. 67-83. (A suggestive critique of Emerson's poetry.)

Kurtz, S. K. *The Sources and Development of Emerson's "Representative Men"* (unpublished doctoral dissertation; Yale, 1947). (Comprehensive and able.)

Lewisohn, Ludwig. *Expression in America* (New York, 1932). (pp. 105-36, on Emerson's poetry and aesthetic theory.)

MacRae, Donald. "Emerson and the Arts," *Art Bulletin,* XX (March, 1938), 79-95.

Matthiessen, F. O. *American Renaissance* (New York, 1941). (Contains much thoughtful criticism of Emerson's poetry and of his aesthetic ideas.)

McDowell, Tremaine. "A Freshman Poem by Emerson," *PMLA,* XLV (March, 1930), 326-29.

McEuen, Kathryn A. "Emerson's Rhymes," *American Literature,* XX (March, 1948), 31-42.

McNulty, John B. "Emerson's Friends and the Essay on Friendship," *New England Quarterly,* XIX (Sept., 1946), 390-94.

Michaud, Régis. *L'Esthétique d'Emerson* (Paris, 1927). (A comprehensive study of Emerson's philosophy of art.)

Miles, Josephine. *The Primary Language of Poetry in the 1740's and 1840's,* University of California Publications in English (Berkeley, Calif., 1950). (Compares Emerson's poetic language and technique with his contemporaries'.)

Miller, Perry. *The Transcendentalists* (Cambridge, Mass., 1950). (Reprints all the major documents which form the background of Emerson's *Nature,* "American Scholar" and "Divinity School Address."

Neilson, W. A. "The American Scholar Today," *American Scholar,* V (Spring, 1936), 149-63. (A reinterpretation.)

Oliver, Egbert S. "Emerson's 'Days,'" *New England Quarterly,* XIX (Dec., 1946), 518-24.

Perry, Bliss. "Emerson's Most Famous Speech"; "Emerson's Savings Bank," in *The Praise of Folly and Other Papers* (Boston, 1923). (Studies of "The American Scholar," and Emerson as Journalist.)

Pochmann, Henry A. "The Emerson Canon," *University of Toronto Quarterly,* XII (July, 1943), 476-84. (Problems of editing or reediting the Emerson manuscripts.)

Smith, Henry N. "Emerson's Problem of Vocation: A Note on 'The American Scholar,'" *New England Quarterly,* XII (March, 1939), 52-67.

Strauch, Carl F. "The Background for Emerson's 'Boston Hymn,'" *American Literature,* XIV (March, 1942), 36-47.

——. *A Critical and Variorum Edition of Emerson's Poems* (unpublished doctoral dissertation; Yale, 1946). (This contains a wealth of new material, both textual and critical.)

——. "The Date of Emerson's 'Terminus,'" *PMLA,* LXV (June, 1950), 360-70.

——. "Emerson's Phi Beta Kappa Poem," *New England Quarterly,* XXIII (March, 1950), 65-90.

Sutcliffe, Emerson G. "Emerson's Theories of Literary Expression,"

*University of Illinois Studies in Language and Literature,* VIII (1923), pp. 9-143. (An early, workmanlike summary of the subject.)

Thompson, F. T. "Emerson's Theory and Practice of Poetry," *PMLA,* XLIII (Dec., 1928), 1170-84. (With special reference to Coleridge and Wordsworth.)

Trueblood, D. E. "The Influence of Emerson's Divinity School Address," *Harvard Theological Review,* XXXII (Jan., 1939), 41-56.

Turpie, M. C. "A Quaker Source for Emerson's Sermon on the Lord's Supper," *New England Quarterly,* XVII (March, 1944), 95-101.

Wahr, Fred B. *Emerson and Goethe* (Ann Arbor, Mich., 1915). (The background of "Goethe; or, the Writer," in *Representative Men.*)

Young, Charles L. *Emerson's Montaigne* (New York, 1941). (The background of "Montaigne; or, the Skeptic," in *Representative Men.* See also Part IV.)

## *PART III*

# EMERSON'S IDEAS[1]

## A. *The Ideal and the Real*

THE CONTRASTING SIDES of Emerson's face which physically reflected the problems and tensions of his life also suggest the logical paradoxes of his thought. In philosophy the parochial citizen of Concord found expression in a homely, Yankee realism, while by contrast the dreamer of things to come found expression in an exalted transcendental idealism. The New England minister often thought and spoke like an oriental mystic, the practical citizen like an impractical visionary, the dry Yankee like a romantic poet, the skeptical individualist like a utopian optimist, and the genteel conservative like the radical prophet of a new America. The man whose heredity and environment linked him to the realities of nineteenth century New England also explored with his mind the mysticism of the ancient East, the categorical imperatives of German philosophy, the subconscious emotionalism of romantic poetry, the ultimate optimism which transcends tragedy, and the equalitarian idealism of an American democracy perhaps never to be realized. Keeping always in mind the known realities of experience, science, politics, morality, and tradition, Emerson also explored in imagination the unknown ideals of religion, philosophy, poetry, myth, and the American dream.

Emerson himself always recognized this dualism between ideal and real, and repeatedly described it. In his *Journals* for 1847 he noted:

1. Part III is concerned with the definition and interpretation of Emerson's ideas. Part IV describes the literary sources of these ideas (his Reading), and the influence which they have exerted on later writers and thinkers.

> Transcendentalism says, the Man is all. The world can be reeled off any stick indifferently. Franklin says, the tools: riches, old age, land, health; the tools . . . A master *and* tools,—is the lesson I read in every shop and farm and library. There must be both. . . .

And in his "Ode Inscribed to W. H. Channing," published the same year, he gave this dualism classic expression:

> There are two laws discrete,
> Not reconciled,—
> Law for man, and law for thing;
> The last builds town and fleet,
> But it runs wild,
> And doth the man unking.

But the "two laws" of Emerson's philosophy always remained "unreconciled." The strong Yankee realism and the ethereal transcendental idealism cohabited in his mind, but never formally joined. And this informality has always troubled critics and philosophers.

Emerson's failure to unite the ideal and the real in the formal bonds of logic has often led to the charge of philosophical inconsistency, and even incompetency. The inconsistency, of course, Emerson admitted, and even boasted. But the apparent logical incompetency he sought to explain and to qualify. "I am too young yet by some ages to compile a code," he excused himself, in his essay on "Experience." And in his last book, he went farther to "suggest that he who contents himself with dotting a fragmentary curve, recording only what facts he has observed, without attempting to arrange them within one outline, follows a system also."[2] Finally, in 1903, John Dewey positively asserted: "When the critic writes of lack of method, of the absence of continuity, of coherent logic . . . and puts Emerson away as a writer of maxims . . . the critic, to my mind, but writes down his own incapacity to follow a logic that is finely wrought."[3] But whether the fault lies with Emerson or with the critic, Emerson's failure to follow the rules of formal logic has caused many to distrust his philosophy.

His reasons for refusing the rules of logic are suggestive, however. Although his personal disinclination was primary, it was

2. *Works*, XII, 11, "Natural History of Intellect."
3. John Dewey, *Characters and Events*, I, 69.

probably the result of deeper causes. Recognizing that he was living in an "age of Revolution,"[4] or transition, he appealed to the future ("I am too young by some ages to compile a code"). Moreover, he emphasized his purpose to use and to interpret the observed facts of experience—to "dot a fragmentary curve," for future "scholars" to fill in. This appeal to the experience of the future relates his thought to pragmatism, and justifies the attempt to interpret his ideas in terms of the modern world, and of their influence on it.[5]

But Emerson also appealed from the lower logic of the human "understanding," to higher logic of the transcendental "Reason." Although he borrowed this distinction from Kant's disciples, Coleridge and Carlyle, and although he never systematized or fully clarified it, he threw out many suggestions which modern thinkers have systematized. Relating "Reason" to the symbolic language of poetry[6] on the one hand, and to the parabolic language of religion and prophecy on the other ("Jesus Christ was a minister of the pure Reason"[7]), he suggested its difference from formal logic. Modern philosophers[8] have developed this distinction between the "discursive" language of science and logic, and the "presentational" language of art, religion, and myth, and have clarified the latter by reference to non-rational psychology and to symbolic logic. And modern scholars[9] are beginning to interpret Emerson's poetry and philosophy in the light of this new logic of poetic symbolism.

Thus the dualism between ideal and real in Emerson's mind may partly be explained by reference to the literature and philosophy of the future. But it also had its sources in the literature and philosophy of the past.

Perhaps the most important, and certainly the most unusual influence on Emerson's thought was exerted by the literature and philosophy of the ancient East. In Emerson's mind a "meeting

4. See "The American Scholar," *Works*, I, 110.
5. See Part IV.
6. See *Nature*, chapter on "Language"; and "The Poet."
7. *Journals*, III, 236 (1833).
8. See Susanne K. Langer, *Philosophy in a New Key* (Cambridge, Mass., 1942).
9. See an unpublished dissertation by Thomas G. Henney, *The Craft of Genius: A Study of Emerson's Poetic Development* (Princeton, 1946).

of East and West" took place which was of historic importance. Although he never fully succeeded in uniting these opposites, he helped introduce the Western mind to Eastern thought, he interpreted and naturalized Eastern thought for modern readers (as in "Brahma"), and he partially assimilated it in his own writing and thinking. Perhaps because Emerson attempted so immense a task, his partial failure has seemed to outweigh the minor successes of lesser men. So his severe critic, George E. Woodberry, suggested in 1907 that:

> His page is as fresh in Japan and by the Ganges as in Boston; and, it may well be that in the blending of the East and West that must finally come in civilization, the limitations that awaken distrust in the Occidental mind may be advantageous when he is approached from the Oriental slope of thought, and his works may prove one of the reconciling influences of that larger world.[10]

The historic dualism of East and West helped to motivate the logical dualism in Emerson's mind and thought.

But this historic dualism of East and West was closely related in Emerson's mind to the philosophic dualism of ideal and real. To Plato he attributed both dualisms, together with his own position of mediator:

> The unity of Asia and the detail of Europe; the infinitude of the Asiatic soul and the defining, result-loving, machine-making, surface-seeking, opera-going, Europe,—Plato came to join, and, by contact, to enhance the energy of each.[11]

And then he went on to describe Plato's dualism between ideal and real and to follow it through the history of European philosophy. In his essay on "Nominalist and Realist," he suggested how Plato's universal "idealism" had, in medieval times, confusingly been called "realism" by technical philosophers, and had been opposed to medieval "nominalism," which resembled our modern naturalism or realism. Now, he concluded:

> If we cannot make voluntary and conscious steps in the admirable science of Universals, let us see the parts wisely, and infer the genius of nature from the best particulars.[12]

10. Woodberry, *Emerson,* pp. 176-7.
11. *Works,* IV, 534; essay on "Plato."
12. *Ibid.,* III, 244.

Thus Emerson sought to mediate between the platonic idealism of "universals" and the scientific naturalism of "particulars." If, like Plato, he also has been charged with having failed to "make the transition from ideas to matter"[13] he clearly recognized his position in the age-old philosophic conflict, and sought to mediate between its extremes.

Finally, the historic dualism between East and West, and the philosophic dualism between ideal and real found new embodiment in the religious dualism between "piety" and "moralism"[14] in the Puritan New England of Emerson's ancestors. As Professor Perry Miller describes it:

> There was in Puritanism a piety, a religious passion, the sense of an inward communication and of the divine symbolism of nature . . . But in Puritanism there was also another side, an ideal of social conformity, of law and order, of regulation and control . . . The New England tradition contained a dual heritage.[15]

This third dualism between religious piety and social moralism Emerson also inherited and sought to mediate. Clearly he sympathized most with the religious enthusiasts, but tempered his own religious emotion with constant reference to "the moral law."

The mysticism of the ancient East, the philosophic idealism of Plato, and the intense religious piety of the Puritan past all contributed characteristically to the formulation of Emerson's ideas; but the opposing pragmatism of the West, the realism of modern science and philosophy, and the moral conservatism of old New England also contributed. Often Emerson merely observed and described the two opposite poles of thought and influence. But often he suggested new syntheses and opened up new avenues of speculation.

The following chapters will consider Emerson's ideas first from the point of view of idealism, then of realism. But his idealism also had practical consequences, and his realism never remained merely prudential. Both sets of ideas had their sources in the past, and both have had their influences on our present;

13. *Works,* IV, 76; essay on "Plato."

14. See Joseph Harontunian, *Piety versus Moralism; the Passing of New England Theology* (New York, 1932).

15. Perry Miller, "Jonathan Edwards to Emerson," *The New England Quarterly,* XIII, 599-600 (Dec., 1940).

each can be understood only by reference to the other and to history. For instance, Emerson's mysticism derived from the Orient, but influenced even the development of Western pragmatism. "To be mystic," said Emerson's friend James Russell Lowell, "is not to be misty." Let us begin with mysticism.

## B. *Transcendental Idealism:*

### 1. *Mysticism*

Underlying Transcendentalism, underlying Romanticism, underlying Emerson's optimism, and underlying the American dream of freedom and democracy, lies the fundamental but vaguely-defined idea of mysticism. To understand Emerson, one must try to define and to understand this idea. From its very nature, mysticism is not susceptible of exact definition: the phrases "union with God" and "knowledge of ultimate reality" are emotional as much as rational. According to the dictionaries, however, mysticism has three fairly distinct and different meanings.

In its first sense, "mysticism" is "a term of reproach"—roughly equivalent to "misty" or "occult." Rufus Jones has pointed out that the Germans have two words: "*Mysticismus* for the occult and the abnormal, and *Mystik* for the theory that God and man are akin and in a reciprocal relationship."[16] Something of the first derogatory meaning undoubtedly influenced Emerson's description of "Swedenborg, or the Mystic." But this concerns us only negatively.

In its second and most specific meaning, "mysticism" is "the doctrine that God or the ultimate nature of reality . . . may be experienced or known in an immediate apprehension or insight, differing from all ordinary sensation or ratiocination; hence, the experience or ecstasy of those mystics who claim to attain this insight. . . ."[17] This definition emphasizes the mystical experience, describes it as "different from all ordinary sensation or ratiocination" (usually as "supernatural," or "transcendental"), and makes the attainment of it the hallmark of mysticism. Since Emerson did not describe the experience as radically different,

16. Rufus Jones, *The Testimony of the Soul* (New York, 1936), p. 200.
17. *Webster's International Dictionary,* and *The Encyclopaedia Britannica,* 14th edition and ff. (article on "Mysticism") combined.

or supernatural, nor claim personally to have attained it in its pure supernatural form, he has often been denied the title of "mystic."[17a]

In its third and most general meaning, however, "mysticism" is "any type of theory asserting the possibility of attaining knowledge or power through faith or spiritual insight."[18] Here the mystical experience is made to include the realm of all religious "faith and spiritual insight,"[19] and the pragmatic use of the experience as a means to knowledge, rather than as an end in itself, is emphasized. And by this general definition, Emerson was clearly a mystic.

But Emerson's "mysticism," like that of many modern, Protestant writers from William Blake to Rufus Jones, was much less vague than that described in the third definition, even if not so specific as that described in the second. Emerson believed that "God, or the ultimate nature of reality, may be known in an immediate apprehension or insight, differing from ordinary experience," in *degree*, but not in kind.[20] So also Rufus Jones has described it:

> The *essentia* of mysticism ought to be thought of simply as the experience of direct communion of the soul with God. As there are great variations of degree in the definiteness of the experience, it would be safer to say that in the mystical experience one finds himself in a direct relationship with an Over-World of reality of the same nature as his own inmost self, and with which he feels himself akin.[20a]

And similarly, Evelyn Underhill has described mysticism as "the art of union with Reality. The mystic is the person who has attained that union in greater or less degree."[21]—Although Emerson personally attained the mystical experience in less degree, and with less definiteness than the pure mystics, he did attain to a "variety of religious experience." And most important, he valued

17a. See Patrick Quinn, "Emerson and Mysticism," *American Literature*, XXI, 397-414 (January, 1950).

18. *Webster's International Dictionary*. (Another definition of purely historical reference is here omitted.)

19. Cf. William James, *The Varieties of Religious Experience*, 424.

20. The disagreement between the strict, Catholic mystics, and the broader, Protestant mystics centers on the interpretation of the mystical experience as absolute and supernatural, or as relative and natural.

20a. Rufus Jones, *The Testimony of the Soul*, p. 202.

21. Evelyn Underhill, *Practical Mysticism* (1915), p. 5.

this experience above all others for the insights which it provided into the conduct of life.

In the history of literature, Emerson belongs clearly to that type of mysticism, or mystical thought, which is distinctively occidental, protestant, and modern. For although he read widely in the mystical philosophy and poetry of the Orient and of Alexandria, he always disagreed with two of its traditional assumptions. First, he never exalted the mystical experience for its own sake as an end in itself, as did Plotinus and the later Neoplatonists.[22] And second, he never even approached the oriental conclusion logically resulting from the exclusive exaltation of the mystical experience,—that all other active and partial experiences are valueless. In a comparative study, Professor Rudolph Otto has described Eastern mysticism as "static," and Western as "dynamic," with the goal of Eastern as "the stilling of all *Karmani,* all works, all activity of will: it is quietism, *tyaga,* a surrender of the will and of doing. . . ."[23] But for Emerson the mystical experience was dynamically a means, rather than passively an end, and the goal of mysticism was insight into the active conduct of life. Emerson always rejected oriental fatalism and quietism.[24]

Just as Emerson rejected the fundamental conclusions of Oriental mysticism, so he rejected the fundamental conclusions of Catholic mysticism,—that the perfect mystical experience is absolutely supernatural, or superhuman, and therefore can never by achieved in this world. Today the official *Catholic Encyclopedia* declares that "the true ideal of Beatific Vision can only be reached in the next life," and by contrast emphasizes that "Protestantism, by advocating a direct union of the soul with God, had its outcome in a mysticism mostly pantheistic."[25] But Emerson, reading widely and sympathetically in the writings of earlier Protestant mystics, such as Meister Eckhart and Jacob Boehme, taught

22. See article on "Mysticism" in *Encyclopaedia Britannica* (14th ed., XVI, 51), by Evelyn Underhill and A. S. Pringle-Pattison. "The system of Neoplatonism culminates in the mystical act, and especially with Jamblichus and the Syrian Neoplationists, mystical practice tended more and more to overshadow the theoretical groundwork." (See also F. I. Carpenter, *Emerson and Asia,* Chapters III and IV.)

23. Rudolph Otto, *Mysticism East and West* (New York, 1932), p. 39.

24. See F. I. Carpenter, *Emerson and Asia,* Chapter II; and Arthur Christy, *The Orient in American Transcendentalism,* Part II.

25. *The Catholic Encyclopedia,* article on "Mysticism," by G. M. Sauvage.

that the mystical vision may be attained in this life and that man may therefore achieve perfection in this world. Because he described the mystical experience as natural rather than supernatural, Emerson's mysticism has often been condemned as "pantheistic" by Catholic and traditional critics.

Emerson knew and valued the mysticisms of the past, but reinterpreted them naturalistically in terms of the active conduct of life in the present. Therefore his mystical thought has been continued by modern writers on the subject. William James interpreted *The Varieties of Religious Experience* in similar terms, illustrating his interpretations by the experiences of several mystics whom Emerson had described in "The Over-Soul," as well as by that of Emerson's disciple, Whitman. Moreover, James declared that "faith-state and mystic state are practically convertible terms,"[26] and described these experiences as the basis of *The Will to Believe,* thereby emphasizing "the paramount importance of their function."[27] Finally, he repeated Emerson's distinction between logical understanding and intuitive Reason, pointing out that mystical experiences "break down the authority of the non-mystical or rationalistic consciousness, based on the understanding and the senses alone."[28]

Finally, Bertrand Russell in his book on *Mysticism and Logic* has continued this realistic interpretation of mystical experiences. William James had suggested that "They offer us hypotheses . . . The optimism to which they would persuade us may, interpreted in one way or the other, be after all the truest of insights."[29] Russell continued:

> Even the cautious and patient investigation of truth by science, which seems the very antithesis of the mystic's swift certainty, may be fostered and nourished by the very spirit of reverence in which mysticism lives and moves . . . At best, science is a continuation of the impersonal disinterestedness of mystics.[30]

Because Emerson taught that the mystical experience did not differ absolutely from other, natural experiences, and that even in

26. *The Varieties of Religious Experience,* p. 424.
27. *Ibid.,* p. 379.
28. *Ibid.,* p. 423.
29. *Ibid.,* p. 428.
30. B. Russell, *Mysticism and Logic* (London, 1921), p. 12.

its less definite forms it might suggest valuable practical insights, his thought has been developed by pragmatic and realistic philosophers.

But neither Emerson's personal experiences of mystical states, nor his thoughts about mysticism differed so greatly from the conventional, Catholic forms as has been supposed. In an unpublished doctoral study: *Emerson's Mysticism* (Western Reserve University, 1941), Dr. Myron F. Wicke has pointed out close parallels between Emerson's own psychological experiences and those of the traditional mystics, and has collected striking quotations both from his *Journals* and *Works* which describe these natural experiences in the language of traditional, supernatural mysticism.

Traditionally, "the mystic way" leads away from the routine life of the senses by means of an "awakening" (or realization of personal inadequacy), through a period of "purgation" (sometimes called "the dark night of the soul"), to a moment of "illumination" (or mystical experience), with its resultant conviction of "union with God," or "knowledge of ultimate reality." Although Emerson did not suffer an absolutely "dark night of the soul," he did pass through a protracted period of personal suffering, combined with mental struggle and self-communion, reaching its "crisis" in 1832,[31] when he retired to the White Mountains and decided to resign his ministry. This period of "purgation" was followed by flashes of mystical insight, which he reported both in his formal *Essays* and his *Journals*. Then he used these insights as the foundation of his book on *Nature*, and of all his later thought.

In the first chapter of his first book, Emerson described most eloquently his own, most intense natural experience:

> Standing on the bare ground,—my head bathed by the blithe air and uplifted into infinite space,—all mean egotism vanishes. I become a transparent eyeball; I am nothing; I see all; the currents of the Universal Being circulate through me; I am part or parcel of God. The name of the nearest friend sounds then foreign and accidental. . . .[32]

Here Emerson did not explicitly claim to have attained a mystical experience, but he did describe this natural experience in the

31. Recorded in his *Journals*, II, 491-503, under the title of "Crisis."
32. Emerson's *Works*, I, 10.

traditional language of mysticism; he placed it at the very beginning of his writing, and from it he developed the fundamental ideas of his philosophy. Later, in his essay on "The Over-Soul" he spoke again in the first person: "There is a depth in these brief moments which constrains us to ascribe more reality to them than to all other experiences."[33]

More informally in his *Journals* and with characteristic self-disparagement, Emerson occasionally described how "a certain wandering light comes to me which I instantly perceive to be the cause of causes."[34] And finally, in 1864 he declared that "The grief of old age is that, now, only in rare moments . . . can we attain those enlargements and that intellectual *élan,* which were once a daily gift."[35]

Clearly, Emerson did not claim to have attained the pure mystical experience, and often he spoke disparagingly of his own illuminations. Moreover, he valued these experiences not so much for their own sake, as for the "enlargement and intellectual *élan*" which accompanied them. Therefore, his attempts to suggest this "*élan*" in his poetry and to develop the implications of it in his philosophy were most important to him. His mystical ideas, rather than his experiences themselves, were the significant elements in his "mysticism."

Although Emerson did not claim to have attained the absolute mystical experience, but rather described his aesthetic, natural experience in mystical terms, his experience was identical with that of all mysticism in two essentials: it was "an ecstasy," and it gave the conviction of "union with God." And from these two essentials, all his mystical ideas followed.

Indeed, all mystical philosophies have in some way developed the implications of the experience of "ecstasy" and "union with God." For "ecstasy" means, literally, "standing outside" the self, or being "beside oneself." In the mystical experience the soul seems to go beyond the body and to achieve identification with God: the individual transcends the limits of his individuality and feels himself part of the whole: the Self sees its partial self in perspective, and shares the omniscience of God, or the Over-

33. *Works,* II, 267.
34. *Journals,* IV, 248-249.
35. *Ibid.,* X, 47.

Soul. Therefore, all types of mysticism have resulted in philosophies which describe things from the point of view of God, rather than of individual man.

But if all mystical philosophies agree on the axiomatic importance of the mystical experience of ecstasy and union with God, and if all agree that this ecstasy outvalues all the routine experiences of daily life, they differ relatively, in relating this experience to daily life. In its extreme, oriental forms, mysticism absolutely denies the value, or reality, of the routine experiences, and calls them "illusions." Subsequently it seeks to destroy the illusion, and to perpetuate the ecstasy. In its extreme occidental forms, however, mysticism merely denies the relative importance of routine experiences, and emphasizes the overwhelming value and authority of the mystical experience for the understanding of routine life.

So Emerson, toward the end of his essay on "Experience," distinguished sharply between these two types of experience:

> We must be very suspicious of the deceptions of the element of time. It takes a good deal of time to eat or to sleep, or to earn a hundred dollars, and a very little time to entertain a hope and an insight which becomes the light of our life.[36]

But he did not deny the value of eating and sleeping. What distinguishes Emerson's mysticism is his attempt to apply his mystical ideas to the philosophy of history on the one hand, and to the daily conduct of life on the other. His emphasis on the supreme value of the mystical experience for the illumination and guidance of practical life in this world differentiates his thought from oriental and from catholic mysticism.

The belief in the supreme value of mystical intuition made Emerson "very suspicious of the deceptions of the element of time." It therefore determined his philosophy of history, which he himself considered so important that he introduced his First Series of Essays with the essay on "History." But only recently has this importance been recognized, because Emerson's approach seemed negative: it asserted the relative unimportance of history; or in mystical language, "the Unreality of Time and Space."[37]

In modern language, Emerson taught that history was less im-

36. *Works,* III, 85.
37. See Bertrand Russell, *Mysticism and Logic,* Chapter I.

portant than "psychology": "history is all to be explained from individual experience. There is a relation between the hours of our life and the centuries of time."[38] Translated into the scientific language of evolution: "ontogeny repeats philogeny." And in the practice of progressive education, this philosophy of history suggested that young children should properly study the primitive, savage cultures, older children Greek civilization, adolescents, the Romantic eras, and so on. "All history becomes subjective; in other words there is properly no history, only biography."[39]

This philosophy of history logically derived from the mystical idea of the insignificance of time and space. But Dr. A. R. Caponigri has shown that it immediately developed from the "ahistorical principle [which] Protestantism possessed in the principle of private judgment."[40] Both the Puritan emphasis on "conscience" and the Quaker doctrine of "the inner light" influenced it. Seeking to discredit the authority of the Catholic past and its historic institutions, Protestantism was led to preach the relative insignificance of history. But this Protestant philosophy of history was also logically based upon mystical premises, as the *Catholic Encyclopedia* (quoted above) emphasizes.

Similarly, modern science has taught the relativity of time and space, and the immutability of the laws of nature. Dr. Caponigri has suggested how Emerson's essay on "Spiritual Laws" related this concept to his mystical philosophy of history by making these eternal laws the direct objects of intuition: "out of time, out of space, and not subject to circumstance."[41]—Like mysticism, science also has sought to discover these "eternal" laws. As Bertrand Russell has written: "at best, science is a continuation of the impersonal disinterestedness of mystics."[42] The mystical idea of the "unreality" of time and space, developed by Emerson as a philosophy of history, is thus related equally to modern religion, education, and science.

But more typical of the stricter type of mysticism than the ideas of intuition, or of the unreality of time and space, is the

38. *Works,* II, 4.

39. *Works,* II, 10.

40. "Brownson and Emerson: Nature and History," in the *New England Quarterly* (Sept., 1945), XVIII, 369.

41. Caponigri, *op. cit.,* 373. Quotation from Emerson's *Works,* I, 122.

42. *Mysticism and Logic,* p. 12.

idea of unity, or identity:—through the mystical experience man achieves "union with God," or a sense of identity with the whole natural and supernatural world. This results in the "Identity-philosophy" common alike to the ancient Hindu scriptures, the German transcendental philosophers, and the more vaguely Romantic poets of Europe and America.

Psychologically, this idea of unity or identity results directly from the mystical experience of ecstasy, in which the individual, escapes the limits of his own individuality to feel himself part of the whole. Negatively, the individual's realization of the relative insignificance of his private self usually involves that agony of "purgation," or "purification" commonly associated with the religious or mystical experience. Before the self can see itself in true perspective, it must renounce its self-importance and its self-love—with all the emotional perturbations usually accompanying this renunciation. Positively, the soul then realizes its real (though relatively infinitesimal) importance as an integral part of the whole, or of God. Identifying itself with God, it achieves that feeling of beatitude or unity which is the goal and reward of all mystics. And recognizing that all other separate selves are equally a part of God's whole, it accepts the brotherhood of man.

The philosophers of mysticism, from the anonymous authors of the Hindu scriptures to Emerson, have emphasized first the negative element of mysticism, which is the detachment of the individual from the "illusions" of the self. And in "Brahma," Emerson translated this idea almost perfectly: all individuals, whether "slayer" or "slain," "know not well" until they learn to identify themselves with God—or the "I" of the poem. But once they find God, and recognize that their own individual lives are but an infinitesimal part of the life of humanity, they achieve perspective and peace of mind. Even if they themselves be slain, their lives contribute to the whole.

This mystical identification, or union of the individual self with God, or the whole, is primary. But after this union, the mystic may follow one of three paths.

First, traditionally, the mystic may celebrate his experience and seek to perpetuate his ecstasy.—He may describe it artistically, for instance, as Emerson did briefly in the first section of *Nature*, and also in several of his poems.—Or he may describe the mechanical pre-conditions of the mystical experience, and seek to re-induce it—like the Yogi and many other mystical and evangelical sects.—Or he may seek to use the experience as a kind of passport to nirvana—as a "liberation from all terrene concerns"—"the flight of the alone to the alone." If he follows the first, traditional path, he will seek to identify himself with God, or the whole, to the exclusion of the world, and his fellow men. But although Emerson described this traditional path—especially in his essay on "The Over-Soul"—he did not follow it.

Second, the mystic may then emphasize the dual experience and consciousness of man.—On the one hand, man is part and parcel of God, and through the mystical experience may be united with Him; but on the other hand, man is selfish and mortal, and divorced from God by his human susceptibility to suffering and error. Plato suggested this dual consciousness in his allegories of the cave, and of the two horses of man's nature. Emerson remembered these, but elaborated a somewhat different image:

> In Flaxman's drawing of the Eumenides of Aeschylus, Orestes supplicates Apollo, whilst the furies sleep on the threshold. The face of the god expresses a shade of regret and compassion, but is calm with the conviction of the irreconcilableness of the two spheres. He is born into other politics, into the eternal and beautiful. The man at his feet asks for his interest in turmoils of the earth, into which his nature cannot enter. And the Eumenides there lying express pictorially this disparity.[43]

The "disparity" between man the suffering, confused, and selfish, actor in the human tragedy, which is also "the divine comedy," and man the ideal made in the image of God, formed the main theme of Emerson's philosophy.

Emerson's place in the philosophy of mysticism explains the fundamental faults and idiosyncracies for which he has usually been criticized. Because Emerson viewed things mystically from the point of view of "the god," rather than tragically from the point of view of suffering humanity, he has been accused of insensitivity to human feeling, and especially to human pain and evil. But this is the very nature of mysticism. And because Emer-

43. *Works,* III, 82; essay on "Experience." See later section on "Experience and Nature."

son judged man by the standard of a god-like ideal of perfection, measuring both man's potentiality and man's failure by this absolute standard, he has been accused both of blind optimism and of heartless perfectionism. But this also is the nature of mysticism. If this mysticism is recognized and accepted, his philosophy becomes simple and logical.

Finally, the mystic who refuses to flee from the concerns of this world, and who describes the disparity between the god-like ideal and the human actual, may turn at times to the interpretation of human life—not in terms of an absolutely god-like perfection, but in terms of that relative excellence which humanity has occasionally achieved. He will see human history not in terms of the years and centuries but of millenniums; he will measure human individuals by the standard of their greatest representative men and heroes; and he will contrast humdrum human experience not only with those intense moments of illumination of which humanity is sometimes capable, but also with the daily conduct of life suggested by those moments of illumination. He will consider man not only absolutely *sub specie æternitatis,* but also relatively in the long perspectives of human history. As an example of this, Oliver Wendell Holmes quoted Emerson's startling assertion: "All that we call sacred history attests that the birth of a poet is the principal event in chronology."[44] "Does this sound wild and extravagant?" asked Holmes. "What were the political ups and downs of the Hebrews?"—In the long perspective of three thousand years we remember Homer and Buddha and Confucius, more than Pericles and Asoka and some Chinese dynast. "Emerson looked along the heights of history and saw mainly the men of faith and insight who moved the masses."[45] This Emersonian quality of perspective has been called "longanimity," as contrasted with the "magnanimity" of men more immediately concerned with the suffering of their fellows. This implies both praise and blame, of course. But again, it is in the nature of mysticism. And in contrast to the oriental and other-worldly mysticism, Emerson's mysticism took an intensely pragmatic interest in the human realities of this world, even if it did not tragically seek to share all human sorrow.

44. *Works,* III, 11; and "Notes," 295, Essay on "The Poet."
45. *Ibid.*

From the mystical idea of unity, or identity, the idea of the relativity of good and evil[46] logically follows. The individual who sees things from the point of view of God, will know that what seems evil to him (the death of his friend) may seem good to God, or to humanity—if for instance, it promotes the laws of evolution and the survival of the fittest. Good and evil are always relative to individuals and to nations, and even the destruction of all humanity might seem "good" to God, if it promoted the evolution of a higher order of beings. This mystical—but not unscientific and not irrational—optimism underlay all Emerson's writing and thinking. Moreover, it underlay the Transcendentalism and the Romanticism of all Emerson's contemporaries—even when they did not understand or express it clearly.

## 2. *Transcendentalism*

"Transcendentalism means, says our accomplished Mrs. B., with a wave of her hand, *a little beyond.*" So Emerson half-humorously described the idea in his *Journals* for October 6, 1836. And five years later, on October 8, 1841, he added a second half-humorous description: "The view taken of Transcendentalism in State Street is that it threatens to invalidate contracts." Somewhere between these two extremes the idea developed in New England. Like the word, "Yankee," "Transcendental" was first applied with mild contempt but soon was accepted with cheerful defiance. If Transcendentalism seemed sometimes vague and immaterial, it also seemed sometimes revolutionary and practical.

Writing of *Transcendentalism in New England,* its first historian thus described the idea:

> With some truth it may be said that there never was such a thing as Transcendentalism out of New England. In Germany and France there was a transcendental philosophy . . . but it never affected society in its organized institutions or practical interests. In old England, this philosophy influenced poetry and art, but left the daily existence of men and women untouched. But in New England, the ideas entertained by the foreign thinkers took root in the native soil and blossomed out in every form of social life.[47]

That is, Transcendentalism in New England took many different

46. See later chapter, "Optimism and Evil."
47. O. B. Frothingham, *Transcendentalism in New England,* p. 105.

forms. First, it paid lip-service to the formal philosophy of Immanuel Kant, but greatly modified it. Second, it developed the Puritan religion of its own New England past in new ways. Third, it applied this philosophic idealism and this religious enthusiasm to the practical reform of American social institutions. And, finally, it stimulated a "renaissance" in American literature—a renaissance whose first exponent was Ralph Waldo Emerson. We shall consider its manifestations in philosophy, in religion, in society, and in literature.

*a. In Philosophy.* In the first paragraph of his famous essay on "The Transcendentalist," Emerson defined the idea as accurately as possible: "What is popularly called Transcendentalism among us is Idealism; Idealism as it appears in 1842."[48] Broadly, he compared it with "the very oldest of thoughts . . . Buddhism is an expression of it." Only later did he specify that:

> The Idealism of the present day acquired the name Transcendental from the use of that term by Immanuel Kant, of Königsberg, who replied to the skeptical philosophy of Locke, which insisted that there was nothing in the intellect which was not previously in the experience of the senses, by showing that there was a very important class of ideas or imperative forms, which did not come by experience, but through which experience was acquired; that these were intuitions of the mind itself; and he denominated them Transcendental forms.[49]

Because the *name* "Transcendentalism" had always been associated with Kant, historians (especially historians of philosophy) have often sought to identify New England Transcendentalism with Kantianism. But Emerson did not make this identification, either in theory or in practice. Only the name was Kantian.

Emerson's Transcendentalism derived from oriental mysticism, from Neoplatonic idealism, and from a diluted form of Kant's philosophy as interpreted by Coleridge, Carlyle, and other amateur philosophers. It included some religious and philosophical elements of mysticism, which were largely lacking in Kant. It included a monistic idealism, which the Neoplatonists had grafted upon Platonism. And it blurred the sharp distinction between "Pure Reason" and "Practical Reason" which Kant had made.

The chief idea which Emerson derived from Kant was the

48. *Works,* I, 329.
49. *Works,* I, 339-40.

distinction between the transcendental "Reason" and the empirical "understanding." "Reason" described "the intuitions of the mind itself," as opposed not only to sensational empiricism but to mechanical logic and rationalism as well. This intuitive "Reason" resembled that perfect "reason" which Swift imputed to the Houyhnhnms, beloved by Gulliver, rather than the logical reason that we now associate with the word. Finding this idea in Coleridge,[50] Emerson elaborated it, first in his Journals and Letters[51] and then in his first book, *Nature.* This intuitive "Reason"–and the religions, poetic, or symbolic "truth" to which it promised access–formed the very foundation of his transcendental philosophy.

But Kant had warned that this "pure" Reason could not be applied practically to the world of the senses. Coleridge repeated this warning[52] and then partially disregarded it, sometimes using the idea for his own purposes. Emerson noted these warnings, and at first heeded them. But soon Emerson began equating transcendental "intuition" with "instinct." And at the end of Nature, he wrote that "if [Man] have elemental power . . . it is not conscious power . . . it is instinct." Thereafter, Emerson often used the words "intuition" and "instinct" almost interchangeably. And practically this confusion converted Emerson's Transcendentalism into a naturalistic philosophy. Disregarding or ignoring the subtle distinctions of Kantian logic, Emerson kept the language and the sanctions of transcendental idealism, but changed their meanings and used them in new ways.

When he equated transcendental "Reason" or intuition with "instinct," Emerson opened a Pandora's box of primitivistic and romantic delusions. For this he has justly been attacked and condemned.[53] But although Emerson's confusion of intuition with instinct was logically dangerous, it also suggested the pragmatic path which modern philosophy has taken in reconciling mystical idealism with empirical naturalism.

50. See Coleridge, *Aids to Reflection,* "On the Difference in Kind of Reason and the Understanding."

51. See *Journals,* III, 235-39; *Letters,* I, 412-13 (1834).

52. See Coleridge, *loc. cit.;* and *The Cambridge History of English Literature,* article on Coleridge, XI, 137.

53. See Yvor Winters, *In Defense of Reason,* chapter on "Jones Very and R. W. Emerson."

If the transcendental "intuitions" are considered as "hypotheses" —to be tested and corrected by later observation and experiment, rather than to be accepted uncritically as absolute truth—they offer the only possible path to discovery of scientific laws. So Charles Sanders Peirce[54] later emphasized and prepared the way for Pragmatism and the modern philosophy of science. So Bertrand Russell suggested when he related the intuitions of the mystics to the hypotheses of the scientists. So George Santayana implied when he first criticized Emerson's idealism as subjective and "genteel," but then added that Transcendentalism "is a plan of those avenues of inference by which our ideas of things must be reached . . . In other words, transcendentalism is the critical logic of science . . . Transcendental logic, the method of discovery for the mind, was to become also the method of evolution in nature and history. Transcendental method, abused, produced transcendental myth."[55]

Emerson's Transcendentalism, therefore, was not philosophically pure but was compounded of "Reason" and of "myth." He lived between two worlds—the supernatural and the natural—striving constantly to reconcile them. If he had not cared so much for the actual "conduct of life," he might have become a pure, logical philosopher. If he had not cared so much for the eternal truths, he might have remained merely a successful pastor, like his father and grandfather before him. As it was, he constantly explored the unknown ways of thought that promised to lead from supernaturalism to naturalism, and often lost his way. But as Joseph Warren Beach has written: "Transcendentalism was an absolutely necessary step in the transition from supernaturalism to naturalism . . . But the transcendentalists themselves did not develop the possibilities of naturalism. They approached it from the wrong side."[56]

Nevertheless, from this "wrong side" Emerson constantly

54. See F. I. Carpenter, "C. S. Peirce: Pragmatic Transcendentalist," *New England Quarterly,* XIV (March 1941), 34-48; and section on "Pragmatism," later.

55. George Santayana, *Winds of Doctrine,* pp. 194-95, essay on "The Genteel Tradition in American Philosophy."

56. J. W. Beach, "Emerson and Evolution," in *University of Toronto Quarterly.*

caught vistas of the truths which modern thinkers have explored, and threw out suggestions which they have followed.[57] Perhaps because Emerson's Transcendentalism was not philosophically pure, it has proved more fruitful than the more logical thought of less imaginative men.

*b. In Religion.* One of the causes of the impurity of Emerson's philosophy was the fact that "Transcendentalism in New England" was a religion before it was a philosophy. Whereas in Germany Kant's logic was the determining element, in America Emerson and his associates were men of religion, both by training and by temperament. Their Transcendentalism developed the religious idealism of their own Puritan past primarily and only borrowed the forms and phrases of German thought secondarily. As O. B. Frothingham justly observed: "It requires an effort to forget that the speculative basis of their faith was not the natural basis of the philosopher but the supernatural one of the believer." Suggesting that Jonathan Edwards himself was "transcendental" in part, Frothingham concluded:

> Indeed, whenever orthodoxy spread its wings and rose into the region of faith, it lost itself in the sphere where the human soul and the divine were in full concurrence. Transcendentalism simply claimed for all men what Protestant Christianity claimed for its own elect.[58]

And H. C. Goddard, the second major interpreter of the movement, emphasized that: "They were Puritans to the core. This . . . was the signally American contribution to transcendentalism."[59]

In other words, American Transcendentalism was primarily religious rather than philosophical. Its inspirational force was what Emerson called "the religious sentiment," rather than the Kantian "Reason" on the one hand, or the merely practical desire to reform society on the other. It developed the "piety" of the early Puritans rather than their logical theology or their social "moralism." When Andrews Norton attacked Emerson's "Divinity School Address," he justly compared its sentiment to the earlier mysticism and emotionalism of Edwards. American Transcen-

57. See, especially, later section on "Pragmatism."
58. O. B. Frothingham, *Transcendentalism in New England,* p. 108.
59. H. C. Goddard, *Studies in New England Transcendentalism,* p. 188.

dentalism was primarily a reassertion of the mystical basis of all religion.

But historically, of course, New England Transcendentalism was a specific reassertion of this religious sentiment, in reaction first against the rationalism of the Unitarians, and second against the pessimism of the Calvinists.

By origin, New England Transcendentalism was merely a branch of Unitarianism. Indeed, the latest *Encyclopædia Britannica*[60] article on "Unitarianism" still describes Emerson as one of the leaders of the "second period" of Unitarianism and goes on to describe "the third period" beginning "about 1885" as one of "recognition of universal religion." Whether Transcendentalism be defined as a separate sect or as a part of Unitarianism, the facts remain that the leading Transcendentalists were Unitarian ministers by training, and that many continued in this profession throughout their lives. It is probable that today Emerson is quoted more often from Unitarian pulpits and from the pulpits of "the Community Church" movement than from academic lecture platforms.

Specifically, Transcendentalism shared three fundamental ideas which Unitarianism had emphasized in its attack on Calvinism. Emerson might even have subscribed to the exact words with which William Ellery Channing, the greatest Unitarian, announced these tenets.

First, Unitarianism, as its name implies, rejected the idea of the Trinity and declared its belief that "there is One God, even the Father; and that Jesus Christ is not this One God, but his son and messenger."[61] By denying the divinity of Jesus and by emphasizing his humanity, Unitarianism and Transcendentalism both implied that human individuals might ultimately hope to realize the Christian ideal in this actual world.

Second, Unitarianism and Transcendentalism both opposed the exclusive and sectarian nature of Calvinism and of Catholicism alike:

60. John H. Lathrop, "Unitarianism: United States," *Encyclopaedia Britannica,* 14th ed.

61. W. E. Channing, address delivered at the dedication of the Second Congregational Unitarian Church, New York, 1826.

Our aim is not sectarian . . . Far from us be this spirit of exclusion, the very spirit of antichrist, the worst of all the delusions of Popery and of Protestantism. We hold nothing to be essential but the simple and supreme dedication of the mind, heart, and life to God and to his will.[62]

Emphasizing that *all* men may hope to realize this Christian ideal through perfect self-dedication, Emerson and Channing both looked forward to an inclusive Universal Religion.

Third, Unitarianism and Transcendentalism both opposed most emphatically the Calvinist emphasis on sin, and on its violent punishment in hell-fire. So Channing attacked the "abject and slavish fear" of one "whose spirit has been broken to this creed"; and in its place emphasized that "the ultimate reliance of a human being is and must be on his own mind . . . Conscience is the highest faculty given us by God."[63] Emerson's "Self-Reliance" stemmed directly from this Unitarian liberalism but placed less emphasis on the "mind," and more on "the religious sentiment."

Indeed, New England Transcendentalism diverged from Unitarianism for the same reason that it diverged from Kantian Transcendentalism: it exalted man's "heart" and soul above his mere "mind" (Hawthorne to the contrary notwithstanding). It reasserted the "piety" of the old Puritan religion and even justified that religious "enthusiasm" which Edwards had shared with Whitefield and the eighteenth century revivalists. In the words of Professor Perry Miller, it declared man's "refusal to live by decorum and sobriety alone."[64]

Specifically, Transcendentalism left behind all the forms and traditions of the Unitarian Church, placing its reliance on the conscience, intuition, or "inner light." In his farewell sermon on "The Lord's Supper," Emerson had borrowed many of his arguments against formal religion from the Quakers.[65] In his "Divinity School Address," he went on to reject "Historical Christianity" itself in favor of "the religious sentiment" in the soul of man. Going beyond Unitarianism and all institutionalized churches, he

62. *Loc. cit.*
63. W. E. Channing, *The Moral Argument Against Calvinism*, 1820.
64. Perry Miller, *The Transcendentalists.*
65. M. C. Turpie, "A Quaker Source for Emerson's Sermon on the Lord's Supper," *The New England Quarterly,* XVII (March, 1944), 95-101.

sought to make religion effective by ending the separation between Sabbath religion and secular life.

Inevitably, since Transcendentalism undermined institutional Unitarianism, even while enlarging many of its religious ideas, many practical Unitarians opposed it. But orthodox Unitarians opposed it for other reasons as well: when Andrews Norton attacked Emerson's "Divinity School Address" as "The Latest Form of Infidelity," he denounced its "pantheistic" ideas. For Emerson not only rejected the authority of the Church as an institution. He also rejected the authority of the Bible as Revelation; and, finally, he even rejected the traditional, anthropomorphic concept of God as a "person," exalting rather the impersonal laws of science and the impersonal beauty of nature. Small wonder that Calvinists gloated:

> Step by step the Unitarian theology has come down from the true position as to the inspiration of the scriptures, and thus having abandoned the only sure footing, those who are foremost in the descent have found themselves among the ooze and quicksands of atheistic philosophy.[66]

But if the orthodox were right in pointing to the non-theistic nature of Emerson's Trandscendentalism, they were wrong in declaring that "there is nothing of the scriptures in it.[67] Transcendentalism merely sought to reassert the mysterious nature of God ("I am that I am") and to rediscover His manifestations in nature and in the soul of man. In so doing, it sometimes rejected and sometimes continued the religious ideas of Puritan and of Unitarian Christianity. But it always went "a little beyond."

*c. In Society.* Emerson's editorial introduction to the first issue of *The Dial* described the social constituency of Transcendentalism perfectly. The passage is worth quoting at length:

> No one can converse much with different classes of society in New England without marking the progress of a revolution. Those who share in it have no external organization, no badge, no creed, no name.

66. From an anonymous review of Emerson's *Essays, First Series* in *Biblical Repertory and Princeton Review,* XIII, 544. The controversy which centered on Emerson's "Divinity School Address" is outlined by Clarence Faust, "The Background of the Unitarian Opposition to Transcendentalism," *Modern Philology,* XXXV, 297-324 (February 1938). Some of these controversial documents are reprinted in Perry Miller, *The Transcendentalists.*

67. C. Faust, *loc. cit.*

They do not vote, or print, or even meet together. They do not know each other's faces or names. They are united only in a common love of truth, and love of its work. They are of all conditions and constitutions. Of these acolytes, if some are happily born and well bred, many are no doubt ill-dressed, ill-placed, ill-made, with as many scars of hereditary vice as other men. Without pomp, without trumpet, in lonely and obscure places, in solitude, in servitude, in compunctions and privations, trudging beside the team in the dusty road or drudging a hireling in other men's cornfields, schoolmasters, who teach a few children the rudiments for a pittance, ministers of small parishes of the obscurer sects, lone women in dependent condition, matrons and young maidens, rich and poor, beautiful and hard-favored, without concert or proclamation of any kind, they have silently given in their several adherence to a new hope, and in all companies do signify a greater trust in the nature and resources of man, than the laws or the popular opinions will well allow.

This spirit of the time is felt by every individual with some differences—to each one casting its light upon the objects nearest to his temper and habits of thought; to one, coming in the shape of special reforms in the state; to another, in modifications of the various callings of men and the customs of business; to a third, opening a new scope for literature and art; to a fourth, in philosophical insight; to a fifth, in the vast solitudes of prayer. It is in every form a protest against usage, and a search for principles. In all its movements, it is peaceable. . . .[68]

Naturally a spontaneous movement as individualistic and anti-institutional as Transcendentalism lacked official, social forms and organizations of its own. Nevertheless, an informal discussion group known afterwards as the "Transcendental Club" had been organized in 1836 to bring together the leaders of the group. And the famous magazine, *The Dial*, gave it a voice from 1840 to 1844. If to these we add Alcott's Temple School, the ideal "communities" indirectly associated with the movement, and various reform "conventions" attended by many of its members, the list is complete.

The "Transcendental Club"[69] originated informally as a group of liberal intellectuals meeting in turn at the various homes of its members. It was first known as "Hedge's Club" after Frederic Henry Hedge, Unitarian minister and later Professor of Ecclesiastical History and German Literature at Harvard. It met first at

68. R. W. Emerson, *Uncollected Writings* (New York, 1912), pp. 32-33.

69. The best, though brief, account of this club occurs in R. L. Rusk's *Life of Emerson*, pp. 243-45 ff.

the home of George Ripley, later the head of Brook Farm, and next at the Boston home of Bronson Alcott. Theodore Parker, Henry Thoreau, Margaret Fuller, and other leading Transcendentalists later attended its irregular meetings irregularly. The "Club," however, did furnish a meeting ground for the discussion of the new ideas, and from it emerged *The Dial* after many uncertainties. Here "the communities" were discussed and partly planned, though with many dissenting voices. Then, after producing these concrete results, it ceased to be.

Probably *The Dial* was the most typical and tangible product of New England Transcendentalism, and certainly Emerson was its leading spirit. Although Margaret Fuller was editor for the first two years, and George Ripley was its first business manager, Emerson contributed more voluminously and more consistently than any other author and also helped continuously with its business affairs. For its last two years he was both editor and business manager, and, finally, even financial "angel."

*The Dial* illustrates both the bad and the good qualities of pure Transcendentalism. It was, as Carlyle (and many others) complained, "too ethereal." It never came to grips with the problems of "the times," in spite of a few topical articles by Emerson and Parker on reform and labor movements, and by Margaret Fuller on women's rights; but it concentrated on "the eternities." It printed many translations, many dull critical essays, and much poor poetry—both in prose and verse. It suffered (partly of necessity) from inbreeding (for instance, printing various excerpts from the writings of Emerson's ill-fated younger brothers and some poems of his first wife, Ellen).

But *The Dial* probably published more famous articles and poems by more famous men of letters than any other American magazine of its small scope and brief span. Besides Emerson, many of whose poems and essays first saw print in its pages, it introduced Thoreau to the reading public, as well as several minor poets like Jones Very and Ellery Channing. It gave Margaret Fuller and Alcott a new voice. And, beyond personalities, it helped to introduce two new realms of literature to the American public: most obviously, the writings of the German romantic poets and Transcendental philosophers; but perhaps more important, the "ethnic scriptures" or religious literatures of the East. Going beyond "the times" to "the eternities," it helped stimulate the American Renaissance.

Meanwhile Brook Farm and Alcott's "Fruitlands" had attempted to institutionalize the social idealism of the Transcendental movement. But Emerson remained skeptical of these and all other utopias. In practice he would go only a "little beyond," although in theory he sympathized with the perfectionists. Perhaps his half-humorous essay reporting the "Chardon Street Convention of Friends of Universal Reform" best suggests his attitude toward social Transcendentalism:

> If the assembly was disorderly, it was picturesque. Madmen, madwomen, men with beards, Dunkers, Muggletonians, Come-outers, Groaners, Agrarians, Seventh-day Baptists, Quakers, Abolitionists, Calvinists, Unitarians, and Philosophers—all came successively to the top, and seized their moment, if not their hour, wherein to chide, or pray, or preach, or protest. The faces were a study.[70]

Although Transcendentalism stimulated social reform, Emerson remained an individualist.

Nevertheless, Emerson remained the leader of the Transcendentalists because he best gave expression to their ideals—both religious and social—even if he did not try to realize them at once. His books became the bible of the social reformers of his day and of many practical-minded men and women who were not interested in philosophy or religion. The testimony of Charles Dickens, novelist and reformer, is perhaps typical of all these:

> There has sprung up in Boston [wrote Dickens in his *American Notes*] a sect of philosophers known as Transcendentalists. On inquiring what this appelation might be supposed to signify, I was given to understand that whatever was unintelligible would be certainly Transcendental. Not deriving much comfort from this elucidation, I pursued the inquiry still further, and found that the Transcendentalists are followers of my friend Mr. Carlyle, or I should rather say, of a follower of his, Mr. Ralph Waldo Emerson. This gentlemen has written a volume of Essays, in which among much that is dreamy and fanciful, if he will pardon me for saying so, there is much more that is true and manly, honest and bold. Transcendentalism has its occasional vagaries (what School has not?), but it has good healthful qualities in spite of them . . . If I were a Bostonian, I think I would be a Transcendentalist.[71]

70. R. W. Emerson, *Works*, X, 374. (First published in *The Dial*, July, 1842).

71. O. W. Holmes, *Emerson*, p. 119.

*d. In Literature.* Although Transcendentalism in America purported to be a logical philosophy and to develop the ideas of Immanuel Kant, and although it did develop the religious ideas and attitudes of Puritanism and Unitarianism, and although it actually contributed to the social reforms and experiments of the times, its greatness lay primarily in its contribution to American literature. Emerson and his associates used the abstract ideas of philosophy, the emotional faith of religion, and the forms of democratic society to create a literature that was new and challenging.

The literary significance of Transcendentalism has only begun to be appreciated, partly because of its confusion with Kantian philosophy and partly because of its confusion with literary Romanticism (which we shall consider in the next section). This significance was suggested by Professor F. O. Matthiessen, who pointed out that Transcendentalism stimulated "The American Renaissance" by calling into question and reexamining all the old assumptions and ideas which Western European civilization had come to consider either axiomatic or proven. And it was first clearly defined by Professor David Bowers,[72] who pointed out that Transcendentalism in America developed a series of "Democratic Vistas," whose framework gave form and meaning not only to the writings of Emerson, Thoreau, and Whitman, who optimistically believed in the actual realization of the democratic dream, but also to the writings of Hawthorne and Melville, who symbolically described its tragic defeat.

Superficially, American Transcendentalism reproduced the literary characteristics of Romanticism, praising intuition rather than logic, poetry rather than prose, and nature rather than the society of man. Moreover it shared the romantic revolt from the past and the romantic idealization of the common man.

But American Transcendentalism converted the romantic revolt from the past into an assertion of the independence of American literature and culture from the European past. And it converted the romantic idealization of the common man into an assertion of the infinite potentialities of all men and of their equality before God. The first assertion received classic expression in Emerson's address on "The American Scholar." The second gave

72. Bowers, "Democratic Vistas," in Spiller, Thorp, Johnson and Canby, *The Literary History of the United States,* I, 345-57.

form and significance to all the literature of "The American Renaissance."

Fundamentally, American Transcendentalism was, as Professor foundations and moral implications of the new democracy."[73] It attempted to explore the "metaphysics of democracy" by developing the equalitarian implications of the doctrine of "the inner light," or the intuitive reason. In Emerson's words, it gave its "adherence to a new hope . . . a greater trust in the nature and resources of man, than the laws or the popular opinions will well allow."[74] Declaring that "all things are possible," it called into question the orthodox dogmas and the classical formulations of religion and philosophy. Believing in the ability of man to govern himself and eventually to determine his own destiny, it suggested a whole new philosophy of life and scale of values, and it explored the implications of this in imaginative literature.

This Transcendental belief in the infinite potentialities of the common man gave greatness to the writings of Emerson—and after him, Thoreau and Whitman. American Transcendentalism first fully explored the psychological implications of this belief, which has also been called "The American Dream." But this complex idea can only be described in a later section.

### 3. *Romanticism*

All the textbooks describe American Transcendentalism as a part of Romanticism, and historically they are right. If Romanticism is defined simply as that literary movement which dominated Europe and America during the first half of the nineteenth century, American Transcendentalism was historically a part of Bowers has described it, "a profound exploration of the spiritual it. Scholars can, and have, described Emerson as a typical example of literary Romanticism.[75]

But the term "Romanticism" covers a multitude of ideas: Professor Lovejoy, after spending much of his life tracking down its many meanings, declared that "next to the word 'nature,' 'roman-

73. Bowers, *op. cit.*, p. 346. See also Henry A. Myers, *Are Men Equal?*
74. See above. From "The Editors to the Readers," of *The Dial.*
75. See C. Cestre, "Le Romantisme d'Emerson," *Revue Anglo-Américaine,* VII, 1-18 (October, 1929).

tic' is possibly the most equivocal in the language."[76] Historically it has had different meanings, and psychologically it has had others still. Historically, for instance, it has meant something very different in America from what it has meant in Europe. In one sense, Emerson was a typical romanticist; in another he was hardly romantic at all; in a third he was an American romanticist with a difference.

Without attempting to discriminate all the multiple meanings of the word,[77] we may cite Professor Lovejoy's historical description of it as that body of ideas first promulgated and named in Germany in the 1780's and 1790's, which protested against the fixed and the finite and praised the individualistic and the infinite.[78]

But Professor Lovejoy's famous article went on to show that historical Romanticism developed many contradictory ideas and that in Germany romantic individualism merged with the idea of "organicism" to produce (illogically) the idea of the organic, or "absolute," state; while the romantic idea of the infinite merged with political nationalism (again illogically) to justify the "infinite" conquests of Hitler. By defining "Romanticism" historically, one may prove that the movement contributed historically to certain modern movements and ideas. And, by selecting the more dangerous modern ideas and by emphasizing the more illogical and extreme elements of Romanticism, one may describe the movement as wholly evil. Certainly in modern times, popular opinion has reacted against historical Romanticism and against Emerson as an exponent of it.

It is also possible, however, to define Romanticism psychologically. Thus defined Romanticism becomes the idealization of all "romance," and of all the youthful, emotional excitement universally associated with romance. But since this psychological romance is also the emotion most characteristic of the historical Romantic period in literature, the two definitions often merge. This second

76. A. O. Lovejoy, "The Meaning of Romanticism for the Historian of Ideas," *Journal of the History of Ideas,* II, 258 (June, 1941).

77. A. O. Lovejoy, "On the Discrimination of Romanticisms," *PMLA,* XXXIX, 229-53 (1924).

78. Lovejoy, "The Meaning of Romanticism. . . ." *loc. cit.*

definition merely emphasizes that Romanticism is a universal element in human experience—and therefore in literature—and that it is not limited to one historical period but recurs constantly (if with different emphases) in every period. But it also suggests that all Romanticism—both historical and psychological—is characterized by youthfulness, and therefore immaturity. "Romanticism" defined psychologically has also become suspect in modern times.

The most brilliant hostile critic of Emerson, Professor Yvor Winters, has defined Romanticism psychologically, and by emphasizing and isolating the illogical and the immature aspects of it, has also made it seem wholly evil.[79] Associating the romantic with the sentimental and the hedonistic, he has described it as "mainly or even purely . . . emotional," has contrasted it with the rational and the moral, and, of course, has condemned it. Emerson, as the epitome of this illogical and immature emotionalism, therefore has received his most absolute condemnation.

Certainly some of Emerson's ideas were romantic—both in the literary and the psychological senses. But other ideas of his were anti-romantic—in both senses. Finally, some of his ideas which have seemed romantic from the European point of view may be interpreted differently from the American.

Analyzing "Le Romantisme d'Emerson," Professor Charles Cestre of Paris has emphasized Emerson's egotism ("la contemplation de son *moi*"), his love of Nature and the woods, his glorification of the instinctive and the subconscious, his praise of intense emotion, and his joyous expansiveness and optimism.[80] Analyzing Emerson's ideas more from the philosophical point of view, Professor Yvor Winters also has declared them to be "the commonplace ideas of the romantic movement."[81] He has emphasized Emerson's exaltation of subconscious instinct and emotion over "Reason," his optimistic assertion that man is fundamentally good, his glorification of infinite change ("an endless seeker, with no Past at my back"), and his exaltation of egotism into a philosophy of pure relativism. It is true that all of these ideas of Emerson were "romantic." If Emerson had not qualified these ideas

79. Yvor Winters, *In Defense of Reason,* p. 8.
80. Cestre, *loc. cit.*
81. Winters, *op. cit.,* p. 578.

radically, if he had not emphasized other ideas equally and if he had not related these ideas to the concrete circumstances of American life so as to suggest their historic relevance and temporal value as well as their "eternal" truth, we should have to call him a pure romantic. But he did qualify and counterbalance these ideas, and he did relate them to American time and place.

Emphatically, Emerson did not consider himself a romantic. Toward the end of his famous address on "The American Scholar," he specifically repudiated the romantic ideal as he understood it:

> I ask not for the great, the remote, the romantic; what is doing in Italy or Arabia; what is Greek art or Provençal minstrelsy; I embrace the common, I explore and sit at the feet of the familiar, the low. Give me insight into today, and you may have the antique and future worlds.

Rather, Emerson considered himself a practical idealist whose primary concern was with American actuality. Certainly he was no "romantic" in the sense of dreamer or escapist.

Moreover, Emerson qualified almost every one of his "romantic" ideas radically. First, he described his "self-reliance" as the opposite of "egotism," and emphasized, not the separateness of the individual "self," but its essential relation to the higher "Self," or God. Second, his exaltation of the instinctive and the subconscious was made in the very name of "Reason"; he wished to integrate the instinctive drives with the conscious reason; and in this his attitude was not greatly different from that of modern nonrational psychology. It is emphatically *not* true that "for Emerson, as for other Romantics, Reason is the source of all evil, is the adversary of Impulse."[82] Third, Emerson qualified his "optimistic" faith that "man is part of God, and so is good,"[83] with the idea: "potentially." His doctrine was one of meliorism—of the potential ultimate perfection of man. He merely accepted the counsel of Jesus: "Be ye therefore perfect, even as your Father is perfect." Fourth, his glorification of infinite "change" always implied this undefined Christian goal of perfection, just as his language ("an endless seeker") implied his religious origins. If these ideas of his

82. Winters, *op. cit.*, p. 578. None of the quotations which Mr. Winters adduces suggest any essential hostility between Reason and Impulse: Emerson's whole effort was to reconcile the two.

83. Winters, *loc. cit.*

were "romantic" and were sometimes stated without immediate qualification, they were always qualified in the next sentence or section, and their language and context always implied this radical qualification.

Moreover, many of Emerson's "romantic" ideas have particularly realistic meanings for the American mind. His love of Nature and the woods, for instance, was part of the American pioneer experience and was not merely a form of escape from industrial civilization, as in Europe it often had been. His "joyous expansiveness" reflected the historic joy in growth and development natural to nineteenth century America. Similarly, his "egotistic" self-reliance was a pragmatically valuable formulation of American experience. In attacking "the dead hand of the past," and "the courtly muses of Europe," Emerson was continuing in literature the political ideals of the American Revolution and was attacking the "colonialism" which continued to follow the alien traditions of feudal Europe. The romantic revolution, which in Europe sought to destroy many of the native European traditions, in America destroyed rather the tyranny of alien traditions.

Thus Emerson qualified his most "romantic" ideas radically and often related them to actual American experience so as to change their meaning. Beyond this, however, Emerson developed other major ideas which were the opposite of "romantic." We shall consider these at length in a later section as "Yankee Realism"; but two of these ideas deserve notice here for their *anti*-romanticism.

First, the idea and the word "moral" probably looms larger and appears more often in Emerson's writing than any purely "romantic" idea or word. "The moral law," "the moral sentiment," and "the moral sense" formed the bed-rock of Puritan conservatism, on which his romanticism was founded. Deriving the idea of a God-given moral law from his Puritan ancestors and reading of it philosophically in Dugald Stewart and other Scottish philosophers[84] in his youth, he later related it to the transcendental "Reason," and made it central in his philosophy. Dr. Myron Wicke has emphasized that "as his mystical attitudes grew stronger, he

84. M. R. Davis, "Emerson's 'Reason' and the Scottish Philosophers," *The New England Quarterly*, XVII, 209-28 (June, 1944).

wrote more and more of the moral sentiment."[85] And Professor Cestre has distinguished "Emerson's Romanticism" from that of Whitman and others by this constant emphasis on morality. To many generations of conservatives this "moralism" has made Emerson appear as a blood brother rather than an enemy.

Second, and more specifically, Emerson also constantly emphasized that other unromantic idea, "discipline." "Discipline" formed the central section of his first book on *Nature* and provided the transition to his "Idealism." And throughout his life he described it as the pre-condition to all mystical intuition and to all radical reforms. So Professor Cestre has emphasized that for Emerson "l'optimisme du 'voyant' n'abolit pas la nécessite de l'effort, il l'organise."[86] And Dr Wicke has devoted a chapter of his study of *Emerson's Mysticism* to this central idea of "discipline."

Indeed, whenever Emerson became most "romantic" and most extreme, he inserted specific warnings emphasizing the constant need for effort and self-discipline. When he exhorted his "American Scholar" to be "free and brave," he specified that "he must be a solitary, laborious, modest, and charitable soul . . . He must embrace solitude as a bride."[87] And when he proclaimed his radical gospel of "Self-Reliance," he warned, first, that it was only for adults who have been "educated." ("There is a time in every man's education when he arrives at the conviction . . . that he must take himself for better for worse"); and second, that this gospel, required strict self-discipline. ("If any one imagines that the law is lax, let him keep its commandments one day.")[88] Only between these warnings did he insert his most "romantic" statement that: "the only right is what is after my constitution; the only wrong what is against it"—and even here the word "constitution" implied a conscious, socially-conditioned law by which the individual must govern himself. Therefore, to assert that Emerson's gospel was mystically immoral ("My impulse to commit incest may horrify you; your impulse to commit murder and

85. Myron Wicke, *Emerson's Mysticism* (unpub. thesis; Western Reserve University), p. 143.
86. Cestre, *op. cit.*, p. 127.
87. Emerson, *Works*, I, 173.
88. *Ibid.*, II, 46, 74.

arson may horrify me; but we should ignore each other and proceed"[89]), is to ignore and distort both the specific warnings and the general context of Emerson's idealism.

Nevertheless, many of Emerson's ideas were "romantic" when stated without qualification, and they have often been interpreted romantically. Sometimes Emerson himself was genuinely "romantic." It is true, for instance, that "Emerson and his contemporaries, in surrendering to what they took for impulse, were governed by New England habit; they mistook second nature for nature."[90] Especially when Emerson developed the ideas of mysticism in the language of naturalism ("impulse," "instinct"), his writing became confused. Perhaps, therefore, the best way to define the extent of Emerson's "Romanticism" is to contrast it with his "Mysticism."

Some critics, like Professor Cestre,[91] have described Emerson's Romanticism and his Mysticism as almost identical. Others, like Professor Winters, have denied Emerson the name of mystic because his "Mysticism" was not of the catholic and traditional type. But we shall rather follow Dean Inge's suggested definition: "In pantheistic mysticism, God is really everywhere; while in ordinary pantheism [or Romanticism], everything is God."[92]

"Mysticism," so defined, teaches that God (or the principle of perfection) exists in all men and *may be* realized in some degree by all. But pantheism, or philosophic Romanticism, teaches that all things *are* infinitely perfect and, therefore, that no laws or standards apply. The mystic *seeks* God and strives for perfection: the romantic believes himself perfectly good and strives only to gratify his own desires. In this sense, Emerson was a mystic but not a romantic.

Mysticism also teaches that God, or the idea of perfection, exists *within* the individual and is not dependent upon society and worldly success: in this mystical sense, Jesus was perfect, even though he failed of worldly success. But Romanticism teaches that perfection consists of self-realization, either through individual self-satisfaction or through worldly success. And in this

89. Winters, *op. cit.*, p. 582.
90. *Ibid.*, p. 587.
91. Cestre, *loc. cit.*
92. W. R. Inge, *Studies in English Mysticism*, p. 178.

sense, Emerson's mysticism was partly romantic. Emerson did not confuse self-reliance with self-satisfaction, but he did believe that perfection should and would be achieved in this world. But this leads us to the subject of Emerson's Optimism.

## Optimism and Evil

The central problem in Emerson's thought—and the problem about which good critics have most disagreed—is that of optimism and evil. What is "evil?" Does good predominate over evil in this world? And will good progressively triumph over evil in history? These are questions which Emerson's writing does not answer simply and clearly. And bound up with these are the problems of tragedy, of war, and "the idea of progress." Were Emerson's eyes "thickly bandaged to the evil and sin of the world,"[93] as Henry James and many others have argued? Or did Emerson merely interpret "evil" differently from other writers?

As a mystic Emerson interpreted evil differently because mysticism has always interpreted evil differently. But as a realist Emerson sometimes slipped back into the conventional interpretation of evil. And as a romantic he often declared that good (in the conventional sense) would surely triumph over evil in history, because Emerson, besides being a mystic, was also a child of the nineteenth century. More often, however, Emerson sought to mediate between the purely mystical and the purely conventional interpretations and to preach the potential inner victory of good over evil in the soul of man or the possible, future victory of good over evil in the life of humanity. The problem can only be solved by reference to the opposing mystical and realistic interpretations, and to the mediating psychological and long-term historical interpretations.

Mysticism denies the reality of "evil" in the conventional sense, and Emerson's interpretation was fundamentally that of the mystic. Of course neither mysticism nor Emerson denies the reality of what men call "evil" or the reality of the feelings of pain and sorrow which accompany the phenomenon of "evil" in individual human experience. But both deny the justice of calling these "evil." They interpret "evil" from the point of view of God or of humanity as a whole, rather than from the point of view of

93. Henry James, *Partial Portraits* (London, 1919), p. 31.

the individual man suffering what he imagines to be evil: the pain or death of the individual man or nation may rather contribute to the development of humanity or of the life-process as a whole. The obvious fact that it is difficult for an individual to look upon his own pain and death with godlike equanimity explains the unpopularity of the mystical interpretation of evil, but in no way invalidates it.

The mystical interpretation of evil is invalidated only when confused with the romantic: the mystic has experienced and understood pain and evil, and having known them, has gone beyond them; but the romantic remains in childlike innocence of pain and evil and imagines that they are unimportant or nonexistent. Emerson, himself, like all mystics, had lived through many long years of pain and tragedy and developed his philosophy as a result: the first section of this *Handbook* has emphasized this all-important fact of personal experience.

In St. Augustine, Florida, where Emerson was recuperating from tuberculosis at the age of twenty-four, he entered in his *Journals:* "He has seen but half the Universe who never has been shown the house of Pain. Pleasure and Peace are but indifferent teachers of what it is life to know."[94] Emerson knew intimately this "house of Pain." And in his writings he constantly repeated that "no theory of life can have any right which leaves out of account the values of vice, pain, disease, poverty, insecurity, disunion, fear, and death."[95] Because he had experienced these "values" at first hand and knew well the fear of death, he could say, unromantically, that pain and death were not "evil." Henry James' description of Emerson's "ripe unconsciousness of evil"[96] ignored these facts.

"Many men can die for their families, many for their country, a few for mankind; Emerson could have died for the universe."[97] Thus Professor Firkins suggested that Emerson's philosophy of evil was derived from and was directed toward active, personal experience. But also he suggested that it was beyond the common

94. *Journals,* II, 180 (1827).
95. *Works,* VII, 165 and XII, 406. See C. E. Jorgenson, "Emerson's Paradise under the Shadow of Swords," *Philological Quarterly,* XI (July, 1932), 274.
96. James, *op. cit.,* p. 7.
97. O. W. Firkins, *Ralph Waldo Emerson,* p. 354.

experience of most men and, therefore, liable to be misunderstood. Emerson himself warned that: "it demands something godlike in him who has cast off the common motives of humanity," and that "to be great is to be misunderstood."[98] But his personal experience of evil has often been forgotten, his warning ignored, and his philosophy misinterpreted.

This was partly Emerson's own fault, of course. For he was guilty of two errors—one verbal and one real. Verbally Emerson sometimes confused conventional "evils," such as pain or insecurity, with Evil in the larger sense, so as to imply that he was denying the fact of evil and of law, nihilistically. And really he sometimes identified himself so completely with a current reform or "cause" that he invoked the name of God to justify his own partisan opinions. The first fault has led to the charges of romanticism, nihilism, and antinomianism. The second has led to the charge of blind optimism and of being a "Militant Pollyanna."[99]

Emerson's first fault involved a problem in semantics or the meaning of words. Using "evil" in the conventional sense but explaining his mystic's interpretation of it, he emphasized "the values of evil": what seems evil to the individual may be really good; it may contribute to his education, or enlarge his experience, or serve as a challenge to overcome. Or, seen from the point of view of God, this "evil" may be merely "fate, or the laws of the world,"[100] which limit the individual and which he cannot understand unless he sees beyond his own selfish interests and achieves a larger perspective. Therefore Emerson wrote in "Uriel": "Evil will bless, and ice will burn"; and in "Experience": "Of course it needs the whole society to give the symmetry we seek. The party-colored wheel must revolve very fast to appear white." That is to say, "evil" in the conventional sense is often not really Evil, but either a possible means to good, or a partial or potential good.

But this is not to say that Evil, in the larger sense, does not exist, or that all is always for the best in the best possible of worlds. Evil exists, although not in the conventional sense of "evil":

> Good is positive. Evil is merely privative, not absolute: it is like

98. *Works,* II, "Self-Reliance."
99. See L. A. Wilkinson, "Emerson: Militant Pollyanna," *The Thinker,* III (April, 1931), 33-44.
100. Essay on "Fate," *Conduct of Life.*

cold, which is the privation of heat. All evil is so much death or nonentity. Benevolence is absolute and real.[101]

That is, true Evil is the denial of life or power. Or, as Woodberry described it:

> Those who receive the most [divine energy] are the greatest men; those who receive and also impart the most are men of genius; those who obstruct and fail of reception are the wicked, for evil is simply the privation of this presence and power.[102]

All of which, perhaps, is merely the amateur philosopher's way of formulating Jesus' parable of the men with the different talents. True Evil[103] consists of burying your one talent—of hiding your light under a bushel.

Therefore, Emerson's was not a philosophy of equivalence or of romantic self-indulgence or of the denial of the values of life and disciplined effort—rather the reverse. But in denying the reality of "evil" in the conventional sense Emerson sometimes seemed to deny all values. And in affirming the supreme importance of self-reliance and of the realization of one's individual potentialities, he sometimes seemed to justify the Nietzschean philosophy of the superman and of immoralism.

On the other hand, Emerson's interpretation of evil was not quite the classical one that some of his apologists have suggested. Dr. Chester E. Jorgenson, who analyzed the problem most thoroughly, concluded that

> Emerson's attitude toward evil has been shown to resemble essentially that of Milton, as well as that basically incarnate in *Macbeth*. Both Milton and Emerson believe in a Beneficent Deity whose unchanging laws lead to happiness if obeyed, and whose laws if transgressed bring immediate retribution.[104]

So far, so good. But Milton accepted the classical-Christian attitude that good and evil are easily distinguished and eternally

101. *Works*, I, 124 ("Divinity School Address").

102. G. E. Woodberry, *Emerson*, p. 111.

103. cf. Emerson's criticism of Swedenborg: "His cardinal position in morals is that evil should be shunned as sins. But he does not know what evil is." (*Works*, IV, 137.) In an unpublished doctoral dissertation, *Emerson and India*, Man M. Singh (Pennsylvania, 1947) has an excellent chapter on Emerson's idea of evil.

104. C. E. Jorgenson, "Emerson's Paradise under the Shadow of Swords," *Philological Quarterly*, XI (July, 1932), 292.

fixed, although he did describe Satan as a noble and heroic figure; but Emerson declared that what men call evil is often really good in disguise, and thus made explicit the moral implicit in Milton's *Paradise Lost*—that the conventional devil was often really a "good, old devil" after all.

This interpretation has seemed antinomian and dangerous. But actually Emerson was closer to the author of "Job"—whose Satan was not merely the "adversary" of God, but also a kind of inspector-general working under the supervision of God—than he was to Milton. And later Emerson's interpretation was more clearly formulated by Whitman in "Chanting the Square Deific," where Satan was made a fourth with the Trinity of Father, Son, and Holy Ghost. The implication was that the Father, or the principle of authority, may sometimes be tyrannical, thus making Satan, or the principle of rebellion against established authority, really good. Thomas Jefferson had said the same thing earlier in political language. But the idea has always remained unpopular with those in authority, whether political or religious. Emerson's interpretation of evil was neither orthodox nor classical.

Emerson's idea of evil, however, was closer to that of Shakespeare's Macbeth, as described by A. C. Bradley: "Evil exhibits itself everywhere as something negative, barren, weakening, destructive, a principle of death."[105] This is especially because both Shakespeare and Emerson refused to specify, *a priori*, exactly what evil was, but rather left the judgment, pragmatically, to future readers or historians. But obviously Shakespeare and Emerson differed radically in their methods of describing evil—Shakespeare describing it dramatically from the point of view of the actor in the human tragedy, but Emerson describing it contemplatively from the point of view of the god sitting detached upon Mount Olympus. To change the metaphor—Emerson, having suffered many of the tribulations of Job, but having regained health and possessions, philosophized upon the problems of humanity, but did not describe them tragically, as did the author of Job. Emerson's philosophy of evil was not that of the dramatist but of the mystic: his point of view was from the high place beyond tragedy.

105. A. C. Bradley, *Shakespearean Tragedy* (London, 1926), p. 35, in C. E. Jorgenson, *op. cit.*, p. 288.

But emphatically Emerson did not deny the values of tragedy, either in life or literature. Rather he considered them preliminary. To argue that Emerson's "formula encouraged him to ignore experience whenever it was in harsh or ugly conflict with his optimism,"[106] as Professor Matthiessen has, is to distort his meaning. For by "Experience," Emerson always meant the particular experiences of individual men who have not achieved the perspective of the mystic philosopher. "In the dark hours" (he wrote in his essay on "The Tragic") "our existence seems to be a defensive war, a struggle against the encroaching All . . . The law which establishes nature and the human race continually thwarts the will of ignorant individuals."[107] But in perspective "the suffering individual finds his good consulted in the good of all, of which he is a part . . . The intellect is a consoler, which delights in detaching or putting an interval between a man and his fortune, and so converts the sufferer into a spectator and his pain into poetry."[108]

Emerson did not ignore or deny the values of tragedy, but, having experienced them, described them as preliminary. In this his mysticism agreed with Dante's, who described all life as a "Divine Comedy" rather than a Human Tragedy, and whose "Paradiso" marked the culmination of his thought. But, if Emerson himself had experienced tragedy and its values, he chose not to realize them in his writing, and therefore his "Paradiso" lacked an "Inferno." Consciously he cut himself off from that tragic area of literary expression which criticism has always considered greatest. For this reason, perhaps, he will never be considered one of the world's great men of letters. But this limitation which diminishes his purely literary importance does not affect his philosophical value.

Indeed, Emerson's conscious rejection of tragic material for his own literary purposes may even increase his value as philosopher and seer. By focusing his attention upon the intellectual meaning rather than the passional feeling of human life, he may have gained sharper perspective and insight. "The life of truth is cold and so far mournful," he wrote in his essay on "Experience," "but it is not the slave of tears, contritions, and perturba-

106. F. O. Matthiessen, *American Renaissance*, p. 52.
107. *Works*, XII, 405, 408.
108. *Works*, XII, 408, 416.

tions." Consciously he chose the philosopher's "life of truth" in contrast to the dramatist's life of tragic experience. But first he had personally experienced and evaluated "the tragic."

More specifically the tragic problem of war engaged Emerson's attention throughout his life and helped make concrete his ideas about evil. Dr. W. A. Huggard,[109] who studied the problem in detail, has pointed out the confused disagreement of his biographers on the subject: Woodberry believed that the Civil War gave Emerson his first real appreciation of "the social unities embodied in the state as a main source of the blessings of civilization"; while Firkins thought that Emerson's approval of the Civil War sprang from "the romantic impulse which had formed his love of Scott and . . . irradiated war with a courtly glamour." But Moncure Conway, who knew Emerson personally in his later years, described the Civil War as a severe ordeal from which he never completely recovered.[110]

The facts are clear that Emerson did approve the Civil War, because he believed it to be for the principle of freedom, and that he did exclaim in 1861: "Ah! sometimes gunpowder smells good."[111] But in a lecture that same year he fully explained the reasons for this approval (summarized by Cabot):

> War universal in nature, from the highest to the lowest race. What does it signify? It covers a great and beneficent principle—self-help, struggle to be, to resist oppression, to attain the security of a permanent self-defended being.[112]

Or, as Dr. Huggard has phrased it:

> Emerson believed that warfare of some sort, either physical or spiritual, is universal . . . the good and useful end is achieved by "the uncivil, unavailable man, who is a problem and a threat to society," the man of faith who attacks the skepticism underlying acquiescence.[113]

To Emerson war seemed one of those social evils which may be turned to the end of good: he opposed the Mexican War because

109. William Allen Huggard, "*Emerson and the Problem of War and Peace,* University of Iowa Humanistic Studies, V, No. 5 (April, 1938), pp. 8-9.

110. Moncure D. Conway, *Emerson,* p. 313.

111. J. E. Cabot, *Memoir,* II, 601.

112. *Ibid.,* II, 772.

113. *Works,* III, 100, quoted in W. A. Huggard, *Emerson and the Problem of War and Peace,* p. 40.

he believed it imperialistic, but he approved the Civil War because he believed it for the cause of liberty. If this was optimistic, it certainly was neither romantic, nor blind. War was an "evil," but in certain cases "evil will bless" and produce good.

Emerson's attitude toward the idea of progress was similar. Although most nineteenth century American thinkers believed enthusiastically in the inevitability of human progress and spoke easily of "manifest destiny," Emerson emphatically did not believe in universal social progress and questioned the right of America to expand indefinitely. Of course he believed that individuals could perfect themselves and that through their influence other individuals might also "progress." But "Society never advances."[114] Dr. Mildred Silver's brilliant study of "Emerson and the Idea of Progress"[115] has done much to correct the exaggerated interpretations of Emerson's optimism.

Emerson's "optimism" can be interpreted either chronologically or logically. Chronologically he passed through four distinct phases.[116] In youth his patroitism was enthusiastic and his *Journals* were filled with flowery prophecies about the future greatness of America—although even these were qualified carefully and almost always criticized the faults of his country and times. Second, about 1838 to 1840, he emphasized "self-reliance" as opposed to "society," and attacked all social institutions and governments as enemies of individual freedom and progress. (Dr. Stephen Whicher[117] has argued that the official attacks on his "Divinity School Address" convinced him of the hopelessness of social progress.) Third, the outbreak of the Mexican War further strengthened his distrust of governmental "progress" at a time when the scientific idea of evolution was becoming most popular. But finally the Civil War roused him again and tempted him to unguarded prophecies about the future "Fortune of the Republic." In youth and in old age Emerson's optimism was sometimes overenthusiastic, but in his middle, most creative years his belief in social and universal human progress was almost *nil.*

114. "Self-Reliance," *Works,* II, 84.

115. Mildred Silver, "Emerson and the Idea of Progress," *American Literature,* XII (March, 1940), 1-19.

116. Silver, *op. cit.,* pp. 17-18.

117. Stephen Whicher, *The Lapse of Uriel* (unpub. doctoral dissertation; Harvard, 1942).

The striking fact is that "Emerson rejected the popular belief of his age that general progress was a law of nature operating automatically and causing an unbroken advancement in the past, present, and future."[118] But, if Emerson usually disbelieved in social progress and even in steady racial progress, he always and emphatically stated his belief in the moral perfectibility of the individual—and through him, potentially, of all men. The individual was the grain of mustard seed—the leaven which might potentially transform this human society into the kingdom of heaven. This Christian belief in moral or psychological perfectibility has often been confused with the "idea of progress."

As usual, Emerson was partly to blame for this confusion, for he often used the language of evolution and natural science to describe his essentially religious ideas, as in his motto for *Nature*. But from 1836 to his essay on "American Civilization" in 1862 he repeatedly asked: "Is this secular progress we have described, this evolution of man to the highest powers, only to give him sensibility, and not to bring duties with it?"[119] And he repeatedly warned: "Don't trust children with edge tools. Don't trust man, great God, with more power than he has until he has learned to use that little better."[120] The secular progress of science and the practical power of man seemed to Emerson significant and challenging but preliminary and dangerous. It might result in human greatness, or disaster.

Dr. Silver has pointed out that the word "progress" occurs several times in Emerson's essay on "The Over-Soul," where it is always used of "a man's improvement in character, of his advance toward a more and more complete incarnation of the Great Spirit, of his absorption of and into the Divine Unity."[121] Of art, Emerson repeatedly asserted that "the ancients have never been surpassed." And in his most optimistic essay, "The Progress of Culture," he asserted that "the world is always equal to itself," and emphasized "a certain equivalence in the ages of history."[122] The individual's powers of perception and creation seemed to

118. Silver, *op. cit.*, p. 2.
119. *Works*, XI, 299.
120. *Journals*, II, 450.
121. Silver, *op. cit.*, p. 11.
122. Silver, *op. cit.*, p. 15.

him all-important. Therefore, his individual's progress was essentially that symbolized in Bunyan's *Pilgrim's Progress.* The progress of humanity was an individual and moral matter.

But from this essentially religious conception of progress Emerson often went on to draw more optimistic implications. Although evolution and scientific progress did not insure psychological and moral progress, they provided the opportunity for it, and victory in the Civil War led Emerson to believe that human freedom was actually being progressively achieved. "The Progress of Culture" would come through the efforts of liberated individuals who would remake institutions and history. In the end individual progress would lead to racial progress. But always he emphasized that, in history, this hope was only a hope—a potentiality, but not an assurance: "Far off . . . is the perfectibility."[123]

In his earlier *Journals* Emerson had described this millennial, Christian hope most vividly:

> The history of Christ is the best Document of the power of Character that we have. A youth who owed nothing to fortune and was "hanged at Tyburn,"—by the pure quality of his nature has shed this epic splendor around the facts of his death which has transfigured every particular into a grand universal symbol for the eyes of mankind ever since.
>
> He did well. This great Defeat is hitherto the highest fact we have. But he that shall come shall do better. The mind requires a far higher exhibition of character, one which shall make itself good to the senses as well as to the soul. This was a great Defeat, we demand Victory. More character will convert judge and jury, soldier and king; will rule human and animal and mineral nature; will command irresistibly and blend with the course of Universal Nature.[124]

Often Emerson the prophet prevailed over Emerson the mystic and declared the actual future realization of the Christian ideal in human history. Often Emerson denied the ultimacy of tragedy and of its values. But the final end of "Victory," he believed, would only be achieved by the Christian means of "Character" or inner progress. Concerning society and its institutions he was never optimistic, but of the redeeming power of individual character in this actual world he hoped much.

123. *Journals*, III, 557.
124. *Journals*, VI, 188-89 (April 6, 1842).

## THE AMERICAN DREAM

Emerson was more optimistic about "America" and its future greatness than about the rest of the world. From the age of nineteen, when he dedicated his youthful *Journal* to: "The Spirit of America . . . to that living soul . . . to whom the Divinity hath assigned the care of this bright corner of the Universe,"[125] to the end of his literary life when he lectured in glowing terms on "The Fortune of the Republic," he idealized his country.

This patriotic enthusiasm has often seemed excessive to modern readers. In an age of internationalism and disillusion his nationalism and optimism have seemed either dangerous or naive, or both. Was he blind to the need and value of international co-operation? Was he foolish to believe that his America could succeed where so many had failed. The answers are not simple.

By "America" Emerson meant much more than his country, "The United States of America." Beyond this physical nation his "America" was "the new world" and, beyond that, the new ideals whose realization this new world made possible. Almost always he meant by "America" not merely the physical country, but also the new ideals of liberty, democracy, and equality to which it was dedicated. In 1851 he wrote: "America is the idea of emancipation."[126] And at other times he phrased it in other terms. But always his "America" was primarily an idea and the opportunity for realizing it.

Moreover, Emerson's idealization of "the Spirit of America" was never narrowly local or temporal but was his way of relating his abstract thought to the physical realities from which it sprang and toward which it was redirected. That his "American" ideals were integrally a part of his fundamental thinking is suggested by a key passage in his *Journals:*

> Democracy, Freedom, has its root in the sacred truth that every man hath in him the divine Reason, or that, though few men since the creation of the world live according to the dictates of Reason, yet all men are created capable of so doing. To this truth we look when we say, Reverence thyself; Be true to thyself.[127]

125. *Journals,* I, 160.
126. *Journals,* VIII, 232.
127. *Journals,* III, 390 (1834).

The American ideals of Democracy, Freedom, and Equality were not separable in his mind from the universal ideals of Reason and Self-reliance.

Perhaps for this reason international-minded critics have sometimes argued that Emerson's idealism really was universal rather than American. George Santayana, who devoted himself to the celebration of "The Life of Reason," declared of Emerson that: "His heart was fixed on eternal things, and he was in no sense a prophet for his age or country."[128] And Matthew Arnold, in the same book in which he attacked the materialism of American democracy, praised Emerson as "the friend and aider of those who would live in the spirit."[129] But Arnold, more perceptive than Santayana, went on to describe Emerson as "the most distinctively and *honourably* American of your writers."[130]

In modern times Emerson's American idealism, both in its patriotic and in its broadly universal aspects, has been characterized as part of "The American Dream." James Truslow Adams, whose *Epic of America* was the first to name and describe this dream clearly, was also the first to identify Emerson with it specifically:

> The American dream—the belief in the value of the common man, and the hope of opening every avenue of opportunity to him—was not a logical concept of thought. Like every great thought that has stirred and advanced humanity, it was a religious emotion, a great act of faith, a courageous leap into the dark unknown. As long as that dream persists to strengthen the heart of man, Emerson will remain one of its prophets.[131]

And following this lead, *Emerson's Americanism* has been analyzed at length by Dr. Ernest E. Sandeen;[132] and the "religious emotion" inherent in his Americanism has been emphasized by Dr. C. H. Foster.[133]

128. George Santayana, *Interpretations of Poetry and Religion* (New York, 1900), p. 233.

129. Matthew Arnold, *Discourses in America* (New York, 1924), p. 179.

130. *Ibid.*, p. 205. (Italics added.)

131. James Truslow Adams, *The Epic of America* (Boston, 1932), p. 198.

132. Ernest E. Sandeen, "Emerson's Americanism," *Critical Studies in Arnold, Emerson and Newman*, University of Iowa Studies, edited by Joseph E. Baker (Iowa City, 1942), VI, 63-118.

133. C. H. Foster, "Emerson as American Scripture," *The New England Quarterly*, XVI (March, 1943), 91-105.

Emerson's "American Dream," like all dreams, was complex and may perhaps be separated into three strands. First, it sprang from and related itself to the concrete realities of nineteenth century American life. The chief characteristic of this life was westward expansion—often described vaguely by the phrase: "the frontier."

Second, the American Dream was influenced by that combination of reality and idea called "the new world." Beyond the physical country and constituted nation the American continent—or rather hemisphere—was a "new" world, offering seemingly endless opportunities for a new life. "America" was "newness" and "opportunity," as opposed to an effete and traditional "Europe."

Third, the American Dream crystallized certain ideals which had originated in Europe but which the conditions of American life made practical and prevalent. These were liberty, democracy, and equality. And these ideals, related to the concrete facts of American life, constituted the core of Emerson's Americanism—as of "The American Dream" as a whole.

Concretely, Emerson's Americanism can best be described in terms of his actual life and of his day-to-day comments on the contemporary events in which he participated and on which he passed judgments. From his earliest youth to his latest age he was fascinated by the phenomena of American life and in his *Journals* often made these phenomena the occasions for his excursions into philosophy. To a surprising degree for a philosopher he participated in this life. But his attitude toward it was not simple: he both idealized it in terms of its potentialities and criticized it for its failure to realize these. As a result two schools of interpretation have arisen: one has described Emerson as the typical American "frontier" optimist whose expansive idealism was largely conditioned by the events of his time; the other has emphasized his New England conservatism and his constant criticism of the excesses of Western and popular American democracy. Needless to say, the truth lies between.

The "frontier" school of interpretation has done well to emphasize Emerson's constant intellectual interest in and (later) physical experience of the American West. Earlier biographers and critics had tended to characterize him as a New England Brahmin and to group him with Holmes, Hawthorne, Longfellow, Lowell,

Thoreau, and Whittier as one of "the New England School." But in sharp contrast to all of these, he constantly turned his attention —and later his steps—to the West. Soon after dedicating his youthful *Journal* to "the Spirit of America," he noted the problem which this West imposed:

> The vast rapidity with which the deserts and forests of the interior of this country are peopled have led patriots to fear lest the nation grow *too fast* for its virtue and peace . . . Good men desire, and the great cause of human nature demands, that this abundant and overflowing richness wherewith God has blessed this country be not misapplied and made a curse of.[134]

From the beginning he turned both his patriotic idealism and his critical intelligence to the "frontier."

As Emerson's lecture tours began to take him in person into Pennsylvania and Ohio and later into Iowa and even California, he had abundant opportunity to observe life on the Western "frontier" at first hand. Much of it he admired, and always he praised its vitality and originality:

> Our eyes will be turned westward, and a new and stronger tone of literature will result. The Kentucky stump-oratory, the exploits of Boone and David Crockett, the Journals of western pioneers, agriculturalists, and socialists, and the letters of Jack Downing, are genuine growths which are sought with avidity in Europe, where our European-like books are of no value.[135]

But as he observed more closely and experienced more personally, his enthusiasm often became diluted and his criticism of America's "wild democracy" sharpened: "The beautiful is never plentiful," he wrote. "Then Illinois and Indiana, with their spawning loins, must needs be ordinary."[136]

The "frontier" critics, rightly, have emphasized the fact of Emerson's constant, deep interest in the West and have shown how this interest distinguished him from most of his New England contemporaries and gave national breadth and perspective to his writing. But the most enthusiastic member of this school, Mrs.

134. *Journals*, I, 247-48 (1823).
135. From an editorial in *The Dial*, April, 1843, quoted in *Works*, I, 416.
136. *Works*, XI, 538.

Lucy L. Hazard, in *The Frontier of American Literature,*[137] allowed herself to quote some of Emerson's ironic "celebrations" of Western life as if they had been serious and in general to distort Emerson's attitude by suppressing the constant critical qualifications with which he balanced his genuinely enthusiastic celebrations of the West. In his most patriotic essay on "The Fortune of the Republic" he wrote:

> In proportion to the personal ability of each man, he feels the invitation and career which the country opens to him. He is easily fed with wheat and game, with Ohio wine, but his brain is also pampered by finer draughts, by political power and by power in the railroad board, in the mills, or the banks. This elevates his spirits, and gives, of course, an easy self-reliance *that makes him self-willed and unscrupulous.*[138]

Thus Emerson connected the American frontier not only with his own ideal of self-reliance but also with the frequent popular abuse of that ideal.

Better balanced in estimating Emerson's frontier Americanism is Professor Ernest Marchand's article on "Emerson and the Frontier."[139] Emphasizing Emerson's personal experiences in the West and the indirect effects of the frontier upon his writing through the psychology which it induced, Marchand has suggested that "the cardinal points of his teaching—optimism, melioration, democracy, individualism, self-reliance—derive their chief sanction and meaning from the psychology bred by the American frontier."[140] Defined broadly enough, this is true: Emerson himself identified the experience and psychology of the new Western frontier with that of the old New England frontier of his ancestors, when he told Bret Harte in 1872 that he (Emerson) "spoke also from Pilgrim experience." His "pilgrim" forebears had also been frontiersmen. And in his own time the rapidly changing conditions of life in his own New England created a different kind of "fron-

137. See detailed criticisms of L. L. Hazard, *The Frontier in American Literature;* by Mildred Silver, "Emerson and the Idea of Progress," *American Literature,* XII (1940), 6; and by Arthur I. Ladu, "Emerson: Whig or Democrat," *The New England Quarterly,* XIII (1940), 434.

138. *Works,* XI, 522. (The final clause—here italicized—was omitted by Mrs. Hazard.)

139. In *American Literature,* III (May, 1931), 149-74.

140. *Ibid.,* p. 174.

tier" between the old order and the new, even if not between the civilization and the wilderness. Emerson's self-reliance was genuinely the product of this larger (but vaguer) American "frontier" psychology.

By contrast other writers have emphasized Emerson's many criticisms of the American West and its materialism, and have defined "the frontier" narrowly so as to suggest his alienation from it. So Dr. Arthur I. Ladu: "Not only did Emerson criticize adversely the frontier conception of democracy, but he stood also against every tenet of the frontier political gospel."[141] The frontier stood for expansionism, seizure of Indian lands, annexation of Texas, and the rest. But Emerson wrote: "*Manifest Destiny, Democracy, Freedom,* fine names for an ugly thing. They call it otto of rose and lavender,—I call it bilge-water."[142]—Clearly he did not like his draughts of "Ohio wine" straight.

Perhaps the estimate of Dr. Ernest Sandeen that "the frontier was a neutral physical fact,"[143] comes nearest to the truth. The modern frontier offered the pioneer opportunity and challenge to which freedom and self-reliance seemed the appropriate answers. But if the American West had been exploited by a feudal or totalitarian government, other answers would have seemed appropriate. And the actual answers of freedom and self-reliance were often translated in practice into terms of aggression, exploration, and self-will.

Just as modern critics mean more by "the frontier" than the physical conditions of Western frontier life, so Emerson meant more by "America" than the physical United States. His "America," like our "frontier," was rather "the new world," both in fact and in idea. Negatively it was freedom *from* the "old world" of "Europe" with its outworn "feudal" institutions and society. Positively it was opportunity *for* the realization of new ideals—first in individual experience, but ultimately in the creation of a new society appropriate to the experience of the new world. To this ultimate society the ideals of freedom, democracy, and equality were all related. But to the individual, freedom was most important.

141. Arthur I. Ladu, *op. cit.*, p. 435.
142. *Works*, XI, 259.
143. In *University of Iowa Studies*, VI, 109.

Therefore Emerson declared of "The American Scholar:" "Free should the scholar be,—free and brave. Free even to the definition of freedom, without any hindrance that does not arise out of his own constitution." And therefore Emerson urged the "American" scholar to listen no longer "to the courtly muses of Europe." For "Europe," also, was not a merely physical country, but also the idea of the past and the tyranny of all past institutions. "Can we never extract this tape-worm of Europe from the brain of our countrymen?" he asked in his essay on "Culture."[144] And he hoped that "one day we shall cast out the passion for Europe by the passion for America."[145] Therefore, finally, he declared "the first danger" to American life to be—not materialism—but "the European influences on this country."[146]

Most spectacular in contrasting this "America," as the idea of newness and freedom from past, with "Europe," as the old world, are two seemingly contradictory entries in Emerson's *Journals* for the same day of February, 1867. In the first, Emerson was critical: "Nationality is often silly," he wrote. "Every nation believes that the Divine Providence has a sneaking kindness for it; as 'God has been received a burgher of Berne.' "[147]—But soon afterward, seemingly forgetting this criticism, he became enthusiastic in praise of the American nation:

> I thought at Chapin's lecture: it is not a question whether we shall be a nation, or only a multitude of people, but whether we shall be the new nation, the leading Guide and Lawgiver of the world.

And then he went on to describe what "the new nation" should do:

> The office of America is to liberate, to abolish kingcraft, priestcraft, caste, monopoly; to pull down the gallows, to burn up the bloody statute book, to take in the immigrant, to open the doors of the sea and the fields of the earth. . . .[148]

—and a good deal more in the same vein.

Even when Emerson spoke of America as a nation, he meant the

144. *Works,* VI, 145.
145. *Works,* VI, 266.
146. *Works,* XI, 533 "The Fortune of the Republic"; see Sandeen, *op. cit.*, p. 87.
147. *Journals,* X, 195.
148. *Loc. cit.*

exact opposite of that narrow "nationality" which he attributed to "the burgher of Berne." His "America" was "*the new* nation," whose "office" was "to liberate" from the old tyrannies and narrow nationalisms. It was, therefore, the office of the "American scholar" to study the "nature" of this new world rather than merely the "books" of the European past and to direct the actions of "the Young American" into ways appropriate to the new conditions of the new world. In Emerson's vocabulary "America" meant the ideals of newness and liberty, rather than merely the fact of political nationality.

The ideal of liberty, or freedom, is so pervasive in Emerson's thought that it is hard to isolate. It was the foundation of his individualism, the *sine qua non* of his Self-Reliance, the absolute of his Americanism. It had been the belief of his pilgrim ancestors, the battle cry of the American Revolution, and the physical fact of frontier life; and it was the ideal most appropriate to "the new world" in all its aspects. The primacy of liberty—both as an historic and as a logical ideal—in Emerson's writing has never been questioned.

But democracy and equality were different. In America "democracy" was a comparatively recent ideal, first attaining general acceptance in Emerson's own time. And "equality" was more doubtful still, associated as it was with the radicalism of the French Revolution—and even in our modern times frequently questioned. Emerson often idealized democracy and equality—and indeed his idealism has been described as "the metaphysics of democracy"—but he also limited and criticized these ideals.

Democracy as a political institution and even more narrowly as a political party was a practical matter which Emerson judged realistically, and which we shall consider in a later section, "Politics and Individualism." But democracy as an American way of life and as a moral ideal was related to the ideal of liberty. In general, Emerson condemned this democracy whenever it involved in any way the tyranny of the majority over the individual. But he praised it when it guaranteed the opportunity of every individual to realize his own potentialities and so to contribute to the common wealth.

In his early address on "The American Scholar," he read with joy "the auspicious signs of the coming days," which included first of all "the elevation of what was called the lowest class in the state." "The literature of the poor, . . . the philosophy of the street," were to be the primary concerns of his democratic American Scholar. And in his essay on "Politics" he explained the logical grounds for his celebration of democracy: "Of persons, all have equal rights, in virtue of being identical in nature." "This interest of course, with its whole power demands a democracy."[149] Emerson's constantly repeated concern for the individual citizen and for his equal rights under a democratic government explain Professor John Dewey's characterization of him as "The Philosopher of Democracy."

But Emerson clearly distinguished between this democracy of equal rights and that of partisan politics:

> When I . . . speak of the democratic element, I do not mean that ill thing, vain and loud, which writes lying newspapers, spouts at caucuses, and sells its lies for gold; but that spirit of love for the general good whose name this assumes.[150]

Specifically he hated "the dictator of our rural Jacobins" because "he cares for nothing but numbers and persons."[151] And he condemned wholeheartedly mere "Majorities, the argument of fools, the strength of the weak."[152]

Finally, in an 1860 essay entitled "Considerations by the Way," Emerson gave vent to his utter condemnation of an American democracy which had not produced self-reliant individuals and leaders, but merely members of "the masses":

> Leave this hypocritical prating about the masses. Masses are rude, lame, unmade, pernicious in their demands and influence, and need not to be flattered but to be schooled . . . Masses! the calamity is the masses. I do not wish any mass at all, but honest men only. . . .[153]

And in his final celebration of "The Fortune of the Republic" he still emphasized that " 'Tis a wild democracy; the riot of mediocrities and dishonesties and fudges."[154] Between the ideal democracy which guaranteed equal rights and opportunities to

149. *Works*, III, 201.
150. *Journals*, IV, 95.
151. *Journals*, V, 76.
152. *Journals*, VII, 148.
153. *Works*, VI, 249.
154. *Works*, XI, 537.

all, and that leveling down process which was to produce endless "George F. Babbits" and "Mr. Zeros," Emerson drew a heavy line.

Always Emerson's idealization of democracy was conditioned by his idea of equality, which in turn was based upon the presupposition of all his thinking: the potential but not actual divinity of every human individual. As we have seen, he emphasized that "Democracy, Freedom, has its root in the sacred truth that every man has in him the divine Reason . . . That is the equality and the only equality of all men."[155] All men, that is, are created equal but subsequently use their talents unequally. The original, potential equality of all men justifies a democracy of equal rights; but the present, actual inequality of all men limits that democracy and puts "equality" into either the past or the future tense.

Nevertheless this ideal of equality remains a presupposition of Emerson's writing as of the Declaration of Independence. In his book on the ideal of equality Professor Henry Alonzo Myers[156] has described Emerson as one of its prophets, although Whitman was to develop the ideal more fully. And he has emphasized that Emerson naturalized this ideal in American life by removing it from the realm of supernatural or otherworldly religion to the realm of daily human life. "Emerson did not deny the divinity of Jesus; he robbed it of unique significance by affirming the divinity and equality of all men."[157] And further Emerson implied the relation of this religious ideal to politics by attacking the "eastern *monarchy* of Christianity" and by describing the ideal democracy which should result from the Christian recognition of the potential equality of all men.

Similarly Professor C. H. Foster has emphasized the religious quality of Emerson's equalitarian idealism and its affinity to mysticism. Continuing the mystical element in American writers as diverse as Anne Hutchinson and Jonathan Edwards, Emerson made the inner light or innate Reason of man the justification of democracy. So his "Divinity School Address" became an attack on authoritarian Christianity and his "Over-Soul" described a democratic deity accessible to all men. Seen in broadest perspective, all Emerson's writings were a kind of "American Scripture,"

155. *Journals*, III, 390.
156. H. A. Myers, *Are Men Equal?* (New York, 1945).
157. H. A. Myers, *op. cit.*, p. 38.

preaching the potential divinity and equality of all men in this new world.

This democratic faith, essentially religious but related to the historic facts of American life, has justified the description of Emerson as "Prophet of America."[158] But Mr. Dillaway's book—like many others which have attempted to relate "prophecies" somewhat too closely to specific later events—in 1937 described Emerson as an enlightened conservative who would have opposed "the New Deal" and other social evils; whereas Emerson's "prophecies" had seldom been either specific or temporal. And as we have seen, even in his own times Emerson often described both the good and the bad aspects of historic American phenomena, such as Western expansion and "the frontier."

Nevertheless Emerson did share "the American Dream," and this dream did dominate the thinking of most Americans of the nineteenth and early twentieth centuries. To Emerson, as Dr. Sandeen and others have emphasized, "America was eminently the country with a future."[159] But time alters both temporal circumstances and philosophic beliefs; and Emerson's dream of America's divine destiny has dimmed somewhat, both as to future fact and as to ideal verity. To what extent has Emerson's American optimism become discredited by the internationalism and disillusion of modern times?

In so far as Emerson was merely nationalistic, his thought has been discredited. But it is important to remember that both in practice and in theory he opposed a blind and imperialistic nationalism. He spoke against the annexation of Texas and disliked the argument of "manifest destiny." Even in celebrating "The Fortune of the Republic" he warned that "The spread eagle must fold its foolish wings and be less of a peacock."[160] And in his Journals he often warned himself that: "A larger state [than America], a prior union, still dearer to the heart and imagination, and much longer to be our country, is the World."[161]

But it remains true that, for America, his optimism was ex-

158. Newton Dillaway, *Prophet of America: Emerson and the Problems of Today* (Boston, 1936).
159. Sandeen, *op. cit.*, p. 107.
160. *Works*, XI, 530.
161. *Journals*, VIII, 203.

cessive. He shared the delusion of Thomas Jefferson and of most leaders of his century that our national land and resources would prove well-nigh inexhaustible. If he did not fully share the nationalistic belief in "manifest destiny," his optimistic belief that "an eternal, *beneficent* destiny is always bringing things right" was an illusion which the twentieth century cannot share. Although he did not dream of an American empire covering all the earth, he did dream of an American democracy whose ideal perfection should make it "the leading Guide and Lawgiver of the world."

In the long run the value of Emerson and of his "American Dream" lies in his celebration of the ideals of liberty and democracy and in his emphasis on the religious foundation of these ideals. The crucial question for our times is whether these ideals —which Emerson believed eternal—will continue to govern our American thought and practice or whether they were the temporal products of a century of peace and prosperity which a later century of war and depression may discredit and even destroy.

In the nineteenth century Melville told symbolically how "Billy Budd," who served on the merchantship "The Rights of Man," was impressed under the articles of war to serve on the warship "Indomitable," and there was put to death. But Emerson believed "The Rights of Man" to be sovereign and eternal. If, under the stress of recurrent wars, America should abandon in practice its constitutional liberty and democracy, Emerson's dream would be discredited. And if America should further abandon in theory its historic ideals of liberty and democracy, believing them to be the temporal products of nineteenth century security, rather than eternal truths, then Emerson's American dream would be destroyed utterly.

## Yankee Realism

### 1. *Pragmatism*

Contrasting with Emerson's transcendental idealism and counterbalancing his mystical flights, a steady Yankee realism kept his mind constantly in touch with the actualities of his own time and place. If he dreamed of an ancient India and of a future America, he also observed and interpreted the events of nineteenth century New England. In philosophy he has been called "a great American mediator,"[162] and this is true in more senses than one. He sought to mediate between mysticism and practicality, between Transcendentalism and science, between romance and politics, between nineteenth century optimism and the old puritan morality, and between the democratic dream of America and the genteel tradition of Europe. If sometimes he merely described the alternatives, often he suggested the grounds for their possible reconciliation.

His realism was partly temperamental, or "Yankee," of course. From his ancestral New England he inherited Franklin's respect for "the tools: riches, old age, land, health; the tools." Mr. Philips Russell introduced his popular biography of *Emerson: The Wisest American* by retelling the story of Emerson's admiration for the Irish serving girl who could manage his balky cow better than he could merely by slipping her finger under its tongue. His ungrudging respect always went to people who could "do things." If he praised an ideal Self-Reliance, he always implemented it with celebrations of prudential wisdoms. Perhaps his most famous epigram described the success story of the man who built the better mouse trap. Emerson was Yankee to the core.

But his realism was partly philosophic also. If he respected "the tools," it was because they also were "instrumental" to the understanding of reality. Although the "uses of Nature" were to the end of "Spirit," men who could "do things" could often interpret the laws of Nature better than their fellows. For ideas were reflections of the patterns and relationships of the world outside the cave of the mind. The realism of Emerson's Yankee common sense paralleled the realism of Plato's universals, and of the medieval scholastics also. Emerson might not have quarreled fundamentally with the modern "Neo-Realists," although he would have agreed more closely with the great American pragmatists: Peirce, James, and Dewey.

That Emerson was a precursor of pragmatism is demonstrably true, not only in theory but in fact also. The first serious study of his philosophy described it in detail as "a Pragmatic Mys-

162. H. W. Schneider, *A History of American Philosophy* (New York, 1946), p. 286.

ticism."[163] And a recent German study of American pragmatism[164] has analyzed in detail the three "pragmatic" philosophies of Emerson, James, and Dewey. But the most important (because the most pragmatic) evidences of the pragmatism latent in Emerson's thought are the written statements of indebtedness and admiration by the great pragmatists themselves: incidental remarks of Peirce; marginal notations of William James; personal statements of O. W. Holmes, Jr.; and the essays on Emerson published on the centenary of his birth by James and Dewey. Professor John Dewey's essay on Emerson remains one of the most enthusiastic ever published. Not only was there "a latent pragmatism in Emerson,"[165] as most philosophers have recognized, but this contributed pragmatically to the later formulation of the philosophy by James and Dewey. We shall consider the various pragmatic ideas of Emerson in relation to those of the later philosophers, thus emphasizing that Emerson's "ideas" have also become "America's."[166]

Like pragmatism itself, Emerson's ideas were of two sorts. The first (and more typically Emersonian) statements emphasized the need of "action" for the true understanding of "ideas." The second (and more typically pragmatic) emphasized the instrumental value of ideas for the rebuilding of the actual world. The first found clearest expression in Emerson's early address on "The American Scholar," and in the philosophy of the first pragmatic philosopher, Charles Sanders Peirce. The second found clearest expression in Emerson's last book on *The Natural History of Intellect* and in the philosophies of James and Dewey.

But all the pragmatists, and Emerson alike, agreed in emphasizing the *interaction* of ideas and materials—of mind and body. A key passage, which James specifically characterized as "prag-

163. Henry D. Gray, *Emerson: A Statement of New England Transcendentalism as Expressed in the Philosophy of its Chief Exponent* (Stanford, 1917), p. 14.

164. Eduard Baumgarten, *Der Pragmatismus: Die geistigen Grundlagen des amerikanischen Gemeinwesens* (Frankfurt, 1938).

165. H. G. Townsend, *Philosophical Ideas in the United States* (New York, 1934), p. 90.

166. The following pages might be included in Part IV, describing the "Influence" of Emerson. However, they also describe, and interpret, ideas which were first of all Emerson's.

matism" in a marginal notation of his copy of Emerson, declared:

> Let the scholar first learn things . . . Let him know how the thing stands; in the use of all means, and most in the reverence of the humble commerce and humble needs of life,—to hearken what *they* say, and so, by mutual reaction of thought and life, to make thought solid, and life wise.[167]

As a practical idealist, Emerson's American Scholar was "to make thought solid." As an enlightened realist, he was also to make "life wise." The "mutual reaction of thought and life" was the theme common to Emerson and to the pragmatists.

The theme of practical idealism, of course, has also been typical of American thought as a whole. So the German philosopher, Eduard Baumgarten,[168] emphasized in his study of *Der Pragmatismus: Die geistigen Grundlagen des amerikanischen Gemeinwesens.* Grouping Emerson with James and Dewey he pointed to their common praise of "the experimental life" and to their emphasis on the idea of "fit action." Indeed, the German was able to understand and even to approve the "liberalism" and "individualism" of these Americans by recognizing it as the pragmatic result of the "frontier situation," which has distinguished historic American life and thought from that of Germany and the Old World. Although Professor Baumgarten's book included other, more questionable, interpretations, his emphasis on the common pragmatic Americanism of Emerson's "Scholar" and of Dewey's "Instrumentalism" remains valid.

Emerson's "American Scholar" had declared that "action" was essential to the understanding of life, but that it was "subordinate": "the true scholar grudges every opportunity of action past by, as a loss of power. It is the raw material out of which the intellect moulds her splendid products."[169] William James later noted that this doctrine was pragmatic, but in a marginal note disapproved of its assertion of "the superiority of what is intellectualized." The basic difference between Emerson and James

167. Emerson, *Works,* I, 180-81. William James's annotated copies of Emerson's writings are preserved in the Houghton Library at Harvard. See F. I. Carpenter, "William James and Emerson," *American Literature,* XI (March, 1939), 39-57.

168. See also Part IV, "Germany."

169. Emerson, *Works,* I, 95.

was that Emerson preferred ideas, whereas James preferred actions. But the first formulator of the philosophy of pragmatism, Charles Sanders Peirce, also preferred ideas above actions and quarreled with his friend James exactly on this point. The pragmatic "idealism" of Emerson's "Scholar" was first translated into the language of philosophy by Peirce.

Charles Sanders Peirce,[170] sometimes called "the grandfather of pragmatism," provides the formal link between transcendentalism and pragmatism—between the thought of Emerson and of James. The son of a Harvard professor, Peirce wrote half-humorously: "I was born and reared in the neighborhood of Concord—I mean in Cambridge—at the time when Emerson, Hedge, and their friends were disseminating ideas."[171] Although he asserted that as a technical philosopher he had developed his own ideas from Kant and Hegel he, like William James and Oliver Wendell Holmes, Jr., did grow up in the shadow of Emerson. And like Emerson his pragmatism was essentially idealistic.

As James later pointed out, Peirce had first announced the principle of pragmatism in 1878 in a paper entitled "How to Make Our Ideas Clear."[172] The pragmatic principle was that ideas, or concepts, can be defined clearly only in terms of their sensible effects in practical experience. Pragmatism, that is, originated as a theory of ideas, or—in Emerson's language of American Scholarship. And so, when James later emphasized the word "practical," Peirce strenuously objected (in a letter to his friend): "Pragmatism is correct doctrine only in so far as it is recognized that material action is the mere husk of ideas . . . the end of thought is action only in so far as the end of action is another thought."[173] Finally, feeling that James had distorted and debased his original idea of "pragmatism," Peirce defiantly changed the name of his own philosophy to "pragmaticism,"[174] in order to emphasize its idealistic nature.

Besides insisting on the idealistic nature of pragmatism in op-

170. See F. I. Carpenter, "C. S. Peirce: Pragmatic Transcendentalist," *The New England Quarterly,* XIV (March, 1941), 34-48.

171. C. S. Peirce, *Collected Papers,* VI, 86.

172. Peirce, *op. cit.,* V, 248-271.

173. Quoted in R. B. Perry, *Thought and Character of William James,* II, 424.

174. Peirce, *op. cit.,* V, 272 ff. (see F. I. Carpenter, *op. cit.*).

position to James, Peirce developed other specific ideas of Emerson in pragmatic ways. He described the intuitive "reason" as the only way in which new ideas can ever be originated, and compared these ideas to the "hypotheses" of science. And he remarked that we "seldom use the word 'reasonable' where the strict logic of our procedure is seen. We call that opinion reasonable whose only support is instinct."[175] But, of course, he went beyond Emerson to recommend that this intuitive "reason" be tested by experiment and be articulated by conscious logic.

Similarly Peirce developed Emerson's transcendental idea of evil, in contrast to the moralism of James. Man should not fight what he believes to be "evil," he maintained, but should seek rather to learn the truth by free experiment. Therefore, he interpreted "self-reliance" as the resolute open-mindedness of the scientist, rather than the self-righteousness of the reformer. And again he clarified Emerson's comparatively vague ideas by reference to the specific techniques of the scientist and of the philosopher. But these ideas remained anti-materialistic in Peirce. Quoting Kant, he insisted that "*praktisch* and *pragmatisch* are as far apart as the two poles."[176] Like Emerson he always opposed the merely "practical," even while emphasizing the "pragmatic" importance of ideas.

But William James converted this idealistic pragmatism into the practical-minded and typically "American" philosophy which most men associate with the name. In doing so, he consciously rejected the "idealism" of Emerson and of Peirce alike. But also he consciously developed and reinterpreted many of their ideas and insights.

Both personally and philosophically William James enjoyed a peculiarly close—even if sometimes rebellious—relationship to Emerson. Henry James, Senior, a lifelong friend of Emerson, a few days after the birth of William, "brought his friend Emerson to admire and give his blessing to the little philosopher-to-be."[177] The two families often saw each other, especially after 1864 when

175. *Ibid.*, V, 107.
176. Peirce, *op. cit.*, V, 274.
177. Henry James, ed., *Letters of William James*, I, 9. The relationship of the two philosophers has been described in detail by F. I. Carpenter, "William James and Emerson," *American Literature*, XI (March, 1939), 39-57.

Henry James moved his family to Boston. The father often read aloud to Emerson letters from his sons in Europe, and himself later wrote an essay "in appreciation" of Emerson. And on the centenary of Emerson's birth William James delivered an oration in praise of Emerson, in which he hailed his "beloved master." Throughout his life the young philosopher occupied the familial relation of a sort of adopted nephew to the older man of letters.

But more significant than this personal relationship is the literary and philosophical relationship of the two. In his youth, William heard the essays of Emerson read aloud by his father. In 1871 he acquired the first two volumes of Emerson's essays for his own library, inscribed them with his own name and date, and marked them heavily with marginal notations. As the years continued he reread these volumes at least three times and acquired six other Emersonian volumes which he also read and marked. His marginalia[178] emphasize the thoroughness of his reading and also make clear his specific reactions to Emerson's various ideas.

Specifically James often commented in the margins of Emerson's essays: "This is pragmatism," and in the flyleaves indexed those passages which he considered pragmatic. These include Emerson's remarks on "Discipline" in *Nature,* his section on Action in "The American Scholar" and several passages from "Literary Ethics." Further, James approved of all Emerson's exhorations to action, such as "build therefore your own world," and his praises of "today," "the present tense" and "the modern majesty consists in work." He liked Emerson's "concrete style," and his treatments of "psychic energy" and "power." His markings make clear that he first read Emerson's essays for general interest, later returned to them critically, and finally analyzed them with relation to his own recently formulated philosophy of "pragmatism."

But together with many Emersonian passages suggesting "pragmatism," James also found many which he indexed as "against my philosophy." These included some which merely emphasized that "ideas" rather than "actions" were the first concern of the "scholar" or "philosopher:" when Emerson said that action was

178. The volumes of Emerson owned by William James are preserved in the Houghton Memorial Library of Harvard University. See Carpenter, "William James and Emerson," *op. cit.*

"the raw material" of intellect and "subordinate" to it James objected. In this respect he merely repeated his opposition to all idealisms, even when the idealism was pragmatic, as in Peirce.

At other times James opposed Emerson's "monism," his "abstract unity," his praise of the "transcendental" and of "the ever-blessed ONE." Whenever Emerson celebrated the "general" tendencies and those "impersonal" laws of life as opposed to the specific facts and personal applications, James resented the denial of "pluralism." He objected to Emerson's transcendental idea of evil because of its danger to humanist morality. But most of all he seemed to hate Emerson's celebration of that purely mystical intuition which "shall exclude example and experience."—Opposite this in the margins James wrote: "the anaesthetic revelation" and "the tasteless water of souls."

But even while James was opposing Emerson's extremes of transcendental mysticism he was finding a place for it in his empirical philosophy, as one of the "Varieties of Religious Experience." And later his book on *Radical Empiricism* was to redefine "experience" so "radically" as to include the mystical experience itself. We have seen[179] how he related mysticism to the universal instinctive feeling that "life is worth living," which Emerson called "the universal impulse to believe." Even in reacting against the transcendentalism of the older man, he thus incorporated it into his new pragmatism. Therefore a recent historian of American philosophy has made the extreme statement that: "William James . . . is the central figure of what should be called neo-transcendentalism in New England. Quite definitely in the line of descent from Emerson, he succeeded to a remarkable degree in translating the aspirations of the older transcendentalism into the language of philosophy."[180]

Historically, the year 1871 first saw the transformation of transcendentalism into pragmatism. In this year the young Peirce and the old Emerson were lecturing in the same course of philosophy at Harvard. One of Emerson's lectures, on the "Natural History of Intellect," contained his final assertion that "my metaphysics are to the end of use." This same year William James was buying Emerson's first two volumes and reading them closely,

179. See section on "Mysticism."
180. H. G. Townsend, *Philosophical Ideas in the United States*, p. 134.

marking those passages which were later to suggest his own "pragmatism." At this time also James was struggling with himself over his problem of vocation, drifting from medicine toward psychology and philosophy.

Most important, 1871 also was the year of the first meeting of "the Metaphysical Club," whose discussions (according to Peirce) resulted in the formulation of the idea of pragmatism. Like the earlier "Transcendental Club" which had met in Cambridge and Boston a generation earlier, this informal discussion group was to influence deeply the future course of American thought. To this "metaphysical" club belonged not only Peirce and James but also Oliver Wendell Holmes, Jr., another son of another close friend and admirer of Emerson.

The future Justice Holmes, called the "Magnificent Yankee" by our twentieth century, is of course less known for his pragmatic philosophy than for his other exploits, although he shared with Peirce and James in the early formulation of pragmatism, and later applied it constantly in his famous legal opinions, as well as in his life and letters. But more important for our purposes, he was closer to Emerson and stated his indebtedness to Emerson more emphatically than any other, except perhaps Dewey. Although no detailed study exists of the influence of Emerson on the younger Holmes, the facts are clear. A constant visitor at the Holmes house, Emerson guided young "Wendell" in the writing of his first published essay on Plato. Later Holmes declared that Emerson had first interested him in philosophy and that the three great intellectual influences on his life had been Plato, Emerson, and his friend William James.[181] Finally in old age, Holmes asserted that "the only firebrand of my youth that burns to me as brightly as ever is Emerson."[182]

What ideas Holmes developed from Emerson cannot be determined exactly, but Emerson's affirmation that "all life is an experiment,"[183] and his repeated rejection of tradition and precedent find application in Holmes. Holmes' lifelong conviction that the

181. See (among others) F. C. Fiechter, Jr., "The Preparation of an American Aristocrat," *The New England Quarterly*, VI (March, 1933), 3-28.
182. Quoted in E. C. Lindeman, "Emerson's Pragmatic Mood," p. 64.
183. See next section, "Experience and Nature."

widest possible range should be allowed to individual states in enacting experimental legislation, and Holmes' repeated assertion that not precedent but the probable future effect of legislation should be the determining factor in its acceptance, were both Emersonian. Moreover, both were pragmatic. Significantly Holmes' early essay on "Plato" had attacked the great philosopher for his lack of connection between ideas and experimental reality; and his early essay on "Books" had repeated Emerson's belief that the authority of the printed word and even of the printed law was not final. Like Emerson, Holmes often opposed the majority, and like Emerson therefore seemed sometimes to oppose "democracy," but neither ever opposed liberty and, above all, both emphasized the right of individuals (and of states) to experiment as freely as possible.

The last of the great pragmatists, John Dewey, has also been the most enthusiastic in his estimate of Emerson. In an address, "Emerson—The Philosopher of Democracy," delivered at Chicago in 1903, and later collected in *Characters and Events*[184] Dewey went beyond statements of personal indebtedness to compare Emerson with Plato:

> Thinking of Emerson as the one citizen of the New World fit to have his name uttered in the same breath with that of Plato, one may without presumption believe that even if Emerson has no system, none the less he is the prophet and herald of any system which democracy may henceforth construct and hold by.[185]

And in a personal letter to the present writer, Dewey reaffirmed his praise: "I have not changed, so far as I am aware, my views on Emerson from those expressed in the article of 1903."[186] Since Dewey's "instrumentalism"—with its emphasis on practicality apparently greater than the "pragmaticism" of Peirce or the "pragmatism" of James—has usually seemed farthest from the "transcendentalism" of Emerson, his views are worth considering in some detail.

First of all, Dewey emphasized that he considered Emerson to

184. John Dewey, *Characters and Events* (New York, 1929), I, 69-77.
185. *Ibid.*, p. 76.
186. Letter to F. I. Carpenter, dated: Columbia University, October 6, 1928.

be "the Philosopher of Democracy"—and thus foreshadowed the interpretations of modern scholars.[187] Quoting Emerson's assertion that "there are degrees in idealism . . . It now shows itself ethical and practical,"[188] Dewey pointed to Emerson's constant reference to "the common experience of the everyday man." Further, Emerson "finds truth in the highway . . . The reputed transcendental worth of an overweening Beyond and Away, Emerson, jealous for spiritual democracy, finds to be the possession of the unquestionable Present."[189] Later Dewey emphasized Emerson's typical Americanism, particularly his faith in the common man, as exemplified by "The American Scholar." Since Dewey's own philosophy has often been called most typically American, this linking of "democracy," "practical idealism," "common experience," and "the strong present tense" is significant.

More technically philosophical, however, Dewey began his essay with an emphatic defense of Emerson's logic: "I am not acquainted with any writer, no matter how assured his position in treatises on the history of philosophy, whose movement of thought is more compact and unified."[190] And he quoted Emerson that: "Logic is the procession or unfolding of the intuition; but its virtue is as silent method; that moment it would appear as propositions and have separate value, it is worthless." Like Peirce, Dewey himself was primarily interested in the logic of discovery and experiment, rather than that of analysis and abstraction. Many years after writing his comments on Emerson's logic, he composed his own *Logic*. Paradoxically the intuitive "reason" of Emerson influenced the mind of Dewey in the creation of a new pragmatic logic—a discipline which might seem farthest from the interests of either philosopher.

A reason for the interest of Dewey, the pragmatist, in logic in general and in Emerson's "logic" in particular is suggested by an article which Dewey wrote on C. S. Peirce— whom we have seen as a kind of transition figure. "Insistence upon ever growing continuity, or *generality* of ways of action," he wrote, "differentiates the pragmatism of Peirce, from that of James . . . To

187. See earlier section, "The American Dream."
188. John Dewey, *op. cit.*, p. 73.
189. *Ibid.*, pp. 73, 75.
190. *Ibid.*, p. 69.

Peirce, habits of reasonable action, or general modes of action, were the end of knowledge . . . Knowledge tends to produce ways of action, and these ways of acting are immensely more important than is any particular result affected by the action."[191] Like Peirce, and like Emerson before him, Dewey constantly emphasized "general ways of action," or rules for "the conduct of life" to be determined by reasonable probability, rather than particular expediency or practicality. In this he returned to the pragmatic idealism of Emerson and Peirce, in opposition to the practicalism or "pluralism" of James.

Both James and Dewey, moreover, developed their pragmatism by way of psychology; both wrote books on *Psychology* in their early years, and both emphasized the supreme importance of mental or "spiritual facts." In these early formulations and analyses of psychology they developed many of the suggestions of Emerson. A modern social psychologist has gone so far as to suggest that Emerson's philosophy was essentially a foreshadowing of pragmatic psychology. Discussing "Emerson's Pragmatic Mood," Professor E. C. Lindeman[192] has declared that: "Since there were no professional psychologists Emerson became one . . . Psychological facts constituted for him the given data from which generalizations were to be drawn . . . It is my contention that the whole of Emerson's psychology is compatible with the pragmatic thesis."[193]

Emerson's "psychology" was, of course, not professional, but his approach was that of the psychological observer and his insights were often developed and applied by the later pragmatists. The present writer has suggested[194] how James' developed and expanded Emerson's psychological approach to reality until he was able to include all "spiritual facts" or "varieties of religious experience" in an inclusive theory of "Radical" or—we might call it—"Transcendental Empiricism."

Just as Emerson's emphasis on the "reality" of religious and

191. J. Dewey, "Charles Sanders Peirce," *The New Republic*, Vol. 89, (February 3, 1937), 416.

192. E. C. Lindeman, "Emerson's Pragmatic Mood," *The American Scholar*, XVI (1946), 57-64.

193. *Ibid.*, pp. 60-61.

194. F. I. Carpenter, "Points of Comparison between Emerson and William James," *The New England Quarterly*, II (1929), 463-64.

spiritual facts, together with his warning that "action" was necessary to every "scholar" who would truly interpret life, contributed to the development of psychology by the later pragmatists; so his emphasis on the creative power of ideas and on the potential ability of every individual to build a new world, contributed to the development of the modern educational theory of the pragmatists. On the one hand, Emerson's "latent pragmatism" crystallized in psychology; on the other, in education.

Emerson's ideas on "education"[195] have been analyzed by three doctoral dissertations and by a scholarly article, but usually from the point of view of the professional educator, rather than the philosopher or literary critic. The educators have pointed to Emerson's anti-institutionalism and his concern with the individual rather than society, to Emerson's idealism and to his optimism. They have agreed that his educational ideas were both progressive and liberal, but have emphasized their unsocial and vague aspects.

But if Emerson's ideas on education, like his psychological insights, were non-professional, they nevertheless inspired powerfully and directly many of the greatest leaders of American education. Horace Mann, leader in the movement for universal and public education, grew up with the transcendental group in New England, married one of the Peabody sisters, and throughout his career referred enthusiastically to Emerson and to his influence.[196] We have seen how John Dewey valued Emerson's ideas. And Edwin D. Mead, another pragmatist, declared that Emerson's late lecture on "Education"[197] "is the most vital, pregnant, and stimulating word upon general education which has been written by an American."[198] Beyond these, many educators have taken their texts from Emerson's "American Scholar"[199] address; and the

195. See doctoral dissertations (all unpublished) by: Hazen C. Carpenter, *Emerson's Views Concerning Education and the Scholar* (Wisconsin, 1938); Mary Mendenhall, *A Transcendental Philosophy of Education* (Yale, 1934); and Albert E. Lewis, *The Contribution of Ralph Waldo Emerson to American Education* (Stanford 1943). See also Virginia Wayman, "A Study of Emerson's Philosophy of Education," *Education*, LVI (April, 1936), 474-82.

196. See Mary Peabody Mann, *The Life of Horace Mann* (Boston, 1891), pp. 51ff.

197. Emerson, *Works*, X, 123-56.

198. Quoted in Henry D. Gray, *Emerson*, p. 93.

199. See Bibliography, and section on "Emerson's Prose."

official magazine of the American Phi Beta Kappa Society was named *The American Scholar*—with a bow to Emerson.

Most pragmatic of Emerson's ideas on education is what may be called "education by experience," first set forth in the chapter on "Discipline" in his first book on *Nature*. All our daily experiences in nature "give us sincerest lessons, whose meaning is unlimited. They educate both the Understanding and the Reason." Education does not begin in school and end with college—it begins in the nursery. The *Oxford English Dictionary* quotes Emerson's essay on "Experience," saying that "The plays of children are nonsense but very *educative* nonsense." And this "education" continues (or should continue) throughout our adult years: formally, the Lyceum movement (to which Emerson repeatedly lectured) developed into our adult education movement. Informally (and more in the Emersonian tradition of self-reliance) *The Education of Henry Adams* described and applied Emerson's theory of education by experience in its widest aspects. In a later statement by John Dewey: "the best thing that can be said about any special process of education . . . is that it renders its subject capable of further education."[200]

Practically, also, Emerson's ideas worked to reform the existing methods of education. His "American Scholar" attacked the American college as "a hospital for decayed tutors," where dead books in dead languages were taught according to a dead system. "The object of education," he had declared, "should be to remove all obstructions, and let this natural force have free play and exhibit its peculiar product."[201] From these ideas developed the educational practices of President Charles W. Eliot of Harvard and particularly the Harvard system of free electives. In his essay on "Emerson" in *Four American Leaders*,[202] President Eliot specified his debt to Emerson.

Finally, Emerson's ideas on education have been subjected in modern times to the same criticisms as those of John Dewey

200. John Dewey, *Reconstruction in Philosophy* (New York, 1920), p. 185.

201. Emerson, *Journals*, III, 4-16 (1834).

202. Charles W. Eliot, *Four American Leaders* (Boston, 1906), pp. 73-126. A recent article by Hazen C. Carpenter, "Emerson, Eliot, and the Elective System," *New England Quarterly*, XXIV, (March, 1951), 13-34, describes this relationship in detail.

and the "progressive" educators. In emphasizing free electives, education by experience, and self-reliance, Emerson assumed a degree of intelligence and a maturity which many children and even adults simply do not possess. In opposing a fixed educational curriculum, he may have advocated too much freedom. In opposing dead languages and arguing that "culture ends in a headache," he may have opened the doors for too practical and experimental an education. In advocating self-reliance, he may have prescribed an education fitted for extraordinary geniuses rather than ordinary citizens.—"There are no 'common' men," he had written.

In the modern "flight from freedom," therefore, critics have often attacked Emerson as a leader of nineteenth century liberalism and progressivism. And in this they have been right. But modern critics have also attacked Emerson as a proponent of vague and transcendental impracticalities—and in this they have been wrong. Emerson's thought was pragmatic and has deeply influenced the pragmatic thinking of the last hundred years.

## 2. *Experience and Nature*

Emerson's first book was entitled *Nature* and one of his best essays, "Experience." John Dewey's greatest book was entitled *Experience and Nature.* Emerson constantly praised science and, in his early *Journals* (March 4, 1831), exclaimed: "The Religion that is afraid of science dishonours God and commits suicide." Pragmatism has been called "the philosophy of science." Emerson repeatedly advocated the experimental life: "All life is an experiment. The more experiments you make the better."[203] William James entitled his final philosophy *Radical Empiricism.*—Was Emerson merely borrowing the scientific jargon of his day and using words like "experience" and "nature" in an attempt to disguise the mystical vagueness of his thought?—Or was his philosophy scientific in any real sense?

On the one hand, Emerson always valued science highly and read much of the scientific literature of his time with enthusiasm.[204] In sharp contrast to many romantic and transcendental

203. *Journals*, VI, 362.

204. See H. H. Clark, "Emerson and Science," *Philological Quarterly*, X (July, 1931), 225-60.

thinkers (Coleridge, for instance), he believed that science—and even the industrial revolution which science had caused—was a positive good both on moral and on material grounds. He adopted the general idea of evolution which was gradually taking shape in his time, although he probably never read Darwin's *Origin of Species.*[205] His philosophy developed some of the implications of scientific thought and has contributed to the naturalistic thought of modern times.

On the other hand, Emerson's transcendental philosophy of intuition, in its pure form, denied the fundamental tenet of modern science—that knowledge can only originate in observation and can only be verified by experiment. Although he broke away from the old fundamentalism which declared that all truth had been revealed, his doctrine of personal intuition was, as H. A. Myers has described it, "only a halfway house between religious dogmatism and the methods of scientific investigation . . . He overlooked the social aspect of knowledge."[206] Moreover, Emerson's readings in science were usually from second-rate thinkers and his formulations of the idea of evolution were never scientific.[207] If Emerson's philosophy developed some of the ideas and implications of science, it was not scientific itself in any strict sense.

Emerson's thinking about nature and experience and his conception of science itself may best be described as prescientific—both in a chronological and in a logical sense. His epistemology (theory of intuition), his theory of evolution, and his philosophy of experience all occupy a middle ground between the unscientific, religious authoritarianism of the past and the careful experimentalism of modern science. The important fact is that science strongly influenced him in his break with the formal religion of his ancestors, and that his own thought in turn has influenced modern scientific philosophers and psychologists.

Professor H. H. Clark[208] has shown that, although Emerson was constantly interested in science from his early youth to his old age, his greatest enthusiasm occurred about 1832 when he was

205. See Joseph W. Beach, "Emerson and Evolution," *University of Toronto Quarterly*, III (1934), 474-97.

206. H. A. Myers, *Are Men Equal?*, p. 44.

207. Beach, *op. cit.*

208. Clark, *op. cit.*, pp. 229-30.

breaking with the Unitarian Church. At this time he was reading many scientific books, especially two by Herschel and Somerville on astronomy. "Indeed is truth stranger than fiction," he exclaimed then. "What is there in *Paradise Lost* to elevate and astonish like Herschel or Somerville."[209] It is clear that the vision of a sidereal universe of impersonal law which astronomy opened to him influenced him to reject the anthropomorphic and personalized religion of his ancestors and led him to the dogma that "the soul knows no persons," stated in the "Divinity School Address."

Meanwhile, after resigning his pastorate, Emerson traveled in Europe, not only to see the cultural monuments of the past, but to learn the scientific theories of the present. In Paris he visited the famous *Jardin des Plantes* and exclaimed to his *Journal:* "I am moved by strange sympathies; I say continually, 'I will be a naturalist.'"[210] Although his sympathies were more important than his accurate understanding of science, he continued to observe and to study. And on his return to Boston he commented enthusiastically on Silliman's "Lectures on Geology" in 1835, and read Lyell's *Principles of Geology,* commenting later on "the correction of our superstitions by the new science of Geology."[211]

This reading in natural science formed the immediate background of Emerson's first book on *Nature* and of his attack on an authoritarian, personal, "superstitious" religion in the "Divinity School Address." Physical science was probably directly responsible for two of his major ideas: first, that God operates through impersonal Law, "whose only adequate symbol is the material laws, the astronomy, etc.";[212] and second, that man is part of the Law of Nature and is not separated off above it. The whole structure of his first book on *Nature* was designed to suggest this continuity of nature and man. If the first motto of *Nature* which was quoted from Plotinus emphasized the difference between inanimate and animate—between "doing" and "knowing"—the motto which he later composed for the second edition emphasized the idea of continuous evolution:

209. *Journals,* II (1832), 487.
210. *Journals,* III, 163.
211. *Works,* X, 336; see Clark, *op. cit.*
212. *Journals,* III, 199.

And striving to be man, the worm
Mounts through all the spires of form.

In his study of "Emerson and Evolution," Professor Beach has pointed out that Emerson's early idea of "evolution" was nothing more "scientific" than the general idea of some "progressive system in nature": "Striving to be man, the worm" did not necessarily pass through any chronological sequence of evolution. Emerson's early idea was essentially the old Platonic concept of the "Great Chain of Being,"[213] which asserted that some scale of being existed, within which all the forms of creation were related, although not necessarily in time or place. Only gradually did Emerson later approach a genuinely evolutionary view—as when he described the "patient periods" of nature in his later essay on "Nature." In his writings after 1850 Emerson more nearly approximated the scientific formulation of the idea, although he never mentioned Darwin and never interested himself in the scientific facts or observations which Darwin and others adduced to prove the theory. Always the ideas or laws of science interested him personally, but the methods and facts of scientific investigation hardly at all.

Emerson's failure to comprehend the scientific idea of chronological evolution (or perhaps his failure to become interested in it) has led Professor Beach to an even more severe criticism: Emerson "never glimpsed the idea that ethical concepts themselves may be the products of evolution . . . This is why his very ethical system is provincial . . . In Emerson, naturalism suffered an arrested development."[214] Besides ignoring the methods by which science proved her own laws, Emerson also ignored the corrollary fact that science was calling into question the old ethical and moral "laws" themselves.

This criticism is largely true. Although "Emerson's Transcendentalism made it possible for him to accept evolution without a qualm," while Coleridge was attacking that "bestial theory,"[215] his Puritan religious heritage did keep him from viewing religion

213. See A. O. Lovejoy, *The Great Chain of Being* (Cambridge, Mass., 1936).

214. J. W. Beach, "Emerson and Evolution." This criticism is repeated and expanded in J. W. Beach, *The Concept of Nature in Nineteenth Century Poetry* (New York, 1936), p. 345.

215. See Beach, *The Concept of Nature . . .*, p. 343.

or morality with scientific objectivity. But this criticism also needs qualification. Emerson did not develop the idea of evolution in temporal and historical terms, partly because he was not interested in history, but in psychology. His theory of nature and of experience was primarily psychological. This fact is all important to an understanding of his philosophy of experience and explains the seeming contradictions in it.

Emerson opposed empirical science only when it interpreted "experience" too narrowly—in terms of past experiences and in terms of mechanical experiences. But nineteenth century empirical science did tend toward the positivism of Spencer and Comte which denied the reality and the value of religious and psychological experiences. Therefore, Emerson, using the language of his day, said of self-reliance that "It shall exclude example and experience."[216] Emerson's whole essay on "Experience," therefore, took on a militantly defensive tone and became an *"apologia pro vita sua."* But this same essay also suggested the reconciliation of the two types of "experience" which the pragmatists and modern philosophers of science have since made clear.

Every serious critic of Emerson, whether hostile or sympathetic, has recognized his primary concern with experience of some sort. Woodberry wrote that "Emerson's thought always works within the limits of human experience."[217] And Santayana repeated that "Emerson traces in every sphere the same spiritual laws of experience."[218] And Santayana, in another book, declared that Emerson "opened his eyes on the world every morning with a fresh sincerity . . . he coveted truth; and he returned to experience."[219] Finally, Firkins described experience as the key to his whole philosophy: "The secret of Emerson may be conveyed in one word, the superlative, even the superhuman, value which he found in the unit of experience."[220]

But Emerson found superlative value only in experience considered qualitatively and related to all the other experiences of

216. *Works,* II, 68 ("Self-Reliance"). William James specifically objected to this passage.
217. G. E. Woodberry, *Emerson,* p. 109.
218. G. Santayana, *Interpretations of Poetry and Religion,* p. 221.
219. G. Santayana, *Winds of Doctrine,* p. 197.
220. O. W. Firkins, *Emerson,* p. 297. See also R. M. Gay, *Emerson,* pp. 8-9.

life. Considered mechanically and isolated from life, "experience" seemed to him valueless and meaningless. The religious experience was supremely valuable because it gave meaning to life. But the experience of scientific measurement was valueless unless it contributed to the understanding of scientific laws. All experience, however, could (and should) contribute to this understanding.

Emerson's essay on "Experience" has been analyzed in detail[221] and is clearly developed. Life seems confused and experience disjointed, Emerson believed, because man sees his experiences separately, *sub specie temporis.* "The party-colored wheel must revolve very fast to appear white." If man will accept and understand his experiences for what they are—fragments of the whole —he may ideally glimpse life *sub specie æternitatis.* Flaxman's picture of the god Apollo viewing the tragic struggle from above and recognizing "the irreconcilableness of the two spheres" is used to illustrate the idea. And finally Emerson personally warns against "the deceptions of the element of time." In a flash of insight, man may suddenly see all the experiences of his life ranged in order, meaningfully. And this sudden experience of illumination— described only in other essays—is the "religious experience," whose value Emerson considered supreme. But this supreme experience is purely inward or psychological and not at all external or scientific in the usual sense of the word.

Nevertheless Emerson made clear that this supreme human "experience" of ecstasy or insight is not really supernatural but natural and integrally related to the daily experiences of worldly life, which often seem confused and meaningless and which, therefore, the Orientals have always described as "illusions." Emerson's final essay on "Illusions" described again this supreme experience of insight, as a vision of "the gods," seen through a snowstorm of illusions, sitting in order on their thrones. But this very mystical experience of illumination seemed to him an integral part of "The Conduct of Life" in the world of Nature.

From Emerson's first book on *Nature,* through his central essay

221. See W. T. Harris in the *Atlantic Monthly,* L (August 1882), 238-52. The present writer made a similar analysis (in, *R. W. Emerson,* American Writers Series [1934], p. 446), before reading Harris's essay: the pattern of Emerson's thought is unmistakable.

on "Experience," to his final essay on "Illusions" his line of thought is direct. His philosophy of nature is of a piece with his philosophy of experience. His book on *Nature,* like "Experience," develops directly from the first material and meaningless "use" of nature as "Commodity" to the final and purposeful concepts of nature as "Idealism" or as subject to comprehension by the mind of man. After "Commodity" came the aesthetic and intellectual uses of nature as "Beauty" and as "Language." Then Emerson's section on "Discipline," like his essay on "Experience," suggests that these daily experiences or uses of nature may—if seen as parts of a larger whole—contribute to the illumination of the mind. This illumination leads to "Idealism" in philosophy, and to a religion of "Spirit." But from "Commodity" to "Spirit" all is natural and all part of the natural experience of man.

The supernatural or "transcendental" interpretation of Emerson's philosophy has been encouraged by his emphasis on the psychological experience of illumination or intuition. If this "intuition" is divorced from nature and from experience—if it is located in the vacuum of a mind undisciplined by nature—it becomes supernatural and merely "transcendental." Emerson's language sometimes seemed to describe it so. But the structure of his essays emphasized that this intuition was rather the highest of the experiences of man in nature.

On the other hand, the "romantic" interpretation of Emerson's philosophy has been encouraged by his emphasis on the divinity or ideal immanent in nature. Sometimes he seemed to idealize nature or make it almost the equivalent of God—just as many romantic poets of his century were doing. Professor Beach has included Emerson with these romantics:

> The sense of oneness with nature is more necessary in proportion as the poet has a weaker sense of the personal identity of God: it is historically the emotional equivalent of the religious sense of oneness with —of sonship to—God. With a pantheist like Emerson, nature and God are virtually interchangeable terms.[222]

But in *Nature* Emerson clearly defined "nature" as the "NOT-ME," and since he always idealized "self" reliance, he clearly implied that God possessed a quality of human consciousness or "self" differing from unconscious nature. Professor Spiller has,

222. Beach, *The Concept of Nature . . .*, p. 354.

therefore, emphasized Emerson's "triangle of relationships"[223] between Nature, God, and the soul of Man. And most critics have agreed that Emerson avoided a romantic pantheism, by describing God as differing from and transcending nature, although as manifesting Himself both in Nature and in man. Emerson's God, or Oversoul, is the principle of perfection, or ideal, immanent in nature and potentially realizable by man in nature, but not realized.

Perhaps the fundamental difficulty in Emerson's philosophy of nature is caused by his treatment of "time" and "history." This difficulty occurs in most philosophies of mysticism which preach "the unreality of time and space";[224] but Emerson now seeks to explain this old mystical idea naturalistically. To Emerson, time is "unreal" because deceptive: "We must be very suspicious of the deceptions of the element of time. It takes a good deal of time to eat or to sleep, or to earn a hundred dollars, and a very little time to entertain . . . an insight which becomes the light of our life."[225] So his essay on "History" emphasizes that "there is properly no history, only biography."[226] That is to say, time and history are unimportant in comparison with man's understanding of the eternal laws and psychological truth. Dr. Caponigri points out that "By his doctrine of intuition as a principle *of nature*, Emerson tries to render the individual independent of history on the level of Truth."[227] Always Emerson was seeking to formulate spiritual laws "out of time, out of space, and not subject to circumstance."[228]

The difficulty is resolved if we accept the suggestion of Professor Lindeman[229] that Emerson was neither a transcendental mystic nor a scientific naturalist, but a psychologist before the time of professional psychologists. Emerson did not set himself above

223. R. E. Spiller, *Literary History of the United States*, I, 369 (chapter on "Emerson").

224. See Bertrand Russell, *Mysticism and Logic*, and William James, *Varieties of Religious Experience*.

225. Emerson, *Works*, III, 85 ("Experience").

226. *Ibid.*, II, 10.

227. A. R. Caponigri, "Brownson and Emerson: Nature and History," *The New England Quarterly*, XVIII (Sept., 1945), 371. (Italics added.)

228. *Works*, I, 122 ("Divinity School Address").

229. E. C. Lindeman, "Emerson's Pragmatic Mood," *American Scholar*, XVI (1946), 57-64.

nature, and on the other hand he did not consider *physical* nature final, but the laws of nature and especially the "spiritual laws" of the mind of man were his subject. And these laws were "eternal" but also natural.

In his excellent early study of "Emerson's Philosophy of Nature,"[230] W. T. Harris (later United States Commissioner of Education) began by describing the enthusiasm of the British scientist, Tyndall, for Emerson. We have already noted the comparison by C. S. Peirce of the transcendental method of "intuition" with the scientific method of arriving at new "hypotheses," and the comparison by Bertrand Russell of the intuitive flashes of the mystic with those of the scientific thinker. Emerson entitled his last book the *Natural History of Intellect.* If he was not a scientist, his philosophy of nature foreshadowed many of the ideas of modern science. And if we think of him as a psychologist ahead of his time, many of his seemingly anti-naturalistic ideas take on new meaning.

### 3. *Politics and Economics*

The "discipline of Nature" whose value Emerson emphasized most in his first book was that of "property and its filial systems of debt and credit. Debt, grinding debt, whose iron face the widow, the orphan, and the sons of genius fear and hate . . . is a preceptor whose lessons cannot be foregone." Of debt Emerson was speaking from experience: while his friend Longfellow had been born into luxury and wrote romantically of the poor, Emerson had been born into poverty and wrote of it at first hand. And partly as a result of this experience he always remained a realist in political and economic practice. Never did he espouse the socialistic theories of Owen or Fourier nor partake in the experiments of his friends at Brook Farm or Fruitlands.

Yet Emerson's idealistic theory logically implied that man should free himself from the compulsions of political authority and of economic necessity. And he did constantly celebrate the extreme ideals of liberty and of individual equality. In England, when Carlyle and others asked him "whether there were any

230. F. B. Sanborn, ed., *The Genius and Character of Emerson,* pp. 339-64.

American?—any with an American idea,—any theory of the right future of that country? . . . I said, 'Certainly yes; but those that hold it are fanatics of a dream.'" And continued: "So I opened the dogma of no-government and non-resistance."[231] Even in his formal essay on "Politics" he argued idealistically that "the less government we have the better . . . The antidote to this abuse of formal government is the influence of private character, the growth of the individual."[232]

The contrast between Emerson's realistic acceptance of "the filial systems of debt and credit" and his idealistic celebration of "no-government and non-resistance" is sharp. If (in the words of one critic) "we may best understand the true nature of Emerson's political ideas if we study them in connection with . . . the *practical* politics of his own time,"[233] we will describe Emerson as a conservative "Whig" and certainly not a liberal "Democrat." But, on the other hand, if we consider only Emerson's extreme celebrations of "no-government" we will call him a political arnarchist, or (in the words of another critic) "Emerson the Nihilist."[234]

The contrast may partly be explained in Emerson's own words by relating Emerson's private Yankee economics to "law for thing," and his public transcendental individualism to the higher "law for man." Dr. Gerber[235] has suggested that Emerson's chapter on "Commodity" in *Nature* implies this; and also that, in his "scale of being" (1. senses, 2. understanding, 3. Reason) economics and politics exist primarily on the level of the senses. In the language of Christianity, Emerson believed in rendering unto Caesar the things that are Caesar's. But Emerson also emphasized the fact that debt disciplined the *intellectual* understanding of man; and he further advocated the gradual improvement and reform of the existing government of Caesar in this world.

231. *Works,* V, 286-87 (*English Traits*).
232. *Works,* III, 215.
233. Arthur I. Ladu, "Emerson: Whig or Democrat," *New England Quarterly,* XIII (1940), 420.
234. C. G. Shaw, "Emerson the Nihilist," *International Journal of Ethics,* XXV (October 1914), 68-86.
235. John C. Gerber, *Emerson's Economics* (unpublished doctoral dissertation; Chicago: University of Chicago, 1941) is the most thorough—and probably the best—study of this subject.

He considered the problems of government and economics both from the pragmatic and from the idealistic points of view. Perhaps we may repeat of him the estimate by Hamilton of Thomas Jefferson—that he was more radical in theory than in practice. Obviously Emerson was far less skilled—and far less interested—in the politics and economics of democracy than was Jefferson; but his liberal theory, like Jefferson's, far outstripped his practice.

To some extent Emerson's conservatism changed with the times and with his own changing circumstances and attitudes. Certainly his youth was dominated by the natural political and economic conservatism of the traditional New England of his fathers, and by his own personal economic insecurity. Until his thirtieth year he was constantly threatened by debt and by ill health, and his personal tastes remained aristocratic. In politics he naturally retained the New Englander's hostility for the "crudeness and coarseness" of Jacksonian democracy, for its anti-intellectualism and for its "spoils system."[236] Even after he inherited his first wife's estate he assumed the expenses of his mother and of his brothers, so that he never achieved freedom from economic insecurity. By necessity he continued to deal realistically with the financial system of industrial America and to depend upon it both for earned and for unearned increment.

But after his break with the Unitarian Church he also broke with many of the conservative traditions of New England. With the enthusiastic radicalism of "The American Scholar" and the "Divinity School Address" a new appreciation of the potential virtues of frontier democracy and of agrarian liberalism appeared. As he became leader of the transcendental idealists, his intellectual sympathy, if not his practice, went out to the economic experiments of his friends and associates at Brook Farm and Fruitlands. Harvard disowned her son for a generation; and Emerson noted that "State Street" feared that "Transcendentalism threatens to invalidate contracts." During this period Emerson gained the reputation of a dangerous radical. Even in later years Julia Ward

236. See R. McQuiston, *The Relation of Ralph Waldo Emerson to Public Affairs* (Lawrence, Kansas, 1923), p. 19.

Howe remembered her trepidation at going to hear such a man lecture.[237]

With the rise of the anti-slavery movement[238] Emerson participated even more actively on the side of the liberals, and opposed more emphatically the conservative elements of his own New England. After Emerson's denunciation of the Fugitive Slave Law, Daniel Webster wrote plaintively to a Concord friend: "Many of those whom I so highly esteemed, in your beautiful and quiet village, have become a good deal estranged, to my great grief, by abolitionism, free-soilism, transcendentalism, and other notions which I cannot [but] regard as so many vagaries of the imagination."[239] And for the next decade Emerson continued active in his support of emancipation.

But after Lincoln's Emancipation Proclamation and victory in the Civil War, Emerson's liberalism went into partial eclipse. The final period of his life expressed a kind of reaction against the radical enthusiasms of his middle years and also the feeling that, since slavery had been abolished, liberty and goodness would be realized automatically. To some extent the provincial prejudices of his youth naturally reasserted themselves. And probably his own comparative prosperity and the happy marriage of his daughter Ellen to the son of Colonel Forbes, "the best of the railroad presidents," influenced him. Certainly his old age showed a loss of liberalism, together with a loss of literary and intellectual power.

From youthful conservative, to radical, to abolitionist, and back to conservative—the pattern seems so natural as to be wholly convincing. But Dr. Arthur I. Ladu[240] has pointed out that even during Emerson's most radical periods he constantly criticized the politics and economics both of the Democratic party in politics and of his radical, reformist friends in economics. It is certainly true that his Yankee conservatism constantly qualified his liberalism, throughout his life.

237. J. W. Howe, "Emerson's Relation to Society," *in* F. B. Sanborn, ed., *The Genius and Character of Emerson.*

238. See Part I, "Reform and Anti-Slavery."

239. Quoted in F. B. Sanborn, *Henry D. Thoreau* (Boston, 1882), p. 94.

240. Ladu, *op. cit.*, pp. 419-441.

First, Emerson always recognized and emphasized the practical necessity of government and the advantages of it under actual existing conditions. "I lose all respect for this tedious denouncing of the State by idlers who rot in indolence, selfishness, and envy in the chimney corner,"[241] he exclaimed in 1845.

Second, although he always advocated "democracy" and although his philosophy always implied a completely democratic metaphysics and ethics, he often opposed violently the practices of the "Democratic" political party, and his New England training made him distrust the uneducated and uncultivated "Democrats." He opposed the "manifest destiny" of mere territorial expansion which the "Democrats" approved. And most of all he opposed the broadly democratic doctrine of the right of the majority to control the minority completely: "Majorities the argument of fools," he exclaimed.[242] Always he tried to distinguish between true democracy and "that ill thing, vain and loud which writes lying newspapers, spouts at caucuses, and sells its lies for gold."[243] Even in 1842 (in his most "liberal" period) he wrote: "Since I have been here in New York I have grown less diffident of my political opinions. I supposed once that the Democracy must be right. I see that they are aimless."[244]

Finally, even while Emerson was encouraging and sympathizing with his transcendental friends at Brook Farm and at Fruitlands, he was emphatic in his opposition to doctrinaire socialism. We have seen[245] how skeptical he was of the practical success of these experiments, even while approving of them as experiments. But he always objected to the imposition of any arbitrary system on individuals: "The mistake [of Fourier's system] is that this particular order is to be imposed, by force of preaching and votes, on all men, and carried into rigid execution."[246] Thus a good case can be made for the argument that Emerson was a conservative, or "Whig," in economics and in party politics.

On the other hand, we have seen that when Emerson did par-

241. *Journals*, VII, 18.
242. *Journals*, VII, 148.
243. *Journals*, IV, 95.
244. *Journals*, VI, 311.
245. See Part I, "Reform and Slavery."
246. *Works*, X, 352-53, "Historic Notes on Life and Letters in New England."

ticipate in public affairs he urged the reform of existing abuses. Beyond this he did constantly criticize the existing order, both generally for its failure to perform the ideal duties of government, and specifically for its failure to free itself from outworn "feudal" laws and customs. In his essay on "Politics" he wrote:

> We think our civilization near its meridian, but we are yet only at the cock-crowing and the morning star. In our barbarous society the influence of character is in its infancy . . . We live in a very low state of the world . . . A man has a right to be employed, to be trusted, to be loved, to be revered.

Modern government seemed to him "barbarous" because it did not guarantee the rights of the individual to physical employment and to spiritual enfranchisement. But more concretely in "The Young American" he argued that: "Feudalism is not ended yet. Our governments still partake largely of that element. . . . In consequence of the revolution in the state of society wrought by trade, Government in our times is beginning to wear a clumsy and cumbrous appearance."[247] Therefore, although he criticized socialism for its rigid system he valued it also for its implied criticism of the existing government: "The Communities . . . proceeded in great part from a feeling that the true offices of the State, the State had let fall to the ground; that in the scramble of parties for the public purse, the main duties of government were omitted,—the duty to instruct the ignorant, to supply the poor with work and good guidance . . . and the mediation between want and supply."[248] These are not the words of a conservative "Whig," nor yet of a vague transcendental idealist.

Nevertheless Emerson was also an idealist, in politics as in religion. In his idealistic mood he argued "the dogma of no-government and non-resistance," admitting himself the "fanatic of a dream." Although he realistically recognized and repeatedly emphasized the practical necessity of government and the practical advisability of progressively reforming the abuses of that government he also argued that "the less government we have, the better."—Idealistically, that is, he was an "anarchist" who believed in the ultimate goal of "no-government."

But even ideally Emerson was not (as he has been called) a

247. *Works,* I, 378-80.
248. *Works,* I, 380-84.

"nihilist."[249] For a "nihilist" believes in "nothing" and in the abolition of all existing institutions and laws. Emerson, even when preaching the ideal of "no-government," emphasized the positive ideal of "moral law" and of cultural and spiritual activity. And even when preaching the ultimate ideal of no-government, he emphasized the necessary expedient of gradual improvement of actual government, through peaceful and democratic processes. Neither idealistically nor pragmatically was Emerson a "nihilist."

But in politics as in religion Emerson was strongly anti-authoritarian. Indeed, his politics and his religion were of one piece: he attacked existing government because it was still "feudal" or "patriarchal," and he attacked orthodox Christianity because it resembled an "eastern monarchy." Christian ministers, like political ministers, appealed to established authority and held office in a hierarchy of authority. Emerson merely denied the final authority of any external government of any kind over the consciences of individuals. Therefore he opposed the tyranny of kings and of democratic majorities equally. In government, as in religion, he believed in the ultimate authority of the individual conscience.

Positively, of course, Emerson's ideal was "Self-Reliance," and in this essay he itemized the practical "revolution" which his ideal should bring about: in "religion," in "education," in "modes of living," in "association," and in "property." And in this essay he also emphasized that self-reliance would not be achieved by some theorist, but rather by some "sturdy lad from New Hampshire or Vermont who . . . *teams it, farms it, peddles* . . . and always like a cat falls on his feet."—That is, Emerson's "anarchist" of self-reliance presupposed an active realistic participation in the economic and social struggles of this world.

It has often been argued that Thoreau realized Emerson's ideal of Self-Reliance at *Walden:* therefore, Emerson's various criticisms of his friends's experiment have seemed both captious and puzzling. In discussing Emerson's attitude toward "the communities," Professor Flanagan has suggested the answer: Emerson's criticism of Thoreau sprang from the same source as his criticism of the "communities"; both tended artificially to isolate and to

249. See C. G. Shaw, "Emerson the Nihilist," *loc. cit.*

compel their participants. Emerson's essay on Thoreau asserted that "the severity of his ideal interfered to deprive him of a healthy sufficiency of human society."[250] Emerson's ideal, that is, differed from Thoreau's in that it criticized the hermit and the primitivist and praised social and economic participation in the modern, industrial world.[251] In politics and in economics Emerson was less revolutionary and more evolutionary than Thoreau.

Compared with Thoreau's political and economic thought, however, Emerson's sometimes seems unrealistic. Critics have pointed to his "almost naive economic optimism based on the belief that America's resources were inexhaustible."[252] Always Emerson defended wealth, using the argument that, in an America of boundless opportunity, wealth was the sure reward of initiative and ability. "The world is all gates, all opportunities,"[253] he wrote.

But Emerson also based his economic optimism on the fact that the industrial revolution was freeing man from serfdom to the soil: "Machinery and Transcendentalism agree well,"[254] he argued. And in so doing he emphasized the positive side of his economic and political ideas, in contrast to Thoreau's primitivism. Where Thoreau's challenging radicalism suggested the ideas of Gandhi, Emerson's merged with the progressivism of modern America.

Even when over-optimistic, Emerson's political and economic thought was sometimes realistic: the Beards have declared that "no one in his time understood better the intimate relation of property and politics."[255] If Emerson was both conservative and liberal at once, he had good reasons. In his speech on "The Fugitive Slave Law" (the occasion is significant), he explained:

> We are all conservatives, half Whig, half Democrat . . . May and Must. In vulgar politics the Whig goes for what has been, for the old necessities,—the Musts. The reformer goes for the Better, for the ideal good, for the Mays . . . But, if we are Whigs . . . let us know that over and above all the *musts* of poverty and appetite, is the instinct of

250. Quoted in John T. Flanagan, "Emerson and Communism," *The New England Quarterly,* X (1937), 258.
251. See *Journals,* V, 128.
252. Gerber, *op. cit.,* p. 15.
253. *Works,* VIII, 137.
254. *Journals,* VI, 397.
255. Charles and Mary Beard, *The Rise of American Civilization,* I, 780.

man to rise, and the instinct of man to love and help his brother . . . The world exists, as I understand it, to teach the science of liberty, which begins with liberty from fear.[260]

Emerson was a conservative, accepting the "musts" of property and poverty and what has been. But he was also a liberal, believing (in the later words of President Franklin Roosevelt) that "we have nothing to fear but fear itself." And, most important, he was a liberal because he believed that industrial America was making liberalism realistically possible. If, conservatively, he advocated a classical economics, with private property, sound money, and free international trade, he also advocated a liberal democracy with a more enlightened cooperation between labor and capital. —Only (and this made his whole political and economic thought seem more transcendentally vague than it really was) he believed that this better society could best be achieved, not by means of politico-economic legislation, but by "the influence of private character."

### 4. *Puritanism and "The Moral Law"*

Emerson's conservatism in economics was undoubtedly influenced by his background of Puritanism, much as Franklin's was.[261] Historians of Puritanism have emphasized its relation to the rise of middle-class economics, and Emerson shared both the fortunes and the economic ideas of the middle class. In his essay on "Wealth" he emphasized that "the subject of economy mixes itself with morals,"[262] and he believed that the "discipline of Nature" largely determines both. Indeed, the old New England proverb: "God helps those that help themselves," expressed the prudential equivalent of Emerson's own "Self-Reliance." But even Emerson's prudential realism appealed to a higher principle than did Franklin's: "Wealth is in applications of mind to nature, and the art of getting rich consists not in industry, much less in saving, but in a better order,"[263] he wrote. In thus relating economy and wealth to "morals" and "a better order" rather than to prudence

260. *Works,* XI, 231-32.

261. See H. W. Schneider, *The Puritan Mind* (Chapter on "Ungodly Puritans").

262. *Works,* VI, 40.

263. *Works,* VI, 86.

and self-interest, Emerson showed himself a true descendant of the Puritans, linking practical affairs with religion.

Emerson's many denunciations of Puritan orthodoxy, Calvinism and its religion of fear, have tended to obscure the great debt which he owed to his Puritan ancestry and its continuing influence. In the persons of his Aunt Mary Moody Emerson and his step-grandfather, Ezra Ripley, this Puritanism effectively influenced his mature life and thought. In one mood he made fun of it, noting that: "Dr. Ripley prays for rain with great explicitness on Sunday, and on Monday the showers fell. When I spoke of the speed with which his prayers were answered, the good man looked modest."[264] But after the death of this same Ezra Ripley three years later he wrote eloquently to his Aunt Mary: "Great, grim, earnest man! I belong by natural affinity to other thoughts and schools than yours, but my affection hovers respectfully about your retiring footprints, your unpainted churches, strict platforms and sad offices, the iron-gray deacon and the wearisome prayer rich with the diction of ages."[265] And his two essays on Aunt Mary and on Ezra Ripley embody this "affection."

It is significant, however, that Emerson's most eloquent celebration of his Puritan heritage is found in one of his most transcendental essays, "The Method of Nature."

> What a debt is ours to that old religion which, in the childhood of most of us, still dwelt like a sabbath morning in the country of New England, teaching privation, self-denial, and sorrow! . . .
>
> And what is to replace for us the piety of that race? We cannot have theirs . . . It is the office, I doubt not, of this age to annul that adulterous divorce which the superstition of many ages has effected between the intellect and holiness . . . I will that we . . . live a life of discovery and performance.[266]

Recognizing his debt to the old religion Emerson thus dedicated himself to the office of becoming philosopher of its "holiness," and of translating its "piety" into terms of modern life.

But usually Emerson's Puritanism remained implicit in his personal temperament and literary style. His was, as George San-

264. *Journals,* August 18, 1838.
265. *Letters,* II, 451.
266. *Works,* I, 220-221.

tayana wrote, a "habit of worship inherited from his clerical ancestors and enforced by his religious education . . . a disposition acquired by too long a discipline and rooted in too many forms of speech, of thought, and of worship for a man like Emerson, who had felt their full force, ever to be able to lose them. . . . His was not a philosophy passing into a religion, but a religion expressing itself as a philosophy. . . . Emerson was indeed the Psyche of Puritanism."[267] This is perhaps an extreme statement—let us consider how far it is true.

In describing the fundamental dualism of Emerson's mind and temperament[268] I have suggested that he reproduced the Puritan dualism between "piety" and "moralism," as well as the historic dualism between East and West, and the philosophic dualism between ideal and real. But he naturally sympathized with the religious "piety" of the Puritans rather than with their theocratic moralism—indeed, his chief effort was to discredit the authoritarian and institutional part of the old religion.

Professor Perry Miller makes this clear in his brilliant essay, which traces the development of Puritan "piety" and religious enthusiam from "Jonathan Edwards to Emerson."[269] The religion of mystical and intuitive faith did not always seem heretical to the Puritans, as it did in the case of Anne Hutchinson and the Quakers, but often became orthodox and central, as in the case of Jonathan Edwards and the eighteenth-century revivalists. Edwards, in his doctrines of the inward communication of God and man and of the immanence of God in nature and, especially, in his literary expression of the ideas of illumination and of the symbolism of nature, was a good deal of a transcendentalist. But "Edwards was particularly careful to hold in check the mystical and pantheistical tendencies of his teaching, because he himself was so apt to become a mystic and a pantheist."[270] That is, Emerson developed the mystical *implications* of Edward's Puritan idealism and gave them full, *explicit* realization.

267. George Santayana, *Interpretations of Poetry and Religion* (New York, 1900), pp. 229-231.

268. See above, "The Ideal and the Real."

269. Perry Miller, "Jonathan Edwards to Emerson," *The New England Quarterly,* XIII (Dec., 1940), 589-617.

270. Miller, *op cit.,* p. 604. See also F. I. Carpenter, "The Radicalism of Jonathan Edwards," *The New England Quarterly.*

But if Emerson developed to the full the old Puritan "piety" and religious faith, he has usually been criticized for ignoring the opposing Puritan heritage of "moralism" and of the "inner-check," which restrained Edwards from heretical pantheism, "antinomianism," and "infidelity." Professor Winters, in his attack on the "Romanticism" of Emerson,[271] has emphasized this criticism: Emerson, by ignoring the social and institutional "moralism" of the Puritans and by advocating a "perfect self-reliance" in opposition to "society," lost sight of his debt "to that old religion" which taught the greatness of "privation, self-denial and sorrow." —Is this true? Did Emerson reject one-half of his Puritan heritage?

Emerson did reject the formalized and institutionalized morality of religious orthodoxy and of social conformity—there can be no question of this. Although in his youth he wrote one good poem, "Grace," to the "preventing God" of the old religion, with His "defences" of "example, custom, fear, occasion slow," Emerson's whole philosophy of Self-Reliance soon opposed this external morality. It is true that he rejected most of the formal, external morality of Puritanism. (We shall consider this in the next section on "The Genteel Tradition.")

But Emerson did not reject the Puritan idea of "moralism," conceived as "a better order" of society. He merely described this morality as one enforced indirectly through the "discipline of Nature" and the intuitive "moral sense" of man, rather than directly through formal law and institutionalized society. Emerson, that is, transformed the old Puritan moralism from a formal and conscious idea to an informal and intuitive one. If he sometimes described this new moralism as merely intuitive and mystical, he usually kept the old word in one form or another, celebrating "moral law," "moral sense," and "moral sentiment."

A recent study[272] has traced this transformation in detail and related Emerson's "moral law" to the Scottish philosophy of "common sense," on the one hand, and to the Transcendental idea of "Reason" on the other. While still in Harvard College, Emerson was reading Dugald Stewart's *Outlines of Moral Philosophy* with enthusiasm, and noting in his *Journals* that Stewart contrasted the

271. Yvor Winters, *In Defense of Reason.*

272. M. R. Davis, "Emerson's 'Reason' and the Scottish Philosophers," *The New England Quarterly,* XVII (June, 1944), 209-28.

"Moral Sense" with the merely rational and logical powers of the mind. This "Moral Sense" described by Stewart was also to be contrasted with the "principles of common sense" described by another Scottish philosopher, Thomas Reid, in that it was "an original and universal principle of the mind that apprehends the distinction between right and wrong." In Dugald Stewart, whose ideas were currently taught at Harvard College, Emerson found not only an "intuitive philosophy which was characteristic of the Scottish reaction to Hume"[273] but also the means of reconciling the Puritan "moralism" of his ancestry with the transcendental "Reason" of Coleridge and Kant, which he was to celebrate later. By making the grounds of morality intuitive, rather than authoritarian, Emerson, at the age of nineteen, had already laid the foundations of his later transcendentalism.

Formally Emerson developed this moral philosophy in two public essays composed at Harvard. The first was his Bowdoin prize essay on "The Present State of Ethical Philosophy" written in 1821. Here he described "the leading characteristics of ethical science as it is represented by *modern* [as opposed to *ancient*] teachers,—by Reid, Paley, Stewart" as its "more practical character" and its emphasis on "the moral faculty, which is recognized as an original principle of our nature,—an intuition by which we directly determine the merit or demerit of an action."[274] And he prophesied that: The first true advance which is made must go on in the school in which Reid and Stewart have labored. Philosophers must agree in terms and discover their own ideas with regard to the moral sense."[275] Later Emerson followed his own advice and "discovered his own ideas with regard to the moral sense" throughout the rest of his life.

The chief difficulties with Emerson's later ideas of "the moral law" are two. First, he never did "agree in terms" with other philosophers, but later adopted the transcendental terminology of Coleridge and Kant to describe as "Reason" what was essentially "conscience," guided by religious intuition. This has proved

273. Edgeley W. Todd, "Philosophical Ideas at Harvard College, 1817-1837," *The New England Quarterly*, XVI, 64 (March 1943), *in* M. R. Davis, *op. cit.*

274. E. E. Hale, ed., "Two Unpublished Essays by R. W. Emerson" (Boston, 1896), *in* M. R. Davis, *op. cit.*, pp. 224-26.

275. Hale, *op. cit.*, p. 226.

confusing to modern readers and has subjected his philosophy to the criticism that it romantically ignored all "morality." Second, because he described "the moral law" in religious rather than scientific terms, he has alienated many modern readers who think of "morality" only in the relative sense of "mores," and who tend to disbelieve in any universal "moral law" or decalogue.

Much has been written about Emerson's doctrine of the intuitive "Reason," which he developed from Coleridge's interpretation of Kant's Critiques of the Pure and the Practical Reason.[276] But very little has been written about Emerson's doctrine of the "moral sense" or "moral law" which he continued to celebrate (although never in systematic terms) through his life. Yet this conservative doctrine was always implicit in his thought and counterbalances its radicalism, just as his idea of the "Over-Soul" and reliance on God counterbalances the radicalism of his idea of "Self-Reliance." Emerson translated all the inherited Puritan "conscience" of his religious nature into the phrase "moral sense" and made it an axiom of all human conduct and psychology. If he was mistaken in imputing to all men as clear a "moral sense" as he himself possessed, it is still true that men do inherit a body of half-conscious moral beliefs and feelings from the society in which they have been reared. Most men share social beliefs and inhibitions which can still fairly be described as a "moral sense."

Nevertheless Emerson's doctrine of "the moral law" was at once too vague and too dogmatic. Although most men, even in our irreligious and skeptical age, still agree that there are some moral laws that are generally accepted; modern anthropology and sociology now emphasize the relativity of morals. Emerson, of course, emphasized this relativity to the point of exaggeration in his essay on "Self-Reliance." But he never specified what was eternal and what was transient in morality. And, worst of all, he assumed that certain of his inherited prejudices, as a Puritan and as a New Englander, were universal moral truths. Therefore, as Professor Beach has charged, his "moral sense" sometimes seemed provincial. His Puritan religious heritage combined with his New England social heritage to influence—and sometimes to bias—his thinking. This social heritage has been called "The Genteel Tradition."

276. See above, section on "Transcendentalism."

## The Genteel Tradition

In his famous essay on "The Genteel Tradition in American Philosophy,"[277] George Santayana described this Tradition as "a survival of the beliefs and standards of the fathers," in contrast to the new democratic philosophy of younger men like Whitman and William James. Specifically, Santayana traced this tradition to Puritanism and described Emerson as its latest spokesman. The present writer[278] has suggested a "Re-interpretation" of this "Genteel Tradition" to describe it as the survival of the moralistic half, only, of Puritanism. And Emerson, by his explicit hostility to all traditionalism, aligned himself clearly with the anti-traditional half of Puritanism. Moreover, Emerson's ideas suggested much of the philosophic pragmatism of William James and helped to inspire the poetic democracy of Whitman.[279] His philosophy always pointed toward the unexplored future rather than toward the traditional past. He was not the spokesman of any tradition, as such.

Nevertheless, Emerson was influenced by this Genteel Tradition: sometimes unconsciously, through his ministerial heritage and his New England temperament; and sometimes consciously, through his belief in the "gentle-man," or the superior, educated man. As Oliver Wendell Holmes pointed out, he did belong by heritage to the "Brahmin caste" of New England, with its Puritan righteousness and its "agonized conscience" on the one hand, and its cultured aristocracy and intellectual superiority on the other. Even if Emerson's philosophy opposed the idea of *tradition*, his social heritage was partly *genteel*.

The most obvious limitation of Emerson's character (and to a lesser degree of his philosophy) was his lack of animal spirits. "I was born cold," he complained. Although this was partly physical, it was also social and psychological: his "New England conscience" inhibited him. Although his ideas anticipated Whitman's in most fields, he opposed Whitman's celebration of sexual love. The story of the co-ed who confided to her professor that Emer-

277. George Santayana, *Winds of Doctrine* (New York, 1912), pp. 186-215.

278. F. I. Carpenter, "The Genteel Tradition: A Reinterpretation," *New England Quarterly*, XV (1942), 427-43.

279. See Part IV.

son's essay on "Love" was very fine but not all that she expected suggests the limitation. Moreover, Emerson's philosophic celebration of the idea of "ecstasy" might have implied something more. Although his "reason" led him to appreciate Whitman and to acclaim Whitman's poetry to the world, his social and moral judgment remained negative and led him to many cautious disclaimers.

This genteel or provincial distrust of animal spirits and sex inhibited him most in the field of art. He shared the traditional New England censoriousness toward the theatre, the dance, the plastic arts, and the novel. His *Journal* on his first trip to Europe reflects his conscientious effort to appreciate the painting and sculpture of Europe, which nevertheless remained alien to him. His occasional successes in overcoming these conscientious inhibitions were sometimes spectacular and sometimes comic. His *Journals* for October 1841 describe in detail his intense appreciation of the beauty of a performance by "Fanny Elssler in the ballet of *Nathalie*" but admit that the theatre may not have been "the safest resort for college boys who have left metaphysics or Tacitus to see these tripping satin slippers." The apochryphal story of his and Margaret Fuller's comments on this same ballet is illuminating: He: "Margaret, this is *Art!*" She: "Waldo, this is *Religion!*"—In moments of aesthetic or religious "ecstasy," Emerson might sometimes overcome his genteel heritage, but a sense of guilt still remained.

This inherited puritanical distrust of sensuous art remains perhaps his greatest fault. In spite of it, he read the novels of Scott "under the desk at Latin School"; and later read "The Golden Asse" of Apuleius, although apologetically, for its philosophy only. He always distrusted novels in general. And in literature his provincial moralism led him to criticize Goethe and even Shakespeare for their lack of moral seriousness. In extenuation it should be emphasized that he did defend Goethe (as he also defended Whitman) against the greater provincialism of his more genteel friends and associates. His poem "To J. W." remains an eloquent rebuke to the captiousness of a minor critic who damned Goethe's immorality; but it still apologizes for the "errors" of the great man. Emerson achieved greatness and a comparative catholicity in spite of the inhibiting gentility of his heritage.

More broadly, his philosophic idealism and his puritan sense of cultural superiority led him to distrust the "materialism" of politics in general, and of Jacksonian democracy in particular. His own sense of democracy was more Jeffersonian and patrician than Jacksonian and popular. Unlike Whitman he could never quite sympathize with "the divine average"—especially in its more concrete manifestations. As an idealist the necessary compromises of practical politics repelled him. Unlike Whitman again he could see only one side of the Civil War: the deeply-felt human sympathy which could transcend partisanship in the emotional sharing of the sorrow of others was denied him.

In pure philosophy also the genteel debasement of "the senses" before "the reason" operated negatively. Although Emerson and William James were both "philosophers," and although James found many "pragmatic" ideas in Emerson, Emerson always remained a transcendental idealist in his exaltation of the generalized and abstracted *idea* above the concrete and particularized illustration of it. James, on the contrary, always emphasized the value of the concrete and the particular, both for purposes of artistic illustration, of scientific verification, and of philosophic clarification. And he specifically criticized Emerson for his "abstract monism," his "intellectualism," and his "rationalist attitude."[280] Although Emerson often recognized the limitations of the intellect he nevertheless overvalued it. And although his celebration of "the Reason" was partly philosophic it was partly temperamental—caused, probably, by his having been born and bred a "Brahmin" and a gentle-man.

The paradox remains: although Emerson revolted from the Genteel Tradition to prophesy the "barbaric yawp" of Whitman and the "radical empiricism" of William James (the two Americans whom Santayana described as most modern, American and anti-genteel) Emerson nevertheless has become a kind of John the Baptist whose severed head modern American critics often exhibit as an awful example of the "Genteel Tradition." Partly because of this modern tendency to overlook the freshness and modernity of Emerson's thought, this study has emphasized his

280. See F. I. Carpenter, "William James and Emerson," p. 52.

pragmatic, democratic, American qualities. And these qualities were dominant in him. Although he was less "modern" and more "genteel" than Whitman and James, his thought remains infinitely more modern and less genteel than that of his contemporaries.

To compare Emerson with his old friend and fellow transcendentalist, Bronson Alcott,[281] is to emphasize the strength of Emerson's thought and the degree to which he transcended his "genteel" heritage. Where Emerson boldly praised self-reliance, Alcott warned himself: "We may have mistaken arrogance for independence. Let us be careful." Where Emerson praised the challenge of the new West for the "American Scholar," Alcott idealized rather the ancient society, the "Old England of New England." Where Alcott used the adjectives "gentle," "pure," "sentimental" and "good" to describe admirable women, and became "the father of *Little Women*" both in fact and in spirit, Emerson sometimes used "gentle" and "pure" in praise, but used "sentimental" and "good" largely in criticism, and often spoke half-humorously of "the good Alcott." Where Alcott opposed the physical labor of gardening "for the appetites" and praised only labor "to beautify," Emerson never undervalued the necessary labor of the earth. Where Emerson was self-reliant, progressive, sometimes coarse, doubtful of the merely "good," and realistic in facing the material world, Alcott was more often cautious, traditional, genteel, sentimental, and absurdly unrealistic.

Emerson recognized clearly and described realistically both "law for man" and "law for thing." Alcott recognized only "law for man" but closed his eyes to "law for thing." If Whitman described the animal instincts far more eloquently than Emerson, and William James described the pragmatic realities far more concretely, their greatest successes merely emphasize the relative failures of Emerson in their particular fields. Usually Emerson's realism was both strong and articulate, and counterbalanced the extreme idealism of his mystical and transcendental thought.

## Selected Bibliography: Part III

The following bibliography includes only items dealing primarily with Emerson's Ideas. Biographies which incidentally inter-

281. See F. I. Carpenter, "Bronson Alcott: Genteel Transcendentalist," *New England Quarterly*, XIII (March, 1940), 34-48.

pret his Ideas are included in Part I: those by Woodberry and Firkins are probably the best. Studies of his Ideas about Literature are included in Part II. Studies dealing primarily with the sources of his Ideas or with their influence on later writers are included in Part IV.

## The Background of Emerson's Ideas

Adams, James T. *The Epic of America* (Boston, 1932). (Relates Emerson to the idealism of "The American Dream.")

Baumgarten, Eduard. *Der Pragmatismus. Die geistigen Grundlagen des amerikanischen Gemeinwesens* (Frankfurt, 1938). (Describes "Emerson, James and Dewey" as the exponents of American Pragmatism. Biased, but interesting.)

Beach, Joseph W. *The Concept of Nature in Nineteenth Century Poetry* (New York, 1936). (Includes two excellent chapters on Emerson's Concept of Nature.)

*The Catholic Encyclopedia* (New York, 1907). Article on "Mysticism" by G. M. Sauvage.

Channing, William Ellery. *The Works of W. E. Channing* (Boston, 1891). (The Unitarian precursor of Emerson's Transcendentalism.)

*The Encyclopaedia Britannica,* 14th ed. and ff. Valuable articles on "Mysticism" by Evelyn Underhill and A. S. Pringle-Pattison; and on "Unitarianism" by J. H. Lathrop.

Faust, Clarence. "The Background of the Unitarian Opposition to Transcendentalism," *Modern Philology,* XXXV (February, 1938), 297-324.

Foerster, Norman. *Nature in American Literature* (Boston, 1928). (Chapter on Emerson is less complete than chapters by Beach, q.v.)

Frothingham, Octavius B. *Transcendentalism in New England* (Boston, 1876). (With Goddard, the best detailed study of the subject.)

Goddard, Harold C. *Studies in New England Transcendentalism* (New York, 1908). (See Frothingham.)

Hazard, Lucy L. *The Frontier in American Literature* (New York, 1927). (Suggestive, but sometimes untrustworthy.)

James, William. *The Varieties of Religious Experience* (New York, 1902). (The chapter on "Mysticism," pp. 379-429, is especially valuable.)

Lovejoy, Arthur O. *The Great Chain of Being* (Cambridge, Mass., 1936). (The philosophical background of Emerson's idea of evolution.)

Matthiessen, F. O. *American Renaissance* (New York, 1941). (Criticizes Emerson's ideas by comparison with those of his American contemporaries.)

Miller, Perry. *The New England Mind* (New York, 1939). (The authoritative analysis of the Puritan background of Emerson's thought.)

——. *The Transcendentalists* (Cambridge, Mass., 1950). (An anthology and brief critical appraisal of the Transcendental background.)

Myers, Henry A. *Are Men Equal?* (New York, 1945). (Includes a brief critique of Emerson's thought in relation to the American idea of equality.)

Otto, Rudolf. *Mysticism East and West: A Comparative Analysis of the Nature of Mysticism* (New York, 1932).

Russell, Bertrand. *Mysticism and Logic* (New York, 1929). (Together with William James, the best brief, modern analysis of mysticism and its corollary ideas.)

Santayana, George. "The Genteel Tradition in American Philosophy," in *Winds of Doctrine* (New York, 1912), pp. 186-215. (Relates Emerson to the Puritan-aristocratic tradition. Brilliant but one-sided.)

Schneider, Herbert. *A History of American Philosophy* (New York, 1946). (Important; strongly anti-Emersonian.)

Spiller, Robert E. "Critical Standards in the American Romantic Movement," *College English*, VIII (April, 1947), 344-52. (Contrasts "Romanticism" in America and in Europe. See also W. F. Taylor.)

Spiller, Robert E., *et al. Literary History of the United States* (New York, 1948). (Includes a brilliant analysis of the democratic implications of Transcendentalism by David Bowers, "Democratic Vistas," I, 345-57; and an excellent essay on "Emerson," by R. E. Spiller, I, 358-87.)

Taylor, Walter F. *A History of American Letters* (New York, 1936). (Includes an excellent chapter on "The Romantic Impulse and the American Environment.")

Townsend, Harvey G. *Philosophic Ideas in the United States.* (The best treatment of Emerson's ideas by a professional historian of American philosophy.)

Winters, Yvor. *In Defense of Reason* (New York, 1947). (A brilliantly destructive criticism of Emerson's ideas and of their influence on Whitman and on Hart Crane; wholly one-sided.)

## Critical Studies of Emerson's Ideas

Arnold, Matthew. "Emerson," in *Discourses in America* (New York, 1924). (The best essay on Emerson by a contemporary of his.)

Beach, Joseph W. "Emerson and Evolution," *University of Toronto Quarterly*, III (1934), 474-97. (Excellent critical study of Emerson's ideas on evolution and of where he got them. See also Beach's book, *The Concept of Nature. . . .*)

Caponigri, A. R. "Brownson and Emerson: Nature and History," *New England Quarterly,* XVIII (Sept., 1945), 368-90. (Thoughtful study of implications of Emerson's ideas. Especially good on "History.")

Carpenter, Frederic I. *Emerson and Asia* (Cambridge, Mass.: 1930). (The oriental background of Emerson's Mysticism. See also Christy.)

——. "C. S. Peirce: Pragmatic Transcendentalist," *New England Quarterly,* XIV (March, 1941), 34-48. (The relationship of Emerson's ideas to early Pragmatism.)

——. "Points of Comparison between Emerson and William James," *New England Quarterly,* II (July, 1929), 458-74. (A general comparison of the ideas of the two.)

——. "William James and Emerson," *American Literature,* XI (March, 1939), 39-57. (A more specific study of James's marginal comments in his volumes of Emerson.)

Carpenter, Hazen C. "Emerson, Eliot, and the Elective System," *New England Quarterly,* XXIV (March, 1951), 13-34.

Cestre, Charles. "Le Romantisme d'Emerson," *Revue Anglo-Américaine,* VII (October, December, 1929), 1-18 and 113-31. (Describes Emerson as a typical European Romantic. Often superficial.)

Christy, Arthur E. *The Orient in American Transcendentalism* (New York, 1932). (The oriental background of Emerson's Mysticism. See also Carpenter.)

Clark, H. H. "Emerson and Science," *Philological Quarterly,* X (July, 1931), 225-60. (A scholarly and illuminating study. See also Beach, "Emerson and Evolution.")

Davis, M. R. "Emerson's 'Reason' and the Scottish Philosophers," *New England Quarterly,* XVII (June, 1944), 209-28. (A thoughtful study of "Reason," "common sense," and "the moral law.")

Dewey, John. "Emerson: The Philosopher of Democracy," *in Characters and Events* (New York, 1929), I, 69-77. (The most enthusiastic appreciation of Emerson by a professional philosopher.)

Eliot, C. W. "Emerson," in *Four American Leaders* (Boston, 1906), 73-126. (Testimony to Emerson's personal influence on a leader in education.)

Flanagan, J. T. "Emerson and Communism," *New England Quarterly,* X (June, 1937), 243-61. (Emerson's ideas on "the communities" and on social reform.)

Foster, C. H. "Emerson as American Scripture," *New England Quarterly,* XVI (March, 1943), 91-105. (The religious and emotional aspect of Emerson's American idealism.)

Gerber, John C. *Emerson's Economics.* (An excellent unpublished doctoral dissertation; Chicago: University of Chicago, 1941).

Gray, Henry D. *Emerson: A Statement of New England Transcendentalism as Expressed in the Philosophy of its Chief Exponent* (Stanford, Calif., 1917). (The most complete discussion of Emerson's philosophy, but not by a professional philosopher.)

Harris, W. T. "Emerson's Philosophy of Nature," in *The Genius and Character of Emerson,* ed. F. B. Sanborn (Boston, 1885). (Harris remains one of the best interpreters of Emerson's ideas. For other articles by him, see G. W. Cooke, *Bibliography,* p. 263.

Huggard, W. A. "Emerson and the Problem of War and Peace," *The University of Iowa Humanistic Studies,* X (April, 1938), 1-76. (Scholarly: condensed from a doctoral dissertation.)

Jorgenson, C. E. "Emerson's Paradise under the Shadow of Swords," *Philological Quarterly,* XI (July, 1932), 274-92. (A study of Emerson's idea of evil. Overemphasizes the classical elements of the idea, as opposed to the mystical.)

Kern, Alexander C. "Emerson and Economics," *New England Quarterly,* XIII (Dec., 1940), 678-96. (See also, Gerber.)

Ladu, Arthur I. "Emerson: Whig or Democrat," *New England Quarterly,* XIII (Sept., 1940), 419-41. (An important but one-sided study, emphasizing Emerson's conservatism.)

Lindeman, Eduard C. "Emerson's Pragmatic Mood," *American Scholar,* XVI (1946), 57-64. (A suggestive essay on Emerson as pragmatist and as psychologist.)

Marchand, Ernest. "Emerson and the Frontier," *American Literature,* III (May, 1931), 149-74. (Thoughtful, but needs qualifications suggested by Ladu, *q.v.*)

McQuiston, Raymer. *The Relation of Ralph Waldo Emerson to Public Affairs,* Humanistic Studies, III, No. 1 (Lawrence, Kansas, 1923). (A good, brief, general summary. See also, Gerber, Ladu, and later special studies.)

Miller, Perry. "Jonathan Edwards to Emerson," *New England Quarterly,* XIII (Dec., 1940), 589-617. (Excellent criticism of Emerson's ideas in relation to their Puritan background.)

Moody, M. M. "The Evolution of Emerson as an Abolitionist," *American Literature,* XVII (March, 1945), 1-21. (Also discusses Emerson's idea of freedom.)

Paul, Sherman. *Emerson's Angle of Vision: Man and Nature in American Experience.* (Cambridge, Mass., 1952).

Perry, Bliss. *Emerson Today* (Princeton, N. J., 1931). (The most readable general interpretation of Emerson's ideas by the dean of Emerson scholars.)

Quinn, Patrick F. "Emerson and Mysticism," *American Literature,* XXI (Jan., 1950), 347-414. (Good discussion of difficult subject, but defines "mysticism" so narrowly as to be largely negative.)

Sandeen, Ernest E. "Emerson's Americanism," in *Critical Studies in*

*Arnold, Emerson and Newman,* University of Iowa Studies (Iowa City, Iowa, 1942), pp. 63-118. (An excellent study of Emerson's ideas on nationalism, democracy, liberty, reform, and "the frontier.")

Santayana, George. "Emerson," *in Interpretations of Poetry and Religion* (New York, 1900), pp. 217-33. (Emerson as "the psyche of Puritanism." See also Santayana on "The Genteel Tradition.")

Shaw, C. G. "Emerson the Nihilist," *International Journal of Ethics,* XXV (Oct., 1914), 68-86. (An extreme, challenging interpretation.)

Silver, Mildred. "Emerson and the Idea of Progress," *American Literature,* XII (March, 1940), 1-19. (An excellent study of a difficult subject.)

Smart, G. K. "A Note on 'Emerson and Communism,'" *New England Quarterly,* X (Dec., 1937), 772-73. (Emerson liked Owen, although not his doctrinaire "communism.")

Turpie, M. C. "A Quaker Source for Emerson's Sermon on the Lord's Supper," *New England Quarterly,* XVII (March, 1944), 95-101. (Quaker background of Emerson's early thought.)

Wayman, Virginia. A Study of Emerson's Philosophy of Education," *Education,* LVI (April, 1936), 474-82. (Brief; see also unpublished doctoral dissertations.)

Whicher, Stephen. *The Lapse of Uriel: A Study in the Evolution of Emerson's Thought* (unpublished; Harvard University, 1942). (A challenging criticism of Emerson's Ideas.)

Wicke, Myron F. *Emerson's Mysticism* (unpublished; Western Reserve University, 1940). (An excellent study and interpretation of the subject.)

Wilkinson, L. A. "Emerson: Militant Pollyanna," *Thinker,* III (April, 1931), 33-44. (Challenging, but one-sided.)

## *PART IV*

# EMERSON AND WORLD LITERATURE

EMERSON was so completely the product of the American nineteenth century that the twentieth century tends to forget that his mind reached deep into the culture of antiquity and that his thought has influenced modern writers in many lands. His optimism and religious faith belonged to a pioneer America and a puritan New England, but his optimism also drew upon the mysticism of the ancient East, and his faith upon the religions of all the earth. If his optimism has been alienated by the tragic experience of our atomic age, his mysticism appeals across the ages to all scientists who think in terms of a truth beyond good and evil. And if modern America has revolted from the religion of Emerson's New England, his pragmatic translation of the old faith into the language of a liberal "conduct of life" has appealed strongly to modern thinkers such as John Dewey and Justice Oliver Wendell Holmes, Jr.

Emerson's "American Scholar" valued "books or the mind of the past" below "nature" or the experience of the present. But his reading of the books of the past has rightly been emphasized by scholars and critics. And since he himself announced that "greatness appeals to the future," his literary influence upon modern writers is also a measure of his importance. If his reputation seems less in mid-century than before, it is the more important to view it in the long perspectives of history.

Emerson's reading was perhaps greatest in contempories like Thomas Carlyle, and his influence was perhaps greatest on contemporaries like Henry Thoreau. But since these were his personal friends even more than his literary acquaintances, we have already considered them as part of his "Biography," in Part I. Older contemporaries like Goethe and younger ones like Whitman, however, were related to him primarily through their books. Similarly Emerson absorbed New England "Puritanism" so naturally that it became part of his own thought, and he suggested the later "Pragmatism" so unobtrusively that even William James did not recognize it until his third reading of the "Essays." Therefore, we have considered these two philosophies as part of Emerson's own "Idealism" and "Realism," in Part III. But his reading of the oriental mystics and Neoplatonists, and his own influence upon later writers like Nietzsche and Maeterlinck was more spectacular. Space and time have never impeded the meeting of minds, and Emerson's reached across the centuries to the mystics of ancient India and across the seas to many modern thinkers.

## SOURCES:

### 1. *The Ancients*

First, both in time and in importance, of the sources which contributed to Emerson's thought were the mystics of the ancient East. Writing before Plato was born and long before Christ preached, the anonymous authors of the Hindu scriptures described a philosophical idealism and a religious faith older and perhaps deeper and more enduring than the familiar classics of the Occident. And among the first major authors of the modern, Western world to read and to assimilate these Oriental books was Emerson. By some strange affinity of the imagination this parochial citizen of Concord, Massachusetts was attracted to the fragments of oriental literature which were being translated for the first time into European languages by scholars in his early youth. And gradually throughout his life he digested and transmuted this oriental idealism with the stuff of Western thought. Historically, this was perhaps his greatest distinction.

The influence of the Orient upon Emerson's thought has been frequently studied,[1] but only recently has it been proved that Emerson read Oriental translations throughout his youthful years. Dr. Man M. Singh[2] has pointed out that *The Edinburgh Review*

1. See especially: F. I. Carpenter, *Emerson and Asia* (Cambridge, Mass., 1930), and Arthur E. Christy, *The Orient in American Transcendentalism* (New York, 1934).

2. M. M. Singh, *Emerson and India* (Pennsylvania, 1947; an unpublished doctoral dissertation).

published many articles on India, and translations of many Hindu scriptures from 1805 to 1818 and later; and that Emerson borrowed many of these periodicals from libraries during the years 1820 to 1825. Moreover, Emerson's unpublished Journals contain many and long quotations from oriental books which were not included in the published *Journals.* At the age of eighteen he was already an "orientalist," and his interest continued steadily throughout his life.

The literature of Asia contributed specifically to certain poems and essays of Emerson. "Brahma"[3] was almost a translation of passages of the Hindu scriptures. "Hamatreya" was half Hindu. The essays on "The Over-Soul," "Fate," and "Illusions" were all strongly influenced by Hindu thought. But more important and more interesting than any specific translation was Emerson's general translation of oriental ideas into the language of his own occidental thought.

The most important idea which Emerson translated is that of "Brahma" itself—the concept of a disinterested and impersonal God whose laws lie beyond human good and evil. To this absolute God, human life and death—human "shame and fame"—are one. Therefore, the human worshiper of Brahma will recognize the relativity of the human laws of good and evil and will accept the scientific laws of the universe.—"Find me, and turn thy back on heaven." Achieving this superhuman point of view, he will join the company both of the religious mystics, and also of the great modern scientists. It is curious that Emerson, by returning to the oldest religious idealism of the East, discovered a philosophy which the latest astronomers and physicists of the West were beginning to formulate in new, scientific terms.

This oriental idea of the relativity of the human point of view is so fundamental, however, that it is hard to describe simply. Emerson emphasized it especially in describing the relativity of human good and evil: "To science there is no poison; to botany no weed; to chemistry no dirt."[4] And by doing so, he drew down the wrath of orthodox Christian theologians—especially for his "Divinity School Address,"[5] where he first expounded the idea.

3. See Part II.
4. *Works,* XII, 55, quoted in Christy, p. 115.
5. See Part II, and Part III.

But Emerson's denial of the orthodox morality of good and evil was specifically suggested by his oriental reading, and has been explained most clearly by reference to it: Dr. Singh's[6] discussion of Emerson's idea of evil is excellent. Moreover Emerson specifically attacked "Swedenborg: or, The Mystic" for his failure to realize this oriental-mystic idea: "His cardinal position in morals is that evils should be shunned as sins. But he does not know what evil is."[7] And he specifically preferred "the more generous spirit of the Indian Vishnu" to this narrower, Christian mysticism.

Emerson's "Over-Soul" also owed much to oriental thought, and W. T. Harris[8] early pointed out that the title was a close translation of the Hindu "adhi atma" or "superior soul." But the idea was even closer, perhaps, to the Neoplatonic idea of "emanation." Further, the relation of the Hindu idea of "Karma" to Emerson's "Compensation" and "Fate," and of "Maya" to Emerson's "Illusions," is both obvious and significant. More superficially, the Hindu idea of "transmigration" appealed to Emerson as a kind of fable of "Immortality," and many of the more primitive gods of the Hindu pantheon offered similarly fabulous illustrations of his own religious ideas.

Besides this fundamental "wisdom of the Brahmins," which helped to form the basic patterns of Emerson's thought, he valued the literatures of the oriental countries for other reasons. Most important was the Persian poetry of Hafiz and Saadi (or "Seyd").[9] Not only did he write an essay on "Persian Poetry" and edit a translation of *The Gulistan or Rose Garden* by Saadi, for which he wrote a "Preface"; and not only did he translate many of the poems of Hafiz and Saadi (via a German translation) into English, but he also imagined a semi-mythical "Saadi" as his own ideal poet, and borrowed many of the symbols and imaginative metaphors of the Persians to enrich his own poetical writing. Dr. Yohannan has shown, for instance, that Emerson's "Bacchus"

6. Singh, *op. cit.*, pp. 243-63.

7. *Works*, IV, 137.

8. W. T. Harris, in *The Genius and Character of Emerson*, ed. F. B. Sanborn, p. 376. See also Christy, *op. cit.*, pp. 73-79.

9. See J. D. Yohannan, "Emerson's Translations of Persian Poetry from German Sources," *American Literature*, XIV, (January, 1943), 407-20; and Yohannan, "The Influence of Persian Poetry on Emerson's Work," *American Literature*, XV (March, 1943), 25-41.

owed much to a poem of Hafiz, as did many of Emerson's other poems in lesser degree.[10] Moreover, the general spirit of imaginative liberation characteristic of these Persians so inspired Emerson that it is often not possible to say exactly whether some of his own poems are "translations," or new expressions of the old spirit. At the opposite pole from his Puritan ancestors, these Persians offered him both the ideas and the images of an imaginative freedom without occidental inhibitions.

Beyond the Hindu scriptures and the Persian poets, Emerson read and borrowed from the literature of Asia widely and for many purposes. The ethical wisdom of Confucius, the moral "Laws of Manu," and the religious commandments of the Koran all furnished him with "lustres," or illustrations for his thoughts, even though he never valued their particular philosophy very highly. The mythical folk-wisdom of the Orient (as also of the Greeks) appealed to him more—perhaps because his mind worked in terms of myths and symbols rather than of explicit morals and commandments. But in every case Emerson read the literature of the East to widen his horizon, to free himself from provinciality, and to achieve the universality and timelessness which characterizes his writing at its best. By returning to the ancient wisdom of the East, he helped prepare the way for that "meeting of East and West" which Whitman later celebrated in his "Passage to India," and which the modern world is slowly beginning to realize more fully.

Besides the ancient East, Emerson also read and absorbed the literature of ancient Greece and Rome from his earliest youth. Trained in the classical tradition of nineteenth century education as embodied in the Boston Latin School and Harvard College, he often read these authors in the original, whereas he read all oriental books in translation only. His works are full of first-hand references to the classics.[11] But for him the figure of Plato so far overshadowed all other classical authors that they seem insignificant by comparison.

Plato served two major functions for Emerson. He was "the Philosopher," who stood first and foremost among all Emerson's

10. Yohannan, "The Influence of Persian Poetry . . .," pp. 25-41.

11. See John P. Pritchard, *Return to the Fountains* (Durham, North Carolina, 1942). The chapter on Emerson includes pp. 44-60.

*Representative Men;* and on him Emerson lavished superlatives: "Plato is philosophy, and philosophy, Plato."[12] But Plato was also "the mystic" who prepared Emerson's mind for the religious idealism of the East: "Mysticism finds in Plato all its texts,"[13] he declared. And he described this Plato as the great mediator between East and West: "The unity of Asia and the detail of Europe . . . Plato came to join, and, by contact, to enhance the energy of each."[14]

If Plato, the father of philosophy, was a historically accurate "representative man," Plato, the mystic and orientalist, was a figure created by Emerson's imagination with the aid of some inaccurate nineteenth-century scholarship. Plato, the philosopher, was the product of Emerson's actual reading of Plato—especially in the original Greek. This Plato's influence has recently been summarized by Dr. S. G. Brown.[15] But Plato, the mythical mystic, was a more exciting figure, resulting from a confusion of Platonism with the later Neoplatonism of Alexandria, abetted by Emerson's reading of the many books of Thomas Taylor—who translated inaccurately and interpreted confusingly both Plato and Plotinus, and the minor Neoplatonists. The influence of this composite, mystical Plato has been studied by Dr. J. S. Harrison,[16] and the relation between this mystical Platonism and Oriental thought, by the present writer.[17]

Emerson's reading of Plato and his philosophic "Platonism" preceded his more mystical Neoplatonism and Orientalism, both in time and in importance. He read Plato in college, wrote his first formal essay on "The Character of Socrates," and studied Plato both earlier and more widely than any other philosophic author. Dr. Brown has suggested that "the fundamental inconsistency in Emerson's thinking lies at the very heart of Platonism"[18]—the inconsistency between the monism of Plato's early works, and the dualism of the *Timaeus* and later works. By con-

12. *Works,* IV, 40.
13. *Loc. cit.*
14. *Ibid.,* IV, 54
15. S. G. Brown, "Emerson's Platonism," *New England Quarterly,* XVIII (Sept., 1945), 325-45.
16. John S. Harrison, *The Teachers of Emerson* (New York, 1910).
17. F. I. Carpenter, *Emerson and Asia,* pp. 39-102.
18. *Loc. cit.*

trast, the purely monistic mysticism associated with "Transcendentalism" was more characteristic of Neoplatonism. Emerson added the doctrines of these more mystical writers to the genuine Platonism of his earlier reading and thought in order to transmute Plato into a mystic.

During the 1830's, when Emerson was rebelling against the orthodox Christian and classical ideas of his boyhood, he was reading widely and deeply in the Neoplatonic translations of Thomas Taylor and their "commentaries" on Plato. This reading might seem abstract and unimportant enough if it had remained "mere" philosophy to Emerson. But it suggested many of his more unorthodox and radical ideas, and channeled his thinking in new directions. "Plotinus, Proclus, Porphyry, Iamblichus" and other more esoteric authors became his familiars for the rest of his life and, with the Orientals, were the most unusual and important of his literary enthusiasms.

First, Emerson credited Neoplatonism (and, in his essay on "Plato," Platonism also) with introducing Oriental thought to the West. "When Orientalism in Alexandria found the Platonists, a new school was produced. The sternness of the Greek school, feeling its way forward from argument to argument, met and combined with the beauty of Orientalism."[19] In Neoplatonism, Emerson found the connecting link between the logic of the West and the mysticism of the East.

This philosophy particularly contributed to Emerson's idea of "The Over-Soul." The idea of emanation—of the "influx of the divine mind into our mind"—is typically Plotinian—and especially so in the language and imagery which Emerson used to expound his idea. God conceived as the source, the fountain, the reservoir of spiritual energy, from whom the individual self derives—was not Platonic but Neoplatonic.

This idea was, of course, monistic—the individual soul being merely an infinitesimal fraction of the Over-Soul. Nature, therefore, was logically also an "emanation" of God—and Emerson (as we have seen)[20] used a motto from Plotinus to introduce his first book. But this idealistic monism of the Neoplatonists easily suggested that—by a reversal of the point of view—Nature might

19. *The Atlantic Monthly*, LI, 826.
20. See Part II.

be interpreted in terms of a materialistic monism, and emanation from above might also be interpreted as evolution from below. So it was easy for Emerson to compose a new motto for the second edition of *Nature,* suggesting this later idea of evolution. The important point is that Neoplatonism, by breaking away from the dualism of Plato, prepared Emerson's mind both for mysticism and for scientific thought, both of which transcended the merely humanistic, or man-centered, point of view.

More specifically, Emerson developed this monism in *Nature,* as the idea of the "correspondence" between moral law and natural law: "The axioms of physics translate the laws of ethics." This idea has been traced both to Neoplatonism[21] and also to Swedenborg, but it is certainly neither Platonic nor orthodox.

Finally, Emerson developed from the Neoplatonists, and not from Plato, his theory that poetry and art may be directly inspired by God, and therefore may express man's highest achievement. Plato, it is well known, distrusted poetic madness, and preferred the rational logic of philosophy. But the Neoplatonists, especially Proclus, exalted the poet, and described his intuitive and symbolic thought as divine.[22]

Thus Emerson's reading of the literature of the ancient Orient, and of Greece and Alexandria, suggested to him many of his major ideas and inspired directly much of his most original writing. This influence of the ancients upon him is significant and unusual, because the ancients have influenced most modern writers toward classicism and traditionalism, but Emerson found in them the seeds of radical, new ideas. If some of these have seemed merely vague and mystical to modern readers, others (like the symbolic philosophy of art, and the idea of relativity of good and evil) have, for better or for worse, contributed significantly to the thought of the modern world.

More important than the ancient books of the East or the classics of Greece and Rome, and more important even than Plato as the primary source of Emerson's thought was, of course, the Christian Bible. But because he had been brought up on it, he revolted against it, exclaiming that "the Bible wears black cloth."[23]

21. See Carpenter, *Emerson and Asia,* pp. 69-70.
22. See Part II.
23. *Journals,* May, 1865.

But he also recognized that "This old Bible, if you pitch it out the window with a fork, it comes bounce back again."[24] Its influence was so fundamental that it is hard to measure—the name of Jesus, as he said in the "Divinity School Address," "is not so much written as ploughed into the history of the world." If Emerson quoted the Bible constantly in his sermons, his published *Works* refer to it rarely by name. His essays on "Swedenborg," and on "Compensation" quote it most frequently.[25] But the Bible had moulded his youthful mind. If he often questioned the dogmas of orthodox Christianity,[26] he still valued the Bible—descendant of the Puritans as he was—above all other books.

## 2. *The Moderns*

Among the moderns Emerson read and valued a few major authors more than all the rest put together.[27] Always a worshiper of greatness, but also trusting his own heart, he chose as his modern literary heroes: Shakespeare, Dante, Milton, Montaigne, Swedenborg, and Goethe. Four of these he described in *Representative Men,* the two others were traditional classics but also genuine favorites of his.

Next to Plato, Shakespeare was Emerson's favorite author—and, of course, Plato was primarily a philosopher. Not only did he nominate Shakespeare as "The Poet," but he spoke of "the transcendent superiority of Shakespeare to all other writers."[28] Besides the famous essay in *Representative Men,* he wrote a second address on Shakespeare in 1864 for the three-hundredth anniversary of the poet's birth.[29] Yet, because of a few sentences of negative criticism in *Representative Men,* the notion persists that Emerson condemned Shakespeare.[30] "He was master of the revels to mankind."

24. *Ibid.*, November 26, 1842.

25. See Harriet R. Zink, "Emerson's Use of the Bible," in *University of Nebraska Studies in Language and Literature* (Lincoln, 1935), p. 58.

26. G. H. Hartwig, "Emerson on Historical Christianity," *Hibbert Journal,* XXXVII (April, 1939), 405-12.

27. "Perhaps the human mind would be a gainer if all the secondary writers were lost,—say, in England, all but Shakespeare, Milton, and Bacon." (*Works*, VII, 194).

28. *Journals,* IX, 187.

29. *Works,* XI, 445-54.

30. R. P. Falk, "Emerson and Shakespeare," *PMLA,* LVI (June, 1941), 523-43. Dr. Falk's essay includes much thoughtful criticism.

The problem of Emerson's criticism of Shakespeare goes to the very heart of his personality and also of his philosophy. Personally, his puritan-religious inheritance made him instinctively distrust Shakespeare, the "player." And, philosophically, his idealism made him criticize Shakespeare, "The Poet," for not also being "The Mystic," or man of religion. But it is infinitely more important to realize that Emerson did consider Shakespeare to be *the* perfect poet in spite of his profane life, that he did value Shakespeare's style as the ideal embodiment of his own theory of symbolic expression, and that he did not seriously question Shakespeare's tragic view of life or his pessimism—both so opposite to his own optimism.

Only because Shakespeare was so perfect a poet did Emerson venture to criticize him as a man, at all. "Had he been less," Emerson explained, "had he reached only the common measure of great authors, of Bacon, Milton, Tasso, Cervantes[31] . . ." his criticism would have been gratuitous. But just because Shakespeare was *the* perfect poet, Emerson did criticize his failure to achieve the absolute human perfection of—say—Jesus (although he never considered Jesus among his Representative Men). Meanwhile, Emerson read and valued the poetry of Shakespeare throughout his life to the very highest degree.

It is significant that Emerson valued both Dante and Milton far below Shakespeare, although both were more religious poets, and Dante somewhat of a mystic also. However, although Emerson was a poor linguist, and theoretically preferred translations, he did learn both Italian and German in order to read both Dante and Goethe in their original languages. For they also were great poets and representative men.

Emerson read Dante[32] in translation in his youth and later learned Italian—as also German—at the instigation of Margaret Fuller. Throughout his life he continued to read translations of *The Divine Comedy,* and was instrumental in the publication of at least one of these. But most extraordinary was his own laborious translation of Dante's *Vita Nuova* into English—partly as an exercise in Italian, but partly also as a labor of love. If

31. *Works,* IV, 218.
32. J. C. Mathews, "Emerson's Knowledge of Dante," *University of Texas Studies in English,* XXII (1942), 171-98.

this translation proves his inadequate knowledge of the language, it proves more significantly his sincere appreciation of the author. Moreover, the year in which he finished his translation—1843—marked perhaps the height of his powers, and proved the maturity of his interest in the great Italian.

Like Dante, Emerson was attracted to Milton as a religious and philosophic poet. He had been brought up on Milton, and lectured on him frequently, both in courses on English literature and on Great Men. From these notes, his essay on "Milton" was published after his death.[33] But because it was so fundamental, the unconscious influence of Milton upon him was perhaps more important than the formal and conscious. Specifically, he praised Milton more often for religious and moral greatness than for the greatness of his poetry.[34]

For Emerson, Milton was the poet and philosopher of freedom. He was the great Puritan, whose ideas Emerson recognized as the antecedents of his own. Moreover, Milton's theory of poetry, with its depreciation of formal rhyme, appealed to him. He borrowed both the title and the idea of "Uriel" from *Paradise Lost*. And he knew many of Milton's early poems by heart. But, in spite of his intimate familiarity with Milton, and of his predilection for Puritan ideas, the significant fact is that—true to his own mature philosophy—he condemned Milton for being "too literary," and preferred the "natural" poetry of Shakespeare to the bookish poetry and allegory of Milton. If Emerson's early poem "Grace"[35] owed much to Milton, his mature essays on "Self-Reliance" and "The Poet" owed little.

At the opposite pole from Milton, Montaigne was anti-Puritan, anti-poetic, and the natural discovery of Emerson's literary maturity. Like Bacon (whom Emerson also read and valued highly) Montaigne was a prose realist, both in philosophy and in literary form; but beyond Bacon, he was also a liberal and lover of man. Without the Machiavellian cynicism of Bacon, his honest skepticism and realism appealed to the Yankee. *Emerson's Mon-*

33. *Works,* XII, 245-80.
34. See R. C. Pettigrew, "Emerson and Milton," *American Literature,* III (March, 1931), 45-59.
35. See G. R. Elliott, "On Emerson's 'Grace' and 'Self-Reliance,'" *The New England Quarterly,* II, 93.

*taigne*[36] has been fully and sympathetically studied, but because Emerson's enthusiasm was so fundamental and so informal, it is harder—and, perhaps, not so important—to define it exactly. "Montaigne, or, The Skeptic" was the Representative Man who related Emerson's ideal philosophy to the common earth; and the essay on "Montaigne" remains the best expression of his enthusiasm both for "the grand old sloven," and for the philosophy which he expressed.

Swedenborg was a stranger enthusiasm of Emerson, and certainly a less popular and less likely choice for *Representative Men.* Moreover, Swedenborg was not even a typical "Mystic," but was a scientist and religious philosopher with highly individual and idiosyncratic theories, and not much literary skill. Yet Emerson read and valued him for many reasons. First, Emerson became acquainted with Swedenborg indirectly through the medium of the minor and periodical literature which contributed so richly to the ferment of New England Transcendentalism.[37] Sampson Reed, an enthusiastic disciple of Swedenborg, early captured Emerson's imagination and introduced him to "the master." Many other Transcendentalists also adopted many vaguely Swedenborgian ideas, often at second or third hand, just as they adopted many vaguely Kantian ideas. Scholars have shown that Emerson often attributed to Swedenborg ideas that were not his, and misinterpreted others.[38] Therefore, Emerson's "Swedenborg" became a kind of semi-mythical figure—and, with Kant, a sort of foster-father of New England Transcendentalism.

Writing of Swedenborg's actual books, Emerson was often apologetic, and almost always qualified in praise. But Swedenborg's personality and philosophy performed a vital function. Because Swedenborg had been a brilliant scientist, who, after his "conversion," devoted himself to explaining and interpreting

36. C. L. Young, *Emerson's Montaigne* (New York, 1941).

37. This Transcendental literature has been studied in detail by Kenneth W. Cameron, *Emerson the Essayist* (Raleigh, N. C., 1945); and in briefer selection and outline by Perry Miller, *The Transcendentalists* (Cambridge, Mass., 1950). Miller reprints significant selections by Sampson Reed, pp. 48-59.

38. See especially many articles by Dr. C. P. Hotson, listed in *Articles in American Literature* . . . (Durham, N. C., 1947), pp. 52-53.

the laws of physical science in "spiritual" terms, Emerson took him for guide in his own interpretation of modern science. His "Swedenborg" became not so much "The Mystic" as the imaginative thinker who reconciled science and religion. Indeed, this Swedenborg suggested to Emerson—and later to William James—a kind of new philosophy of science.

This reconciliation of science and religion Swedenborg accomplished by means of the doctrine of "correspondence,"[39] or analogy. Accepting this doctrine, Emerson fathered upon Swedenborg the whole monistic (and vaguely "mystical") philosophy which attempted to reconcile "law for man" with "law for thing." This, of course, made "Swedenborg" seem a very great and "representative" man to Emerson.

Last and most modern of Emerson's favorite authors and *Representative Men* was Goethe. As with Dante, Margaret Fuller helped Emerson learn the language in order to read this great "Writer" in the original. But in this case Emerson's effort was the more surprising, because Goethe was neither an established world classic nor a religious philosopher. Moreover, Emerson never read *Faust* with enthusiasm, but concentrated on the earlier, romantic and minor works of the great German.[40]

Goethe, more than any author except Montaigne, freed Emerson from the narrow puritanism and provincialism of his New England heritage. Goethe was never popular in New England, and was famous (or infamous) for his paganism, worldliness, and utter flouting of "the moral law." Inevitably, therefore, Emerson was influenced by his own background and often became the moral apologist for Goethe, as in his poem "To J. W.," where he excused "the errors of a sage sublime" on the grounds of his still greater achievements. And it is true that his criticism of Goethe remained somewhat puritanic—especially since he never fully recognized the higher social idealism of the second *Faust.* But the mere fact that Emerson read and appreciated the modern writer as fully as he did is evidence of the catholicity of his tastes.

Positively, Goethe (like Swedenborg) suggested to Emerson

39. See Part II, *Nature,* for a discussion of the idea of "correspondence."

40. See F. B. Wahr, *Emerson and Goethe* (Ann Arbor, Mich., 1915). Many of the following facts are documented by Dr. Wahr's book.

a possible philosophic reconciliation of science and religion. "He married Faith and Reason, for the world,"[41] Emerson noted. Moreover, many of his aesthetic ideas influenced Emerson,[42] although the essay on "Goethe; or, The Writer" criticized his overemphasis of "Culture." Goethe's proverbial wisdom and "Conversations"[43] appealed to Emerson much as Franklin's had. As "The Writer" whose mind ranged broadly and variously over all the phenomena of the modern world, Emerson appreciated greatness in spite of barriers of language, of temperament, and of religious heritage.

Besides his favorite major authors and *Representative Men,* Emerson, of course, read widely in the literature of the modern world. Most important was the purely contemporary literature which he found both in current magazines and in books. But three groups of earlier writers deserve separate mention. From the metaphysical poets Emerson derived inspiration both for the form and the content of his own poetry.[44] In the Cambridge Platonists, especially Cudworth, Emerson found many of the ideas, with which he had been acquainted by his reading of Plato and the Neoplatonists, developed in new ways.[45] And in the various formal philosophers which he studied in college and in divinity school, especially the Scottish,[46] he found many ideas sometimes credited to other sources.

The vast body of minor contemporary literature which every man of letters reads in his formative years probably constitutes the most important element in his education; and Emerson, in spite of his puritan heritage and philosophic bent, read widely and miscellaneously. Later he emphasized the great value of "some idle books under the bench in Latin School," and always remembered the novels of Scott with particular affection. Even more important were the romantic poets of his youth—especially

41. *Letters,* I, 354.

42. Vivian Hopkins, "The Influence of Goethe on Emerson's Aesthetic Theory," *Philological Quarterly,* XXVII (October, 1948), 222-44.

43. Wahr, *op. cit.*

44. See N. A. Brittin, "Emerson and the Metaphysical Poets," *American Literature,* VIII (March, 1936), 1-21.

45. J. S. Harrison, *The Teachers of Emerson;* see Index for references.

46. See M. R. Davis, "Emerson's 'Reason' and the Scottish Philosophers," *New England Quarterly,* XVII (June 1944), 209-28. See also Part III.

Scott, Byron, and Wordsworth. Inevitably, he was a product of the Romantic era.

Of more particular interest, however, was the contemporary periodical literature which led Emerson toward Transcendentalism. This has been studied in detail,[47] and is of importance to special students, both of Emerson and of Transcendentalism. But to the general student, his major literary contemporaries, Carlyle, Coleridge, and Wordsworth, and the German transcendental philosophers whose ideas these English men of letters translated (in every sense of the word), are of primary interest.

Wordsworth[48] and Coleridge were early favorites of his, and he was reading the *Lyrical Ballads* as early as 1826. Wordsworth particularly, seemed to him the greatest English poet since Milton and he read the "Immortality" ode for comfort after Ellen's death The "Ode to Duty" and many other poems appealed to his puritan temperament. But most important, of course, was the poetic theory, expressed in the "Preface" to the *Lyrical Ballads* and embodied in all of Wordsworth's poetry—the simplicity, the high seriousness, and the honest treatment of common and rural life. Both the philosophy and the diction of "Good-Bye, Proud World" and of many of Emerson's later poems owed much to his reading of these poets.

But Coleridge[49] was more important to Emerson's development than Wordsworth, because Coleridge was to him the modern philosopher and psychologist, rather than merely the poet. If Coleridge together with Wordsworth suggested many of the ideas of his theory of poetry, Coleridge alone suggested many of the basic ideas of his transcendental philosophy. He was reading Coleridge's *Aids to Reflection* and *Friend* in 1829—a year before discovering Carlyle—and for the next seven years Coleridge remained perhaps the most important single influence on his literary life. He valued

47. Kenneth W. Cameron, *Emerson the Essayist* (Raleigh, N. C. 1945). This two-volume study includes and/or summarizes the material of Dr. Cameron's earlier study, *Ralph Waldo Emerson's Reading* (Raleigh, N. C., 1941). See also Perry Miller's anthology and notes in *The Transcendentalists;* and J. W. Beach's study of Emerson's reading in the literature of science (and pseudo-science) in "Emerson and Evolution."

48. F. T. Thompson, "Emerson's Theory and Practice of Poetry," *PMLA,* XLIII (December, 1928), 1170-84.

49. F. T. Thompson, "Emerson's Indebtedness to Coleridge," *Studies in Philology,* XXIII (January, 1926), 55-76.

Coleridge not for any one work or any one idea, but as the "mouthpiece of the mind of man," who had probably "put more ideas into circulation" than any Englishman living.

For Emerson, Coleridge (and Carlyle to a lesser degree) interpreted the Transcendentalism of Kant. Of course Coleridge often misinterpreted it (as we have seen in Part III), but Emerson was no purist, and valued ideas primarily for their power of suggestion. Coleridge's distinction between "Reason" and "Understanding" (which was only vaguely Kantian, being much closer to his own earlier distinction between "Imagination" and "Fancy") particularly influenced Emerson's philosophy of Nature.[50] And in spite of occasional disagreements and criticisms, Emerson continued to value Coleridge's philosophic prose throughout his later years.

Carlyle,[51] of course, was primarily a friend, and as such was more to Emerson than Coleridge could have been. He valued Carlyle also as a literary artist and stylist. But Carlyle had first been a translator of German thought, and a minor philosopher. Emerson had first read his translation of Goethe's *Wilhelm Meister* in 1830, and his *Life of Schiller*. Then the *Corn Law Rhymes* caught Emerson's attention, and led to his historic visit to their author. Immediately after this, *Sartor Resartus* seemed to speak directly to Emerson's own experience of loss and inner struggle, with its chapters on "The Everlasting No" and "The Everlasting Yea." But Carlyle's many articles and books dealing with German literature and thought continued to nourish Emerson's interest in the German philosophers.

The last important group of writers to influence Emerson's thought were the German Transcendentalists, but all the evidence leads to the conclusion that their influence was also the least.[52] Emerson read several discussions and digests of Kant's philosophy, but seems to have read little of Kant at first hand and that little late. His effective reading of it was largely at

50. See Part II.

51. See Part I, "Friendships." For literary influence, see F. T. Thompson, "Emerson and Carlyle," *Studies in Philology*, XXIV (July, 1927), 438-53.

52. René Wellek, "Emerson and German Philosophy," *New England Quarterly*, XVI (1943), 41-62. This article restudies the subject and summarizes the results of many earlier books and articles (see its footnote 1, p. 41).

second and third hand, as it appeared refracted through the minds of Coleridge and Carlyle. And more important, his development of "Transcendentalism" was almost entirely un-Kantian, following rather the philosophic principles of Neoplatonism, and the literary romanticism of Goethe, Schelling, and Novalis.

Only Hegel, among the genuine philosophers of German Transcendentalism, exerted direct influence on Emerson, and that so late in his life as to be of minor importance to him. Professor Henry A. Pochmann[53] has suggested that the years after 1850 constituted a "Hegelian period" in Emerson's thought, and during those years Emerson read increasingly in Hegel, largely at the urging of his friends J. E. Cabot and W. T. Harris. On a late lecture tour of the West he met several times with the group of "St. Louis Hegelians" for discussion, although showing little skill or interest in Hegelian dialectics. Later these "Hegelians" flocked in turn to Emerson and Alcott's "Concord School of Philosophy." Meanwhile Emerson developed some typically Hegelian ideas—especially from his *Philosophy of History.* But for Emerson "Hegel pre-exists in Proclus,"[54] and certainly he owed far more to the Platonists and to the Orientals than to the German Transcendentalists.

## Influences

### 1. *America, Nineteenth Century*

Just as every man of letters is most influenced by the vast body of minor miscellaneous literature of his own early years, he in turn influences most the many minor, younger writers of his own later years. Emerson's personal and literary influence upon these younger men was often very deep, and very wide, as their many explicit personal statements attest.[55] Some of the younger men were also his friends who, like Thoreau, have been considered in Part I in relation to "Emerson's Biography." But others, like Whitman, were influenced most by their reading of Emerson's books.

53. In his comprehensive study of the influences of German culture on America, as yet largely unpublished. H. A. Pochmann, *New England Transcendentalism and St. Louis Hegelianism* (Philadelphia, 1948), studies one phase of the subject.
54. *Works,* VIII, 180.
55. See, for instance, "Notes" and "Index" in Rusk's *Life of Emerson.*

Certainly Thoreau and Whitman were the two major writers who can fairly be called disciples of Emerson, and who developed his literary ideas most effectively. Because they were major writers, they developed his ideas in new ways, often disagreeing with them and changing them. But these three belonged to what Sainte-Beuve called one "family of minds." And where Thoreau grew up almost within Emerson's physical family, Whitman belonged to a different environment and to a different moral tradition. Therefore Emerson's great influence on him is the more remarkable.

Whitman's literary relationship with Emerson was complex, presenting many problems and contradictions, and it has been studied and analyzed in detail.[56] The fundamental document is Emerson's famous letter of 1855, welcoming the first edition of *Leaves of Grass* as "the most extraordinary piece of wit and wisdom that an American has yet contributed," and greeting its author "at the beginning of a great career."[57] But Emerson somewhat qualified his opinion in the course of later years. And Whitman, in his efforts to emphasize his own originality and to magnify his own greatness, later made statements about their relationship, some of which were false and some exaggerated.

Whitman undoubtedly read Emerson, and was deeply influenced by him, before writing the first edition of *Leaves of Grass* in 1855. But in middle life he denied this: to his friend Kennedy he declared "positively" that he had not read Emerson before 1855, and he repeated to John Burroughs that he had not read Emerson until 1856, and then "by the seashore."[58] But more

56. Besides chapters in the different biographies, three articles have studied this relationship in detail: 1. J. B. Moore, "The Master of Whitman," *Studies in Philology*, XXIII, 77-89 (Jan., 1926), considers primarily the literary relationship from the point of view of Whitman (as the title indicates). 2. Clarence Gohdes, "Whitman and Emerson," *Sewanee Review*, XXXVII, 79-93 (Jan., 1929), considers primarily the facts of their personal relationship, presenting the conflicting evidence. 3. Finally, Carlos Baker, "The Road to Concord: Another Milestone in the Whitman-Emerson Friendship," *The Princeton University Library Chronicle*, VII, 100-117 (April, 1946), prints a new letter of Emerson's, recommending Whitman to Secretary Salmon P. Chase, and summarizes the other "milestones" of their personal friendship.

57. Reprinted in full in H. S. Canby, *Walt Whitman* (Boston, 1943), pp. 120-121.

58. For these and following references, see C. Gohdes, *op. cit.*

honestly he later admitted to his friend Trowbridge that in 1854, "I was simmering, simmering, and Emerson brought me to a boil." And these facts are certain: that Whitman's early manuscript notebooks contained snatches of "embryonic verse" with references to Emerson—especially one to "Emerson lecturing"; that in 1847 the *Brooklyn Eagle* contained a review by Whitman of Emerson's "Spiritual Laws"; and that the *Democratic Review*, at the time when Whitman was contributing frequently, contained many digests, quotations, and reviews of Emerson's essays. In spite of disclaimers, Whitman's first *Leaves of Grass* owed a very great deal to Emerson.

Indeed, Emerson's ideas furnished many of the seeds from which Whitman's *Leaves* sprang—Emerson helped Whitman do almost everything but limit his plot and cut his lawn. Professor Moore (who had minimized Emerson's influence on Thoreau) declared that "there is no doubt that Whitman was more indebted to Emerson than to any other for the fundamental ideas in even his earliest *Leaves of Grass*."[59] We have already quoted some of the passages of Emerson's "Poet"[60] which prophesied Whitman's practice of poetry: the American inspiration, the absence of metres, the originality, the love of wild nature, and the "excited" use of mere catalogues of words. But the whole Emersonian philosophy so pervades Whitman's *Leaves* that it can hardly be differentiated clearly.[61] Even those major ideas which Whitman developed and celebrated in opposition to Emerson—such as sexuality, "en masse," and "the divine average"—all found earlier theoretical justification in Emerson's writing.

After Emerson's famous letter in praise of the 1855 *Leaves of Grass*, Emerson was led to qualify his praise by the many and often violent objections of his friends; and Whitman in turn was led to disclaim Emerson as "Master," partly because of Emerson's own criticisms, and partly because Whitman's "eidolon," or ideal of himself, demanded an absolute self-reliance and originality. From the beginning, indeed, Emerson's praises had often been qualified, as when he described the *Leaves* to Sanborn as "a

59. J. B. Moore, "The Master of Emerson," *loc. cit.*
60. See Part II, p. 95.
61. See, for instance, the attack of Yvor Winters in *In Defense of Reason* on the ideas of Emerson and Whitman as indistinguishable.

singular blend of the Bhagvat Ghita and the New York *Herald.*"[62] Later Emerson's visit with Whitman and his Bohemian colleagues in 1857 accentuated the difference of their tastes. After 1860, when Whitman visited Boston and discussed at length with Emerson the question of sex in the *Leaves,* their disagreements became clearer to both (although Emerson's opposition was not emotional nor moralistic, as has often been implied). But a recently discovered letter from Emerson recommending Whitman to the Secretary of the Treasury dispels all question of any serious quarrel: to Secretary Chase Emerson wrote in 1863 that "Whitman is known to me as a man of strong original genius, combining with marked eccentricities, great powers and valuable traits of character . . . If his writings are in certain points open to criticism, they . . . are more deeply American, democratic, and in the interest of political liberty than any other poet."[63]

Nevertheless, Emerson's many critical remarks, even when fair and just, disturbed Whitman, and from the years 1860 to 1880 he sought to minimize his debt and to criticize Emerson in turn. Sometimes (as we have seen) he denied Emerson's early influence; sometimes, on the other hand, he described Emerson's influence as only temporary. His 1880 article on "Emerson's Books (the Shadows of Them)," although often critical, was at least objective: "The best part of Emersonianism is, it breeds the giant that destroys itself . . . No teacher has ever taught, that has so provided for his pupil's setting up independently."[64]

After 1880, when Emerson was very old, Whitman became purely laudatory. His visit to Emerson at his Concord home in 1881 seemed to weave a spell about their relationship, and after Emerson's death there was nothing but praise. The three volumes of Traubel's intimate memoirs *With Walt Whitman in Camden* which Boswellize Whitman's later years, begin with an account of his relationship with Emerson, and mention Emerson more often than any other writer. They quote Whitman as describing Emerson as "far above other giants," and "a born democrat," and as saying that "after every heresy I go back to Emerson," and

62. Quoted in Carlos Baker, *op. cit.,* p. 102.
63. Reprinted by Carlos Baker, *op. cit.,* p. 108.
64. Whitman's *Prose Works* (Philadelphia, no date), p. 322.

"I look in all men for the heroic quality I find in Emerson."[65] And Whitman concluded: "Emerson was a far-reaching force: a star of the first, the very first magnitude maybe: without a doubt that."[66]

Besides Thoreau and Whitman, and the Transcendental group that lived near Concord and Cambridge,[67] Emerson influenced most of the important New England writers of his time to a lesser degree. Lowell, Holmes, and Whittier were enthusiastic admirers. Longfellow remained aloof. Hawthorne let himself be attracted by his wife towards the Emersonian orbit, but soon found himself repelled by an instinctive antagonism. And Melville, like Hawthorne, became an effective critic of Emerson.

James Russell Lowell was inspired by Emerson in his youth, and for many years with the encouragement of his young wife devoted himself to the transcendental and literary forms of the time. His half-humorous description of his own "bundle of 'isms," and his wholly serious tribute to the great Emerson, constituted the beginning and the end of his famous *Fable for Critics.* In later life he recalled more humorously his own youthful enthusiasms in his essay on "Thoreau," and paid final homage to the personal influence of Emerson in "Emerson the Lecturer."[68] But whether in his own personal experience, or in his critical judgment of his literary contemporaries, Emerson came first:

> There comes Emerson first, whose rich words, every one,
> Are like gold nails in temples to hang trophies on.

Oliver Wendell Holmes was less affected by Emerson's ideas, but equally by Emerson's personality. Together with Lowell, he both experienced and described in vivid detail the stimulation and liberation of "The American Scholar"[69] address at Harvard. Later Emerson became a frequent visitor at Holmes' Boston house, and during this relationship advised and inspired the young Oliver Wendell Holmes, Jr.[70] And in old age, Holmes wrote a sympa-

65. Quoted in Carlos Baker, *op. cit.*, pp. 115-16, with references.
66. Quoted in J. B. Moore, *op. cit.*, from Traubel, III, 185.
67. See Part I, "Loves and Friendships."
68. See Part I.
69. See Part II.
70. See Part III, "Pragmatism."

thetic and readable biography of his friend—although not of his friend's ideas.[71]

John Greenleaf Whittier never knew Emerson closely, being separated both by space and by difference of background. Obviously Whittier had neither the education nor the inclination really to study Emerson's philosophic ideas. But as poet he was deeply influenced by Emerson, and often illustrated in his own homely and popular terms some of the philosopher's poetic ideas—as, for instance, in "Snowbound," whose motto and basic idea were:

> . . . enclosed
> In a tumultuous privacy of storm.[72]

Writing on Emerson in 1880, Whittier finally asserted that "no living poet of the English-speaking tongue has written verses bearing more distinctly than his the mark of immortality."[73]

Hawthorne, however, belonged to the loyal opposition. No complete study has been made of the curiously ambivalent relationship of the two men, but the outlines appear clearly in Hawthorne's Journals. Beginning with his marriage to one of "The Peabody Sisters of Salem"[74] (all of whom were enthusiastic Emersonians), Hawthorne was attracted to the Transcendental orbit and lived for a time at Brook Farm. Then he spent the better part of three years in Concord, during which his Journals record many visits, walks, and talks with Emerson. The two men never became close friends (although Emerson tried), but the Emersonian ideas affected Hawthorne deeply.

The influence of Emerson's ideas on Hawthorne appears in several instances. Most important and interesting is their embodiment in the character of Hester Prynne in *The Scarlet Letter.*[75] Following the exhortation of Emerson's poem "Give All To Love," Hester achieved in almost complete self-reliance and a genuine heroism, although Hawthorne felt the need of condemning her in his moralistic "Conclusion." The conflict of the novel

71. See Part I.
72. Emerson's "Snow-Storm." See Part II.
73. J. G. Whittier, *The Literary World,* XI (May 22, 1880), 182.
74. Louise H. Tharp, *The Peabody Sisters of Salem,* Boston, 1950.
75. F. I. Carpenter, "Scarlet A Minus," *College English,* V, 173-180 (Jan., 1944).

is that between individual "self-reliance" and a moralistic "society," and Hawthorne here described this ideal conflict clearly and fairly. But in *The Blithedale Romance* he distorted his plot to describe the idealistic Hollingsworth as a megalomaniac, and the self-reliant Zenobia as a scarlet woman. Finally Hawthorne focused the conflict between transcendental self-reliance and puritan moralism on the actual person of Margaret Fuller (who is generally considered the prototype of his fictional Zenobia). Whereas Emerson apotheosized Margaret (or so Hawthorne believed), Hawthorne damned her self-reliance as "defective and evil."[76] But in all instances the influence of Emerson on Hawthorne appears in the ideal definition of those basic conflicts and problems which Hawthorne's novels and tales embodied in their plots and characters.

Even more than Hawthorne, Melville stood in ideal opposition to Emerson, for Melville expressed most clearly in the American nineteenth century that "modern" pessimism which most distrusts Emerson's optimism. Moreover, Melville came under Emerson's influence later than did Hawthorne, and reacted more emphatically, more specifically, and more articulately. Melville's comments on Emerson's ideas found expression first in his letters and conversation; second, in his fictional satires upon the transcentental philosophy; and finally in his marginal comments on Emerson's *Essays*. Since Melville's criticism of Emerson was not merely personal but also universal, and has been studied in detail, it is worth emphasizing.

Emerson never read Melville with any interest, nor did Melville read Emerson effectively until after he heard him lecture in 1849.[77] Then he characterized Emerson as "this Plato who talks through his nose," but praised him as "more than a brilliant fellow . . . Swear he is a humbug—then he is no common humbug . . . To my surprise, I found him quite intelligible."[78] Following this, Melville focused his attention on Emerson's philosophy, both in

76. See *The Heart of Hawthorne's Journals*, ed. N. Arvin, Boston, 1929, pp. 113, 271 ff.

77. William Braswell, "Melville as a Critic of Emerson," *American Literature*, IX, 317-334 (Nov., 1937).

78. Quoted in Braswell, *ibid.*, pp. 317-318. See also: Egbert S. Oliver, "Melville's Picture of Emerson and Thoreau in 'The Confidence Man,'" *College English*, VIII, 61-72 (1946).

conversations with Hawthorne, and later in reading Emerson carefully; and made Emerson the mouthpiece and symbol of that transcendental optimism which he opposed most violently.

The most famous and significant satire upon Emerson's Transcendental philosophy is probably that contained in Melville's *Pierre,* and embodied in the character of Plotinus Plinlimmon. Indeed, the whole idea of Plinlimmon's famous pamphlet on "Chronometricals and Horologicals" was the conflict between Transcendental Idealism and realistic common sense. Melville, of course, preferred common sense and distrusted idealistic philosophy, and his Pierre suffered defeat because of excessive idealism. But more specifically, Melville attacked "certain philosophers" who have pretended to have found "the talismanic secret . . . Plato, and Spinoza, and Goethe and many more belong to this guild of self-impostors, with a preposterous rabble of Muggletonian Scots and Yankees, whose vile brogue still the more bestreaks the stripedness of their Greek and German Neoplatonical originals."[79]—The significant fact is that Melville here attacked the whole philosophy of idealism, that he included Emerson with Plato and Goethe, and that he recognized him to be "no common humbug."

As Melville's personal despair deepened, however, he attacked Emerson's Transcendentalism more specifically and more savagely. In "The Confidence Man" he drew fictional caricatures of Emerson and Thoreau, as Mark Winsome and his ugly follower Egbert, which now declared the "humbug" of these "confidence-men," and the actual evil effects of their false idealism.[80] And in his short stories "Cock-a-Doodle-Doo" and "Bartleby," he satirized Emerson's self-reliance by the process of *reductio ad absurdum,* the one story describing the absurdly tragic results of an active absolute idealism (like *Pierre),* and the other the tragic results of a passively "self-reliant" withdrawal from society.[81] But these stories were all so exaggerated as to destroy much of their effect.

Finally, Melville read Emerson more fully and criticized him

79. Quoted in Braswell, *op. cit.,* 318.

80. See Egbert S. Oliver, "Melville's Picture of Emerson and Thoreau in 'The Confidence Man,'" *College English,* VIII, 61-72 (1946).

81. See Egbert S. Oliver, "'Cock-a-Doodle-Doo' and Transcendental Hocus-Pocus," *New England Quarterly,* XXI, 204-216 (June, 1948).

more temperately in the 1860's. His marginal comments[82] praise Emerson's concern with the inner meaning of things, as opposed to the mere forms of art and poetry. These comments emphasize the fact that for Melville, as also for Hawthorne, Emerson had first defined those fundamental problems and ideal conflicts which the two novelists then embodied fictionally in their plots and characters. But Melville went on to criticize Emerson's optimism, his puritanism, and most of all his defective realization of the evil of life. His most judicious marginal criticism of Emerson may be cited in full:

> This is admirable, as many other thoughts of Mr. Emerson's are. His gross and astonishing errors and illusions spring from a self-conceit so intensely intellectual and calm that at first one hesitates to call it by its right name. Another species of Mr. Emerson's errors, or rather blindness, proceeds from a defect in the region of the heart.[83]

Of course this criticism of Melville's merely emphasizes the vital fact that Emerson was a philosopher and mystic, rather than a tragic novelist or dramatist; but it states the criticism fairly, and by implication defines Melville's opposite position. If Emerson suffered from "a defect in the region of the heart," caused by his adoption of a mystical philosophy "beyond tragedy,"[84] Melville suffered from a parallel defect in the region of the head, caused by his preoccupation with his own bitterly tragic emotional experiences.

Last and not least of the younger contemporaries whom Emerson influenced was Emily Dickinson. On one of his visits to Amherst he stayed at her brother's house, and she probably heard him lecture more than once.[85] She read his Essays and Poems appreciatively, and referred specifically to "The Humble-Bee." But more important than anything specific was the pervasive and formative influence of the Emersonian ideas. As Professor Whicher has put it: "Her sole function was to test the transcendental ethic in its application to the inner life, which was after all the key to the position."[86] In contrast to Whitman's expansive

82. See William Braswell, *op. cit.*
83. Quoted in Braswell, *op. cit.*, p. 331.
84. See Part I, "Beyond Tragedy."
85. See George F. Whicher, *This Was a Poet*, New York, 1938. The chapter on "Emerson" and his influence occupies pp. 189-205.
86. G. F. Whicher, *op. cit.*, p. 200.

social transcendentalism, her poetry developed the tragic, individualistic implications of these ideas. And perhaps even more important, she developed the poetic symbolism, the metrical irregularity, and the imperfect rhymes, which Emerson's poetry had used more or less tentatively, into an effective modern poetic technique.

## 2. *American Reputation*

Beyond Emerson's influence on individual authors of importance, his general influence on the culture and thought of America was, of course, tremendous. This can hardly be measured, except vaguely in terms of miscellaneous critical references on the one hand, and of numbers of editions of his books and collected works on the other. *The Literary Reputation of R. W. Emerson: 1882-1945* has been studied by Dr. R. E. Amacher[87] and others: before considering his influence on the major writers of modern America, this "reputation" may be summarized.

Emerson's death in 1882 naturally evoked a chorus of praise. We have already seen how Whitman stopped criticizing in 1881, and how Whittier paid high tribute. Besides the many biographical and critical studies, the distinguished collection of addresses on *The Genius and Character of Emerson,* edited by his friend F. B. Sanborn, appeared in 1885. Most critical references were laudatory, and Matthew Arnold's judicious mixture of praise and blame evoked heated American replies. Frequent editions of both individual books and complete works appeared between 1882 and 1903.[88] In 1900 Emerson was officially voted into the American Hall of Fame. And finally, the centenary in 1903 stimulated another outburst of critical praise, and of new editions. Nevertheless, Emerson's reputation was still limited largely to America and England, and, of course, many voices dissented, or qualified the praise. Until 1903, Emerson's reputation remained unsure, and limited.

But after 1903, Emerson became progressively accepted as an American classic, and his name continued to grow outside the

87. R. E. Amacher, an unpublished doctoral dissertation (Pittsburgh, 1946).

88. See G. W. Cooke, *A Bibliography of R. W. Emerson,* Boston, 1908.

English-speaking countries. The centenary produced not only the definitive edition of his *Works,* but a volume of addresses[89] including one by William James, and many uncollected addresses including the highest praise by John Dewey. In 1907, the distinguished critical biography by George E. Woodberry described Emerson's as "the only great mind that America has produced in literature"; and this statement was argued pro and con in a whole series of articles and books. In 1909 the publication of the ten volumes of *Journals* enhanced Emerson's reputation still further.

The First World War caused only a slight lessening of interest, and following it the 1920's marked perhaps the high point of Emerson's reputation: in America S. P. Sherman and Bliss Perry helped spread his fame, and in France Régis Michaud and Charles Cestre. But the depression decade of the 1930's caused a revulsion from "Emerson's optimism," and the publication of his collected *Letters* in 1939 proved of interest more to scholars than to the general public. The decade of disillusion beginning with the Second World War continued the decline. Today Emerson seems less popular than at any time since his death. And yet, during the last six years three popular "libraries" have issued inexpensive editions of his writing.[90]

It is significant that the relative decline in Emerson's reputation is recent, that it is explained by obvious historical and psychological causes, and that it clearly marks a backward swing of the pendulum from an earlier extreme of blind faith in "the American dream." And more important perhaps than popular reputation, Emerson's influence upon leading writers of the twentieth century has continued unabated.

### 3. *America, Twentieth Century*

The most important American writers of the twentieth century whom Emerson deeply influenced were probably the pragmatists: James, Dewey, and Holmes. The first two affirmed this influence in addresses on the Emerson centenary of 1903, and all continued progressively to develop the pragmatic implications of Emerson's

89. *The Centenary . . . of R. W. Emerson,* Concord, Mass., 1903.

90. Penguin Books, ed. by E. C. Lindeman, 1947; The Viking Portable Library, ed. by Mark Van Doren, 1946; and Rinehart Editions, ed. by R. L. Cook, 1950. See also The Modern Library, earlier.

ideas. But this influence has already been considered in the section of "Pragmatism," Part III.

After Emily Dickinson, the two major poets of twentieth-century New England—E. A. Robinson and Robert Frost—both affirmed Emerson's deep influence upon them, and developed the implications of his poetic ideas for the modern world—the one in terms of transcendental tragedy, the other in terms of realistic Yankee humor.

E. A. Robinson's narrative poetry, like Emily Dickinson's lyric poetry, emphasized the fact that transcendental "optimism" did not deny human tragedy, but rather reaffirmed it.[91] Robinson was deeply affected by his reading of Emerson, especially in his early years: "He [Emerson] really gets after me,"[92] he wrote. And many of his poems subsequently developed Emerson's abstract ideas. Particularly his Arthurian cycle illustrated the three types of human love which Emerson had named: "Initial, Daemonic, and Celestial Love." "Merlin" described the purely sensuous love of an older man for a younger woman; "Lancelot" described a deeper love which failed because of a divided loyalty; while "Tristram" described an ideal love. But more important, "Tristram" radically altered the pattern of the old myth in order to describe this love as "ideal"; it described the actual realization of this "ideal" love in the most passionate terms; and it described its tragic fulfillment as bringing a victorious ecstasy transcending space and time.[93] In "Tristram" Robinson wrote the most perfect transcendental poetic tragedy, and in so doing produced his poetic masterpiece.

Robert Frost developed in his poetry the opposite aspect of Emerson's thought: its pragmatic realism and Yankee humor. Like Robinson, Frost read Emerson early and enthusiastically,

91. See Floyd Stovall, "The Optimism behind Robinson's Tragedies," *American Literature*, X, 1-23 (March, 1938); and F. I. Carpenter, "Tristram the Transcendent," *New England Quarterly*, XI, 501-523 (Sept., 1938).

92. In a letter to D. G. Mason, *Yale Review* (June, 1936), 861. Robinson's remarks on Emerson have never been collected, but are quoted in various biographical studies. See also F. I. Carpenter, "Tristram the Transcendent," *loc. cit.*

93. See Part III, "Mysticism." This interpretation is documented in F. I. Carpenter, "Tristram the Transcendent."

especially his poetry.[94] He developed the human Yankee realism of "Bulkeley, Hunt, Willard, Hosmer, Merriam, Flint," and the colloquial accents of many other poems of Emerson, rather than any transcendental mysticism. But always as a kind of background for all of Frost's poetry and implying a contrast with the immediate human foreground, is the suggestion of a deeper meaning and symbolism in such prosaic events as, say, "Mending Wall."[95]

Beyond New England Emerson has influenced many modern American authors, although often less directly, and often together with Whitman. Hart Crane developed the most extreme of the Emersonian ideas, without their necessary counterbalance of common sense.[96] And Robinson Jeffers has described in tragic, narrative poetry the consequences of that extreme self-reliance which dares absolutely to defy society and its taboos.[97] In his first published volume, Jeffers took one of his poetic mottoes from Emerson. In conversation with the present writer he affirmed his continuing admiration of Emerson. And many of his later poems attempted to define the "transcendental" values of "integrity and organic wholeness." Finally, the present writer's interpretation of Emerson's biographical and psychological outlook as being "Beyond Tragedy" was suggested by Jeffers' "The Tower Beyond Tragedy."

In prose as in poetry, Emerson's ideas have continued to stimulate modern American writing. So John Steinbeck's preacher,

94. H. H. Waggoner, "The Humanistic Idealism of Robert Frost," *American Literature*, XIII, 207-223 (Nov., 1941). Professor Waggoner not only describes the Emersonian aspects of Frost's poetry, but also quotes frequently from an interview with Frost:

> "Emerson's poetry, he discovered and learned to love, Mr. Frost says, very early in life . . . In one talk . . . he quoted Emerson twice and referred to him again when the subject being discussed was not philosophers but relativity." (p. 209.)

95. See T. K. Whipple, *Spokesmen:* "Frost has not a little of the transcendentalist in his make-up" (p. 102, quoted in H. H. Waggoner, *op. cit.*, p. 208).

96. See Yvor Winters, *In Defense of Reason,* "The Significance of *The Bridge* by Hart Crane."

97. See F. I. Carpenter, "The Values of Robinson Jeffers," *American Literature,* XI, 353-366 (Jan., 1940).

Jim Casey, in *The Grapes of Wrath,* preached the Emersonian doctrine of the Over-Soul in colloquial language: "Maybe it's all men an' all women we love; maybe that's the Holy Sperit—the human sperit—the whole shebang. Maybe all men got one big soul ever'body's a part of."[98] (The novel also ends with a mystical affirmation of faith by Tom Joad.) And so Thomas Wolfe, in the whole series of his "autobiographical" novels, ending with his "Credo" in *You Can't Go Home Again,* embodies the same transcendental philosophy—although in Wolfe's case more specifically inspired by Whitman.[99]

Beyond these major authors, many other Americans in many different fields have paid tribute to Emerson in many different ways. George Santayana's essays on Emerson have already been quoted. Edgar Lee Masters edited a volume of selections, with a personal introduction which bears witness to Emerson's great influence on Masters' youth.[100] Professor Harry Overstreet has emphasized Emerson's influence on his early thinking leading to *The Mature Mind.* Harry Emerson Fosdick, named after Emerson, has constantly quoted him. And many others have shared his influence.

### 4. *England*

For obvious reasons, Emerson never became as popular in England as in America. The advocate of American cultural independence, the opponent of orthodoxy, the prophet of individualism, could hardly expect to find general acceptance in the old mother-country with its Anglican religion and traditional social order. Nevertheless, in a century of social change and industrial revolution Emerson's specific challenge to the old order and his general philosophy of liberalism found many enthusiastic disciples. Although he lectured for only a year in England, he spoke before many "mechanics' institutes" and popular audiences in Manchester and Liverpool which the aristocratic Carlyle, for example, scorned. And although he never achieved a wide popular

98. See F. I. Carpenter, "The Philosophical Joads," *College English,* II, 315-325 (Jan., 1941).

99. See F. I. Carpenter, "Thomas Wolfe: The Autobiography of an Idea," *University of Kansas City Review,* XII, 179 ff. (Spring, 1946).

100. *The Living Thoughts of Emerson,* "presented by Edgar Lee Masters" (New York, 1940).

reputation in England, he made a deep impression on many representative men.

The first biography of Emerson was written by an Englishman, George Searle Phillips, in 1855.[101] One of the biographies occasioned by his death in 1882 was by Alexander Ireland, an old Scotch friend who had first met him in 1833, and had been chiefly instrumental in arranging his lecture tours of 1847-8 in England and Scotland. In 1888, Richard Garnett wrote a fair biographical-critical study of him. Meanwhile many editions[102] of his individual works had been published in England under the sponsorship of Carlyle, together with a good many reprints in the cheaper "libraries."

But Emerson's English influence was probably less great on the popular audiences than on the leading literary men of the day. Carlyle, although older than he, felt his personal inspiration. And Arthur Hugh Clough was drawn by his friendship[103] to live for a time in New England. Others, like Harriet Martineau, both visited him in New England and welcomed him to England. There were many true friends and personal disciples. But the reaction to Emerson's personality and philosophy by the younger literary men of nineteenth century England was probably typified by Matthew Arnold.

Arnold's characterization of "Emerson," in *Discourses in America* is famous:[104] "He is the friend and aider of those who would live in the spirit." But modern readers remember Arnold's words as damning with faint praise: "We have not in Emerson a great poet, a great writer, a great philosophy-maker." Arnold, however, did not thereby intend faint praise.

In the first place, Arnold was making a personal statement of deep indebtedness to Emerson. His "Discourse" continued: "His . . . is a relation of, I think, even superior importance." In a personal letter in 1864 he had testified to "the refreshing and quickening effect your writings had upon me at a critical time in

101. *Emerson: His Life and Writings,* by January Searle [pen name], London, 1855.

102. See Clarence Gohdes, *American Literature in Nineteenth Century England,* New York, 1944; pp. 145-148.

103. See Part I, "Friendships," for Carlyle, Clough, and others.

104. M. Arnold, *Discourses in America,* New York, 1924; pp. 138-208.

my life."[105] Rereading the *Essays* later, his "strong sense" of the value of their author had "deepened." In his "Discourse," Arnold was personally expressing the attitudes of deep, but (of course) not uncritical admiration characteristic of many of his young compatriots.

But Arnold was also expressing relatively high praise. He believed that Emerson's spiritual "friendship and aid" made his *Essays* greater, *as literature,* than any other prose in English of his time:

> As Wordsworth's poetry is, in my judgment, the most important work done in verse, in our language, during the present century, so Emerson's *Essays* are, I think, the most important work done in prose. His work is more important than Carlyle's. . . .

Both personally and judicially, Arnold bore witness both to the historic influence, and to the literary excellence, of Emerson's *Essays.*

Like Arnold, a group of younger men of letters had read Emerson's *Essays* before 1847, and/or heard his lectures and met him personally during his year in England. Arthur Hugh Clough was the moving spirit who invited Emerson to visit at Oxford. James Anthony Froude wrote: "He broke the fetters. I owe my freedom to him."[106] John Tyndall, the scientist, declared: "Whatever I have done, the world owes to him."[107] Max Müller, the orientalist, dedicated his *Lectures on Science and Religion* (1873) to Emerson, "in memory of his visit to Oxford, and in acknowledgement of constant refreshment of head and heart derived from his writings during the last twenty-five years."[108] Herbert Spencer eagerly sought Emerson's advice. And the young Mary Ann Evans (later George Eliot), after meeting Emerson exclaimed of him: "The first *man* I have ever seen."[109] These are high testimonials from major writers.

105. Quoted in C. Gohdes, *op. cit.*, 146.
106. Quoted in Gohdes, *op. cit.*, 145; see Herbert Paul, *The Life of Froude,* New York, 1905, p. 41.
107. Quoted in Rusk, *Life of Emerson,* 457.
108. Quoted in Gohdes, *op. cit.*, p. 146.
109. Quoted in Rusk, *op. cit.*, p. 356; from J. W. Cross, *George Eliot's Life,* London, 1885; I, 191.

Besides a host of lesser admirers,[110] many English authors reacted strongly to Emerson's influence, in different ways. John Ruskin, who met him at Oxford, wrote late in life that he "never cared much for Emerson," but nevertheless cited him twenty-eight separate times in his collected works.[111] Charles Kingsley discussed Emerson in three works, and made him the exponent of "Transcendentalism" in *Phaëton; or Loose Thoughts for Loose Thinkers* (London, 1852). William Butler Yeats criticized his friend George Russell (the poet "A.E.") for being too enthusiastic about Emerson and Whitman, "writers who have begun to seem superficial precisely because they lacked the Vision of Evil."[112] But Yeats also testified to Emerson's deep influence, and thanked him for introduction to the Hindu scriptures. And Alfred Noyes, as we have seen,[113] paid the highest tribute to Emerson's theory and practice of poetry.

## 5. *France and Belgium*[114]

The pattern of Emerson's influence was much the same in France as in England. His popularity was never very widespread, but he influenced deeply many important teachers, writers, and thinkers.

As early as 1838 two professors at the Collège de France—Edgar Quinet and the Polish liberal Adam Mickiewicz—were discussing a "volume of Emerson"; and in 1844 Quinet copied many passages

110. See Gohdes, *op. cit.*, and Townsend Scudder, *The Lonely, Wayfaring Man*, New York, 1936. See also R. E. Amacher, *The Literary Reputation of Emerson, 1882-1945* (Pittsburgh, 1947, unpublished).

111. See "Index," *Collected Works of John Ruskin.* I owe this and the following items to Professor W. E. Houghton of Wellesley.

112. W. B. Yeats, *Autobiographies* (London, 1938), p. 211.

113. See Part II, "Poetry."

114. The French influence has been studied in detail by: Hans Keller, *Emerson in Frankreich: Wirkungen und Parallelel* (Giessen, 1932). Only part of this doctoral dissertation was published at Giessen, however; the rest was announced as to be published in *Beitragen zur Philosophie* by Winter in Heidelberg. Whether or not this actually appeared I have not been able to determine. This perhaps unpublished study included chapters on Emerson and: Amiel, symbolism, protestantism, Guyau, Bergson, Maeterlinck, Oltramare, and other general subjects.

from Emerson into his notebooks.[115] During the 1840's these two, together with their friend Michelet, quoted and praised Emerson frequently in their lectures and writings.

The first French essay published on Emerson[116] appeared in 1846, and is interesting because it remains one of the best. It was written by the Comtesse d'Agoult, mistress of Liszt, mother of Cosima Wagner, and a leading salonière of the time, under the pen name of "Daniel Stern." It praised Emerson as "the personification of the American genius, impatient of all authority and disdainful of all tradition," and described him as the prophet of a future American literature and poetry. A second essay, by Émile Montégut a year later, described Emerson more conventionally as a moral philosopher and idealist.

In spite of these early essays, Emerson remained comparatively little known in France for the next few decades. Although he visited France in 1847-8 he made comparatively little personal impression there (unlike England). On his third European trip, in 1871, he was welcomed by Rénan, Turgenev, and Taine; and gradually his influence increased. In 1907 Marie Dugard's critical biography was published. Maeterlinck's enthusiastic essay added to Emerson's fame. In the 1920's a sympathetic biography and many critical articles appeared by Michaud and Cestre; and Emerson's reputation as a leading American writer, and as a thinker of world importance, became firmly established.

Meanwhile, Emerson influenced several major French writers and thinkers more directly. Most extraordinary was the appreciation of Baudelaire,[117] both because of the latter's enthusiasm for Poe (who hated Emerson) and because of his own anti-moralism and pessimism. Nevertheless, Baudelaire referred to Emerson in 1852, and read him more thoroughly during the 1860's, when he cited him frequently. He valued particularly Emerson's practical

115. Maurice Chazin, "Quinet, an Early Discoverer of Emerson," *PMLA*, XLVIII, 147-163 (March, 1933); and Chazin, "Extracts from Emerson in Quinet's Cahiers," *Revue de Littérature Comparée*, XV, 136-149, 310-326 (Jan.-March, April-June, 1935).

116. Bessie D. Howard, "The First French Estimate of Emerson," *New England Quarterly*, X, 447-463 (Sept., 1937).

117. See Margaret Gilman, "Baudelaire and Emerson," *Romanic Review*, XXIV, 211-22 (Oct., 1943).

advice and psychological encouragement, particularly as expressed in *The Conduct of Life.* He also valued Emerson's development of Swedenborg's idea of "Correspondence." In general, Emerson seemed to him "propre à aiguilloner la meditation."[118]

More to be expected—and also deeper and more important—was Emerson's influence on the Belgian mystic Maurice Maeterlinck.[119] Not only did Maeterlinck read Emerson's works many times and annotate them carefully, but he wrote an enthusiastic introduction to a French translation of Emerson's essays (Brussels, 1894).[120] And frequently he praised Emerson highly: he found in him a fellow spirit, and he valued his mysticism above that of Whitman and other less "controlled" writers.

Last major French writer to read Emerson widely and develop his ideas effectively was Henry Bergson, the philosopher. No scholarly study has yet been published to define the actual extent of Emerson's influence;[121] but Bergson affirmed his debt to Emerson in conversation with Professor Bliss Perry, and the close similarity of many of Bergson's ideas to Emerson's has often been remarked. Bergson's philosophy of "intuition," his emphasis on the relativity of the concept of "time," and his ideas on "the comic"[122] all may fairly be described as embodying the definition, qualification, and systematization of Emerson's ideas. In his essay on "Experience," Emerson had prophetically italicized the phrase "*vital force*" (cf. *élan vital*), and had emphasized its fundamental importance.

Other modern French writers, such as Amiel, Oltramare, Guyau, and Sartre, have either praised Emerson, or developed ideas strikingly similar to his. But the quality of their relationship remains for future scholarship to define.

118. M. Gilman, *op. cit.*, p. 221.

119. G. R. MacMinn, "Emerson and Maeterlinck," *Sewanee Review* (July, 1916). Maeterlinck's appreciation was reprinted as the title piece in *On Emerson and Other Essays,* New York, 1912.

120. Translated by an enthusiastic disciple of Emerson, Marie Mali. See Maurice Chazin, "Emerson's Disciple in Belgium: Marie Mali (1855-1927)," *Romanic Review,* XXIV, 346-349 (Oct.-Dec., 1933).

121. Unless the chapter of Hans Keller, *Emerson in Frankreich,* dealing with Bergson, has been published.

122. See Joseph Jones, "Emerson and Bergson on the Comic," *Comparative Literature,* I, 63-72 (Winter, 1949).

### 6. *Germany*

In Germany, Emerson was accepted somewhat more widely than in France (although somewhat later), and his influence on Friederich Nietzsche was perhaps deeper than on any philosopher in any country. But this was only natural, considering that transcendental philosophy had originated in Germany, and that Emerson had valued Goethe highly as representative modern "Writer."

Herman Grimm—scholar, essayist, and son of the younger of the brothers Grimm famous for their collection of fairy tales—was one of the first Germans to read Emerson enthusiastically, about 1855. Soon afterwards he began a fruitful correspondence with Emerson,[123] and was instrumental in the translation and publication of his essays in Germany.[124] Together with his wife, Gisela von Arnim, daughter of Goethe's correspondent Bettina, he helped spread Emerson's fame. During Emerson's last European trip, in 1873, the three met and visited in Italy.

From the 1860's to the end of the century Emerson's popularity in Germany steadily increased, and reached its climax following the centenary in 1903. At that time two eminent German-born scholars at Harvard University testified to his influence in the Germany of their youth, which had inclined them later to accept appointment in America. Kuno Francke described the American's appeal to the German mind in an address later reprinted in *German Ideals of To-day*.[125] And Hugo Münsterberg, psychologist and disciple of William James, testified to his constant rereading of the *Essays* from the age of fourteen (from 1869) on.[126] Emerson's appeal to the liberal Germans of the generation before the First World War was immediate and great.

From 1918 to the beginning of the Second World War much excellent critical interpretation of Emerson appeared, including the best book of criticism by any European: *Emersons Geistes-*

123. *Correspondence between Emerson and Herman Grimm,* ed. F. W. Holls, Boston, 1903.

124. Julius Simon, *Ralph Waldo Emerson in Deutschland, 1851-1937* (Berlin, 1937) gives detailed bibliographical information concerning the German translations of Emerson, and the critical discussions of his work in Germany.

125. Kuno Francke, *German Ideals of To-day,* Boston, 1907; pp. 93-126.

126. In *The Centenary of . . . R. W. Emerson* (Concord, Mass., June, 1903), pp. 113-119.

*welt*, by Paul Sakmann. Typical of German scholarship, Sakmann's method was to compare Emerson's various ideas with those of the great German philosophers, from Kant and Hegel to Nietzsche and Spengler. Sakmann, however, largely avoided the tendency of much German scholarship to convert his subject into a typical German (as Shakespeare had often been converted into an *Ur-Deutsch*). Rather he defined similarities and differences, pointing out how Emerson's optimism and attitude toward evil paralleled Goethe's and Hegel's, and how his doctrine that "Fate," or "the beneficent necessity," included moral freedom, paralleled Spinoza's "*libera necessitas.*"

Most interesting and most important, however, because it goes to the very heart of all Emersonian criticism and interpretation, is the reception given to Emerson by the Nazis. In the late 1930's, three scholarly volumes[127] interpreting Emerson were published in Nazi Germany, and later two critical articles by Germans were published in American magazines. Of course all of these pointed to the close interrelationship between Emerson and German philosophy. But three different attitudes emerged. Simon and Schottlaender declared almost the identity of the two, and Simon typically asserted that "Emerson is representative of the Germanic nature. . . . His political views, to be sure, must be partially subordinated for the moment."[128] Baumgarten and Hildebrand, on the contrary, emphasized the typically American characteristics of Emerson, interpreting them historically as caused by the peculiar circumstances of life in the new world. Baumgarten[129] particularly attacked Santayana's dictum that Emerson "was in no sense a prophet for his age or country." And Hildebrand, discussing specifically Emerson's attitude toward Europe as "the old world," emphasized the connection between Emerson's philosophy of "History" and his hostility toward European traditionalism; and contrasted sharply his attitude toward heroes with Carlyle's. (But, of course, both writers interpreted many of Emerson's ideas as Germanic, and some as racial.) Finally, the ex-

127. By Julius Simon, Eduard Baumgarten, and Hedi Hildebrand (see Bibliography). Also articles by Rudolf Schottlaender and Hermann Hummel.

128. Quoted by Hermann Hummel in "Emerson and Nietzsche," *New England Quarterly*, XIX, 69 (March, 1946).

129. It is perhaps significant that Baumgarten "disappeared" in 1938, after being forced to leave Goettingen (see H. Hummel, p. 70).

patriate German democrat and member of the Reichstag until 1930, Hermann Hummel, interpreted Nietzsche as an Emersonian liberal, and perhaps overemphasized Emerson's influence on him.

All modern German interpretation of Emerson has focused upon the influence of Emerson upon Nietzsche.—And quite properly so; because his influence was greater than upon any other major writer (excepting, of course, his friends Thoreau and Whitman), because Nietzsche remains a major figure in world literature and philosophy, and, most important, because Nietzsche has been described as a precursor of Nazism. If Emerson's ideas, developed by Nietzsche, resulted in Nazism, the conclusion is obvious and damning. But if Emerson's ideas differed radically from Nietzsche's, or if Nietzsche's differed radically from those of Nazism, an opposite conclusion is indicated. Only gradually have most of the facts of Emerson's influence on Nietzsche been made public, and gradually the relationship of their ideas has been clarified.[130]

Nietzsche's works published under his supervision contain only two comments on Emerson, although the motto of his *Froehliche Wissenschaft* was closely adapted from a sentence of Emerson's essay on "History." His letters and posthumous works, however, contained many and enthusiastic comments on the American. And his unpublished papers, including detailed marginalia in three volumes of Emerson's essays, were even more enthusiastic. In 1920, Charles Andler's study of *Nietzsche: sa vie et sa pensée* described Emerson as the last of the "*précurseurs*" of the German, and first used the unpublished materials to suggest the extent of Emerson's influence. In 1938 Baumgarten used this unpublished material more thoroughly. And in 1946 Hummel concluded that "Emerson must be regarded as the teacher and master rather than a '*précurseur*' of Nietzsche."[131]

130. The following writers have published detailed studies of the Emerson-Nietzsche relationship, either in the form of separate magazine articles, or as chapters of books: Charles Andler, Régis Michaud, Rudolf Schottlaender, Julius Simon, Eduard Baumgarten, Hermann Hummel, and Grace R. Foster (see Bibliography for details). The recent article by Hummel summarizes the factual evidence most completely; that by Foster interprets the philosophical relationship most reasonably.

131. H. Hummel, "Emerson and Nietzsche," *New England Quarterly,* XIX, 84 (March, 1946).

These facts are established: that Nietzsche always carried a volume of Emerson with him when he traveled, beginning about 1862 and continuing for more than twenty years until 1882; that Nietzsche owned at least four volumes of Emerson which he annotated heavily, and is known to have borrowed others; that he actually composed the first drafts of fragments of his works in the margins of Emerson's books; and that many sentences of his have been identified as free adaptations of Emerson's.

Nietzsche's letters refer to "our glorious friend Emerson."[132] His notebooks speak of "Emerson, the most gifted of the Americans," as having been "seduced" by Carlyle. They exclaim: "Emerson. I have never felt so much at home in a book, so much in my own house as,—I ought not praise it; it is too close to me." They add: "The author as yet the richest in ideas of this century has been an American (unfortunately clouded by German philosophy)." Finally Nietzsche wrote to a friend in 1883: "Tell your dear wife that I feel in Emerson a brother soul (but the mind is badly formed)." And in 1884 he was having "a long essay of Emerson's" translated into German.

During the most creative years of his life Nietzsche read Emerson more frequently, continuously, and deeply than any modern writer after Goethe; and he praised him more enthusiastically.—But what ideas did Emerson suggest to Nietzsche? And did these ideas lead toward Nazi nihilism?

Many fundamental ideas of Nietzsche's are closely similar to Emerson's, and many others seem similar. The list of parallels is impressive. Emerson's idea of "power" was developed enthusiastically by Nietzsche, who praised the American as a fellow "dionysian"[133] (cf. Emerson's poem "Bacchus"). Emerson's revolt against the ministry and against orthodox Christianity was repeated by Nietzsche, both in life and in philosophy: Nietzsche's father was a minister, who died when his son was young, and the son studied theology for a time, but later rebelled. Emerson's rejection of "official goodness" was carried to its logical conclusion by Nietzsche's philosophy: *Beyond Good and Evil.* Emerson's praise of "Self-Reliance," and his attack on "Society," was carried

132. For these and following references, see Hummel, *op. cit.*, 65-66.

133. See R. Schottlaender, "Two Dionysians: Emerson and Nietzsche," *South Atlantic Quarterly*, XXXIX, 330-343 (July, 1940).

to the extreme by Nietzsche's exaltation of the "Superman," and his attack on all social institutions and regulations as for "slaves." Emerson's revolt against "the dead hand of the past," and much of his philosophy of "History," was continued by Nietzsche. Emerson's praise of intuition and instinct, and his derogation of the conscious will (see "Spiritual Laws") were strongly Nietzschean. And finally, Nietzsche's conception of his role as philosopher-prophet, and the very name "Zarathustra" which he adopted were Emersonian, as was the aphoristic style, and the form of prose essay which he used to express his ideas.

Many of Nietzsche's fundamental ideas either paralleled or developed logically from similar ideas of Emerson's; but a radical difference remained. Emerson's ideas were always qualified by other equally important ideas, and balanced against them, and justified by them; but Nietzsche's were not. In Nietzsche's philosophy:

> The expression of ideas was radicalized . . .; certain restrictions were abolished; themes previously hinted slightly were developed to the extreme . . . Criticism of the religious, of politics, of science, of social life, became more and more caustic and finally destructive to the point of nihilism.[134]

Moreover, in Emerson's philosophy the restrictions were seldom described as merely negative, nor were the criticisms merely destructive; rather they implied an underlying "moral law," and a new tradition of democracy based on an assumption of the dignity and worth of the common man. Nietzsche[135] did not seek to change the old values: rather, he described in new, somewhat romantic terms the old feudal struggle between the overlord and the under-privileged serf; whereas Emerson sought to open all men's eyes to the opportunity of freedom offered by the new world and its democracy.—The parallel but contrasting development of two particular ideas by the two men will illustrate:

Emerson revolted against orthodox Christianity and in his "Divinity School Address" attacked it for speaking "as if God were dead." Nietzsche also revolted against orthodox Christianity; but in so doing denied the truth of Christianity as a whole, and pro-

134. Hermann Hummel, *op. cit.*, pp. 79-80.

135. This distinction is effectively developed by Eduard Baumgarten, *Der Pragmatismus* . . ., II, 406-7.

claimed that "God is dead." Emerson, in the same breath, had celebrated "the Moral Nature" as "that Law of Laws"; but Nietzsche exalted the Superman as above and beyond all human laws. Emerson, true descendant of the Puritans, sought to purify Christianity; but Nietzsche, in respect to Christianity at least, was wholly the nihilist.

More subtly, Emerson's doctrine of the unconscious "Will"[136] differed from Nietzsche's. Both men celebrated the instinct, or unconscious will, and placed it above the conscious will, or "understanding." But Emerson sought to incorporate the unconscious will in the higher "Reason," while Nietzsche denied the ultimate value of rationality. Moreover, Emerson praised the unconscious will only when it was good-will: "So much benevolence a man hath, so much life hath he." But Nietzsche disagreed, saying: "So much kindness, so much weakness."[137] Emerson's higher "Reason" was the disciplined and educated instinct; but Nietzsche's "will" was the totality of irrational impulses.—In the later language of Freud, Nietzsche rejected the "super-ego" in favor of the "id"; whereas Emerson described the ego (or "Self") as related to both the "id" and the "super-ego," and praised "Self-Reliance" only when disciplined by "Nature," and when nourished by the "Over-Soul." Nietzsche rejected both the transcendental "Reason" and the Emersonian "Over-Soul."

Thus far we have emphasized the nihilism of Nietzsche's ideas, as contrasted with the progressivism of Emerson's. In one respect, however, Nietzsche was clearly the greater writer and thinker: where Emerson was a mystic on the one hand, and a pragmatist on the other, Nietzsche was a tragic writer. Emerson dealt with wrong ideas about God as a psychologist and educator would do, but Nietzsche's method was that of the tragic "poet."[138] Nietzsche's whole philosophy of the Dionysian described the god who had learned wisdom through suffering; whereas Emerson's philosophy often ignored "the troubled pre-history of wisdom,"[139] which in life he had nevertheless experienced.

136. See Grace R. Foster, "The Natural History of the Will," *American Scholar*, XV, 277-290 (Summer, 1946). See also Part III.
137. Quoted in G. R. Foster, *op. cit.*, p. 283.
138. See Eduard Baumgarten, *op. cit.*
139. See R. Schottlaender, *op. cit.*

### 7. *Other Countries*

In the other countries of Europe, in Asia, and in Central and South America, Emerson's influence has been much less than in England, France, and Germany; but often it has been surprisingly great on individuals, and often it has been much more widespread than might be expected. Very little is known accurately, but its probable extent may be inferred from the one thorough bibliography which has been published.[140] Moreover, the great interest in and study of American literature following the Second World War promises to increase both our knowledge of Emerson's past influence, and the extent of his future influence.

In Japan, Emerson has undoubtedly been read less than in India (whose philosophy he so loved), yet the bibliography[141] of Japanese translations, biographies, and articles, runs to seventy pages. A Japanese student at Amherst, Baron Naibu Kanda, heard Emerson lecture in 1879, was deeply impressed, and during his later life as teacher of English in Japan often spoke and lectured on Emerson. The earliest Japanese translations date from 1890. In 1912, Goro Takahashi published his *Memoirs of Emerson,* which remains the best Japanese biography. In 1917, Emerson's *Works* were translated, in eight volumes. Since then the increased Japanese interest in things American has resulted in an increased reading and study of Emerson, obviously encouraged by the Oriental cast of Emerson's own thought.

In India, Emerson has always attracted readers because of his own absorption in Hindu philosophy, but no study has been published of the extent or degree of his influence there. Many Indian scholars and literary men have written informally bearing witness to their own and to their countrymen's enthusiasm, but these articles have usually been general and vague.[142] In modern times eminent Indian writers have praised Emerson and affirmed his

140. B. Jugaru, *A Bibliography of R. W. Emerson in Japan from 1878 to 1935,* Kyoto: The Sunward Press, 1947. Pp. xx, 70. See review in *American Literature,* May, 1949.

141. B. Jugaru, *op. cit.*

142. Perhaps the least vague is that by H. Maitra, "Emerson from an Indian Point of View," *Harvard Theological Review,* IV, 403-417 (Oct., 1911). M. M. Singh's doctoral thesis, *Emerson and India* (Pennsylvania, 1947), lists the Indian bibliography, but, in spite of its title, does not study Emerson's influence *on* India.

influence on their thought—most notably Rabindranath Tagore—but the extent of this influence remains to be defined and documented. In America, the Theosophical Society has published a good deal relating to Emerson written by Hindus, but usually of a non-scholarly nature. Finally, the great influence of Thoreau upon Gandhi may partly be credited to Emerson's teaching, even if indirectly.

Chinese scholars—notably Dr. Hu Shih, formerly Chinese ambassador to Washington—have described Emerson's popularity with the Chinese; but, again, details are lacking.

Among European countries other than England, France and Germany, Emerson's influence was perhaps most considerable in Scandinavia. Recently, professorships of American literature have been founded in Norway, in Sweden, and in Finland, and students have begun to read and study Emerson much more widely than heretofore. But as yet his earlier influence in these countries has barely been suggested. In his inaugural address, Professor Sigmund Skard[143] of Oslo has outlined its history in Norway. In the 1890's, N. Tambs Lyche, editor of *Kringsjaa,* wrote and printed much concerning American intellectual life, and particularly his favorite, Emerson. And the Nobel prize winner, B. Björnson, admired and praised Emerson and Whitman as liberators, and defended them against the attacks of his famous compatriot, Knut Hamsun, later a Nazi.

In Italy, where Margaret Fuller had been the close friend of the republican leader Mazzini, Emerson was often read, and at least two translations of the *Essays* appeared before 1905, but his influence has not been studied.[144]

Most interesting among the European countries, perhaps, is Russia. The Russian cosmopolitan novelist, Ivan Turgenev, was an admirer of Emerson who met and talked with him in France. Tolstoi, although corresponding with the utopian New England idealist Adin Ballou, apparently did not read the heterodox Emerson widely. Nevertheless, several Russian translations appeared,

143. Sigmund Skard, *The Study of American Literature* (Philadelphia: University of Pennsylvania Press, 1949).

144. Emilio Goggio, "Emerson's Interest in Italy," *Italica,* XVII, 97-103 (Sept., 1940), does not consider Emerson's influence in Italy at all. I have happened upon only one Italian study of Emerson: C. Formichi, *Scienza e Féde nell' Opera di R. W. Emerson,* Rome, 1922.

including in 1902 a translation of the complete *Works.* In Soviet Russia, however, Emerson's "idealism" has proved an obstacle to official acceptance, although Whitman has often been praised. A chapter on Emerson from a Soviet *History of Philosophy*[145] (Moscow, 1943), gives the verdict: "American transcendentalism is a post-revolutionary reaction to the trend of ideas in the American Enlightenment." "The idealist ethic of Emerson," however, "is free of the vicious reaction and mystic asceticism of Kirkegaard's ethics." But "Emerson's ethics are profoundly individualistic," he praised "the right to property," and he attacked the "masses."—"Such is the ugly materialist lining of Emerson's beauteous idealist front."[146]

Emerson's influence on, and popularity with the European immigrants who flocked to America in the early twentieth century is suggested by the publication of a Dano-Norwegian discussion of his writings in Chicago in 1910.[147] And Bliss Perry reported how a Finnish immigrant girl spoke to him enthusiastically of reading *The Heart of Emerson's Journals* in a Finnish language newspaper in Fitchburg, Massachusetts.[148] But these are only straws in the wind.

In the Americas a former vice-president of Cuba published an enthusiastic biographical study of Emerson, in Costa Rica.[149] An Argentine scholar named Sarmiento, visiting Boston in the 1860's, had met and been deeply impressed by Emerson: fifty years later an Argentine philosopher recalled this relationship, and interpreted the Emersonian philosophy in a series of lectures: *Hacia una moral sin dogmas: Emerson y el eticismo.*[150]

### *Conclusion*

In general, Emerson's influence and reputation was greatest in the generation between his death and the First World War. In America, where his personal magnetism was felt at first hand,

145. "A Soviet View of Emerson," translated by Sidney L. Jackson, *New England Quarterly*, XIX, 236-243 (June, 1946).
146. All the above are quoted from: S. L. Jackson, *op. cit.*
147. *Ralph Waldo Emerson: En Fremstilling,* af Oscar Gundersen (Chicago: John Anderson Publishing Co., 1910). 156 pp.
148. Bliss Perry, *Emerson Today,* p. 114.
149. Enrique José Varona y Pera, *Emerson,* San José, Costa Rica, 1917.
150. By José Ingenieros, Buenos Aires (2nd ed., 1919).

and where he became spokesman of nineteenth century liberalism, it was stronger earlier. In Europe, it was less before 1900, strongest around 1910. In modern Europe, it has become more wide-spread with the increase of interest in American culture following the Second World War. But this also seems less important, because Emerson's greatest influence has always been exerted upon a comparatively few kindred minds interested in ideas: his world influence must be measured rather by depth and intensity than by breadth and popularity, although in America throughout the second half of the nineteenth century his popular influence was very great indeed.

—And today, and tomorrow? Emerson's historic position as spokesman of nineteenth century American liberalism seems secure. But, as a corollary, because his thought was conditioned by the optimism of his time and place, the modern pessimistic temper has made it suspect. Certainly he is less popular now than at any time since his death. Further, many of his basic ideas, such as self-reliance and the cultural independence of the American writer, have been attacked as romantic and nationalistic. These attacks have been described most clearly and specifically by Professor Yvor Winters,[151] and most generally by T. S. Eliot—whose whole philosophy of tradition and pessimism may fairly be described as anti-Emersonian. But many modern critics who began by attacking Emerson most violently have ended by praising him: H. B. Parkes,[152] whose early attack in 1932 inspired the extreme criticism of Yvor Winters, later described him as a liberating spokesman of "The American Experience."

But if Emerson's optimism and liberalism made him spokesman of nineteenth century America, it also appealed beyond time and place to those minds of every century and every country who have sought to see things under the aspect of eternity. His disciples have included not only mystics and philosophers, but also scientists and scholars who have sought to achieve a supra-personal and supra-national point of view. His optimism, even though conditioned by his own time and place, became also that of the mystic who has seen beyond tragedy; his liberalism became also

151. See Part III, "Romanticism," for a summary and counter-statement.

152. See H. B. Parkes, *The Pragmatic Test* (San Francisco, 1941), pp. 39-62; and *The American Experience* (New York, 1947), pp. 188-192.

that of the scientist who has gone beyond dogma to a freedom conditioned only by ultimate truth. He was philosopher not only of the over-soul but of the pragmatic experience; he was prophet not only of the American dream of democracy but of the universal religion of human brotherhood and individual integrity.

## SELECTED BIBLIOGRAPHY: PART IV

The following Bibliography includes only items concerning Emerson's reading of, and influence upon, world literature. For items concerning his Biography, his Prose and Poetry, and his Ideas, see Bibliographies at ends of Parts I, II, and III.

Amacher, R. E. *The Literary Reputation of R. W. Emerson, 1882-1945* (University of Pittsburgh, 1947; unpublished doctoral thesis).

Andler, Charles. *Nietzsche, sa Vie et sa Pensée.* Paris, 1920. (Chapter on "Emerson," I, 340-371.)

Arnold, Matthew. *Discourses in America.* London, 1885. ("Emerson," pp. 138-207.)

Baker, Carlos. "The Road to Concord: Another Milestone in the Whitman-Emerson Friendship," *The Princeton University Library Chronicle,* VII, 100-117 (April, 1946).

Baumgarten, Eduard. *Der Pragmatismus. Die geistigen Grundlagen des amerikanischen Gemeinwesens.* Frankfurt, 1938. (Contains a chapter on the Emerson-Nietzsche relationship.)

Beach, J. W. "Emerson and Evolution," *University of Toronto Quarterly,* III (1934), pp. 474-497. (Emerson's reading in nineteenth century science.)

Braswell, William. "Melville as a Critic of Emerson," *American Literature,* IX, 317-334 (Nov., 1937).

Brittin, N. A. "Emerson and the Metaphysical Poets," *American Literature,* VIII, 1-21 (March, 1936).

Brown, S. G. "Emerson's Platonism," *New England Quarterly,* XVIII, 325-345 (Sept., 1945).

——. "John Jay Chapman and the Emersonian Gospel," *New England Quarterly,* XXV, 147-180 (June, 1952).

Cameron, Kenneth W. *Emerson the Essayist.* Raleigh, N. C., 1945. 2 vols. (Reprints and discusses many articles and fragments of contemporary literature, especially dealing with Transcendentalism and Swedenborgianism, which influenced Emerson. Supersedes Mr. Cameron's *Ralph Waldo Emerson's Reading* [Raleigh, N. C., 1941].)

Carpenter, F. I. *Emerson and Asia.* Cambridge, Mass., 1930. (Emerson's reading of Oriental literature. See also Christy.)

——. "The Philosophical Joads," *College English,* II, 315-325 (Jan.,

1941). (Emersonian ideas as developed by John Steinbeck.)

——. "Scarlet A Minus," *College English,* V, 173-180 (Jan., 1944). (Emersonian ideas in the *Scarlet Letter,* and Hawthorne's novels.)

——. "Tristram the Transcendent," *New England Quarterly,* XI, 501-523 (Sept., 1938). (Emerson and E. A. Robinson's Arthurian poems.)

——. "The Values of Robinson Jeffers," *American Literature,* XI, 353-366 (Jan., 1940). (Emerson and Jeffers. )

*The Centenary of the Birth of R. W. Emerson.* Concord, Mass., 1903. (Contains addresses by William James, Hugo Münsterberg, and many others.)

Chazin, Maurice. "Emerson's Disciple in Belgium: Marie Mali (1885-1927)," *Romanic Review,* XXIV, 346-349 (Oct.-Dec., 1943).

——. "Extracts from Emerson by Edgar Quinet (1844-1845)," *Revue de Littérature Comparée,* XV, 136-149, 310-326 (Jan.-March, April-June, 1935).

——. "Quinet, an Early Discoverer of Emerson," *PMLA,* XLVIII, 147-163 (March, 1933).

Christy, A. E. *The Orient in American Transcendentalism.* New York, 1932. (The section on Emerson, pp. 61-185.)

Cooke, G. W. *A Bibliography of Ralph Waldo Emerson.* Boston, 1908. (Lists many reviews, articles about Emerson, and poems addressed to him: documents his "influence.")

Davis, M. R. "Emerson's 'Reason' and the Scottish Philosophers," *New England Quarterly,* XVII, 209-228 (June, 1944).

Elliott, G. R. "On Emerson's 'Grace' and 'Self-Reliance,'" *New England Quarterly,* II, 93-104 (Jan., 1929). (The Miltonic influence.)

Falk, R. P. "Emerson and Shakespeare," *PMLA,* LVI, 523-543 (June, 1941).

Formichi, C. *Scienza e Féde nell' Opera di R. W. Emerson.* Rome, 1922.

Foster, Grace R. "The Natural History of the Will," *American Scholar,* XV, 277-287 (Summer, 1946). (A comparison of Emerson's and Nietzsche's ideas, with special reference to Nazism.)

Francke, Kuno. *German Ideals of Today.* Boston, 1907. (Essay on "Emerson," pp. 93-126.)

Gilman, Margaret. "Baudelaire and Emerson," *Romanic Review,* XXIV, 211-222 (Oct., 1943).

Goggio, Emilio. "Emerson's Interest in Italy," *Italica,* XVII, 97-103 (Sept., 1940).

Gohdes, C. H. *American Literature in Nineteenth Century England.* New York, 1944. (Emerson, pp. 145-148 especially.)

——. "Whitman and Emerson," *Sewanee Review,* XXXVIII, 79-93 (Jan., 1929).

Gundersen, Oscar. *Ralph Waldo Emerson: En Fremstilling.* Chicago, John Anderson Publishing Co., 1910.

Harris, W. T. "Emerson's Orientalism," in F. B. Sanborn (ed.), *The Genius and Character of Emerson*. Boston, 1885. (Pp. 372-385.)

Harrison, J. T. *The Teachers of Emerson*. New York, 1910. (A study of Emerson's reading of Plato and the Neo-Platonists.)

Hartwig, G. H. "Emerson on Historical Christianity," *Hibbert Journal*, XXXVII, 405-412 (April, 1939).

Hildebrand, Hedi. *Die amerikanische Stellung zur Geschichte und zu Europa in Emerson's Gedankensystem*. Bonn, 1936.

Hopkins, V. C. "Emerson and Cudworth," *American Literature*, XXIII, 80-98 (March, 1951).

——. "The Influence of Goethe on Emerson's Aesthetic Theory," *Philological Quarterly*, XXVII, 222-244 (Oct., 1948).

Hotson, C. P. "Emerson and the Swedenborgians," *Studies in Philology*, XXVII, 517-545 (July, 1930). (For many other articles by Dr. Hotson on Emerson and Swedenborg, see: *Articles in American Literature . . . 1920-1945*, Durham, N. C., 1947, pp. 52-53.)

Howard, B. D. "The First French Estimate of Emerson," *New England Quarterly*, X, 447-463 (Sept., 1937).

Hummel, Hermann. "Emerson and Nietzsche," *New England Quarterly*, XIX, 63-84 (March, 1946).

Ingenieros, José. *Hacia una moral sin dogmas: Emerson y el eticismo*. Buenos Aires, 1919.

Jackson, S. L. "A Soviet View of Emerson," *New England Quarterly*, XIX, 236-243 (June, 1946).

Jones, Joseph. "Emerson and Bergson on the Comic," *Comparative Literature*, I, 63-72 (Winter, 1949).

Jugaru, B. *A Bibliography of R. W. Emerson in Japan from 1878 to 1935*. Kyoto, The Sunward Press, 1947. Pp. xx, 70.

Keller, Hans. *Emerson in Frankreich: Wirkungen und Parallelen*. Giessen, 1934.

Koht, Halvdan. *The American Spirit in Europe: A Survey of Transatlantic Influences*. Philadelphia, 1949.

MacMinn, George R. "Emerson and Maeterlinck," *Sewanee Review*, July, 1916.

Maeterlinck, Maurice. *On Emerson and Other Essays*. New York, 1912.

Maitra, Herambachandra. "Emerson from an Indian Point of View," *Harvard Theological Review*, IV, 403-417 (Oct., 1911).

Masters, Edgar Lee (ed.). *The Living Thoughts of Emerson*. New York, 1940.

Mathews, J. C. "Emerson's Knowledge of Dante," *University of Texas Studies in English*, XXII, 171-198 (1942).

Michaud, Régis. *Autour d'Emerson*. Paris, 1924. (Includes studies of Emerson's relations with Swedenborg, and with Nietzsche.)

Miller, Perry. *The Transcendentalists*. Cambridge, Mass., 1950.

Moore, J. B. "The Master of Whitman," *Studies in Philology*, XXIII, 77-89 (Jan., 1926).

Münsterberg, Hugo. In *The Centenary of R. W. Emerson* (*q.v.*), 113-118.

Oliver, E. S. "'Cock-a-Doodle-Doo' and Transcendental Hocus-Pocus," *New England Quarterly*, XXI, 204-216 (June, 1948). (Melville and Emerson.)

——. "Melville's Picture of Emerson and Thoreau in 'The Confidence Man,'" *College English*, VIII, 61-72 (1946).

Parkes, H. B. *The Pragmatic Test*. San Francisco, 1941. ("Emerson," pp. 39-62.)

Perry, Bliss. *Emerson Today*. Princeton, 1931.

Pettigrew, R. C. "Emerson and Milton," *American Literature*, III, 45-59 (March, 1931).

Pochmann, H. A. *New England Transcendentalism and St. Louis Hegelianism*. Philadelphia, 1948.

Pollitt, J. D. "Ralph Waldo Emerson's Debt to John Milton," *Marshall Review*, III, 13-21 (Dec., 1939).

Pritchard, John P. *Return to the Fountains*. Durham, N. C., 1942. (Pp. 44-60. Influence of the classics on Emerson.)

Rusk, Ralph L. *The Life of Emerson*. New York, 1949. (Details and documents Emerson's literary relationships with his contemporaries.)

Sanborn, F. B. (ed.). *The Genius and Character of Emerson*. Boston, 1885. (Includes many testimonials of Emerson's influence on his younger contemporaries.)

Scudder, Townsend, III. *The Lonely Wayfaring Man: Emerson and Some Englishmen*. New York, 1936. (Emerson's influence in England.)

Schottlaender, Rudolf. "Two Dionysians: Emerson and Nietzsche," *South Atlantic Quarterly*, XXXIX, 330-343 (July, 1940).

Simon, Julius. *Ralph Waldo Emerson in Deutschland*. Berlin, 1937.

Singh, M. M. *Emerson and India*. (An unpublished doctoral thesis, Pennsylvania, 1947.)

Skard, Sigmund. *The Study of American Literature*. Philadelphia, 1949. (Pamphlet, pp. 31.)

Thompson, F. T. "Emerson and Carlyle," *Studies in Philology*, XXIV, 438-453 (July, 1927).

——. "Emerson's Indebtedness to Coleridge," *Studies in Philology*, XXIII, 55-76 (Jan., 1926).

——. "Emerson's Theory and Practice of Poetry," *PMLA*, XLIII, 1170-1184 (Dec., 1928). (Wordsworth and Coleridge.)

Varona y Pera, Enrique José. *Emerson*. San José, Costa Rica, 1917.

Waggoner, H. H. "The Humanistic Idealism of Robert Frost," *American Literature*, XIII, 207-223 (Nov., 1941). (Frost's debt to Emerson and to William James.)

Wahr, F. B. *Emerson and Goethe*. Ann Arbor, Mich., 1915.

Wellek, René. "Emerson and German Philosophy," *New England Quarterly,* XVI, 41-62 (March, 1943).

Whicher, George F. *This Was a Poet.* New York, 1938. (Emily Dickinson and Emerson, pp. 189-205.)

Winters, Yvor. *In Defense of Reason.* New York, 1947. (Two chapters attack Emerson's influence on the modern world, pp. 262-282 and 575-604.)

Yohannan, J. D. "Emerson's Translations of Persian Poetry from German Sources," *American Literature,* XIV, 407-420 (Jan., 1943).

——. "The Influence of Persian Poetry on Emerson's Work," *American Literature,* XV, 25-41 (March, 1943).

Young, C. L. *Emerson's Montaigne.* New York, 1941.

Zink, H. R. "Emerson's Use of the Bible," *University of Nebraska Studies in Language. . . .* No. 14. Lincoln, Neb., 1935. Pp. 61-74.

# INDEX

# INDEX

Abbreviations: "n" indicates footnote; "b," bibliography.


Adams, Henry, 10, 177
Adams, James T., 10, 154, 204b
Adams, John Q., 14
Adkins, N. F., 86n, 104b
Agoult, Countess d', (D. Stern), 242
Albee, J., 45b
Alcott, Bronson, 19, 24, 26, 30-32, 33, 37, 45b, 70, 132, 133, 203, 225
Amacher, R. E., 81, 234, 241n, 254b
"American Civilization," 68, 151
"The American Scholar," 14, 16, 21, 36, 51, 54-56, 58, 94, 95, 135, 139, 159, 160, 166, 170, 176, 177, 188, 209
Amiel, 241n, 243
anarchism, 191, 192
Andler, Charles, 246, 254b
Anglican, 19, 238
Anglo-Saxon, 93
Anthony, Susan, 16
'Apology," 80
Apuleius, 201
architecture, 99
Argentina, 252
Arnim, Gisela von, 244
Arnold, Matthew, 34, 96, 154, 205b, 234, 239-240, 254b
"Art," 69
Asia (see orientalism)
Asoka, 123
astronomy, 180
Babbitt, Irving, 82, 102
"Bacchus," 85, 94, 212, 247
Bacon, Francis, 77, 217n, 218, 219
Baker, Carlos, 35n, 49b, 226n, 228n, 229n, 254b
Ballou, Adin, 251
Barker, Anna, 23
Baudelaire, 242, 243
Baugh, Hansell, 34n, 49b
Baumgarten, Eduard, 166n, 167, 204b, 245, 246, 248n, 249n, 254b
Beach, J. W., 84, 85n, 127, 179n, 181, 184, 199, 204b, 205b, 223n, 254b
Beard, Charles, 193
"Beauty," 67
Beecher, H. W., 16
Belgium, 243
Benton, Joel, 104b
Bergson, Henri, 241n, 243
*Bhagavad Gita*, 87, 228
Bible, 216-217
Björnson, B., 251
Blair, Walter, 61, 74n, 75, 81n, 86n, 104b
Blake, William, 114
Bliss, D., 6
*Blithedale Romance*, 33, 37, 231
Boehme, Jacob, 115
Booth, R. A., 45b
"Boston Hymn," 20, 36, 40, 87
Bowers, David, 135, 136
Boynton, P. H., 49b
Bradley, A. C., 147
"Brahma," 60, 80, 81, 82, 86-87, 88, 94, 111, 121, 211
Braswell, William, 231n, 232n, 233n, 254b
Brittin, N. A., 222n, 254b
Brokmeyer, H. C., 19
Brook Farm, 37, 70, 134, 186, 188, 230
Brooks, Van Wyck, 3, 9, 10, 36, 44, 45b, 46b, 84n
Brown, John, 40, 68
Brown, S. G., 214, 254b
Brownell, W. C., 77, 78, 104b
Bruel, André, 27n, 46b
Bryant, W. C., 17, 18
Buddha, 123, 125
Bulkeley, Peter, 6
Bunyan, John, 152
Burke, Kenneth, 60, 104b
Burns, Robert, 20, 21
Burroughs, John, 226
Byron, 12, 13, 222
Cabot, J. E., 8n, 39n, 42-43, 44, 46b, 69, 73, 91n, 149, 225
California, 6, 20, 156
Calvinism, 129, 195
Cambridge Platonists, 222
Cameron, K. W., 54, 104b, 220n, 223n, 254b
Canby, H. S., 27n, 28, 226n

Caponigri, A. R., 58, 104b, 120, 185, 206b
Carlyle, Jane, 25
Carlyle, Thomas, 19, 24-27, 28, 30, 31, 33, 34, 40, 52, 55, 61, 63, 64, 65, 66, 68, 70, 71, 73, 74, 79, 110, 125, 133, 134, 186, 209, 223, 224, 225, 238, 239, 240, 245, 247
Carpenter, F. I., 31n, *passim*, 206b, 254b
Carpenter H. C., 176n, 177n, 206b
Cary, E. L., 46b
Catholicism, 114, 115, 116, 117, 119, 120, 129, 206b
Celtic, 93
Cervantes, 218
Cestre, Charles, 27n, 29n, 49b, 84, 104b, 136n, 138-139, 141, 142, 206b, 235, 242
Channing, W. Ellery (1818-1901), 20, 35, 133
Channing, William E. (1780-1842), 129, 130, 204b
Chapman, J. J., 76
"Chardon St. Convention," 62, 68, 134
"Character," 63
Chazin, M., 242n, 255b
China, 251
Christy, A. E., 115n, 206b, 210n, 211n, 255b
Cincinnati, 17, 18
"Circles," 77
"Civilization," 67
Clark, H. H., 178n, 179, 180n, 206b
Clough, A. H., 24, 34, 71, 239, 240
Coleridge, S. T., 25, 65, 82, 110, 125, 126, 179, 181, 198, 199, 223-224, 225
Commager, H. S., 58n, 104b
"The Comic," 67, 243
"Compensation," 58, 59-60, 212, 217
Comte, 182
"Concord Hymn," 35, 36, 80, 81, 87, 94
"Concord School of Philosophy," 19, 225
*The Conduct of Life*, 66-67
Confucius, 123, 213
"Considerations By The Way," 67, 161
Conway, M. D., 46b, 149
Cooke, G. W., 45b, 46b, 102, 234n, 255b
Correspondence, doctrine of, 53, 63, 216, 221, 243
Costa Rica, 252
Crane, Hart, 237
Cuba, 252
Cudworth, 222
"Culture," 67, 159
Curtis, G. W., 17, 49b
Curtis, M. A., 17
Dante, 32, 148, 217, 218-219
Darwin, 179, 181
Davis, M. R., 140n, 197, 198n, 206b, 222n, 255b
"Days," 80, 81, 84, 88
Democracy, 153-164, 188, 190, 202, 248
Democratic Party, 187, 189, 190, 193
Dewey, John, 19, 99, 109, 161, 165, 166, 167, 172, 173-175, 176, 177, 178, 206b, 209, 235
*The Dial*, 26, 28, 32, 38, 43, 69, 81, 131, 132-134
Dickens, Charles, 16, 134
Dickinson, Emily, 233-234, 236
Dillaway, N., 46b, 163
"Discipline," 23, 53, 141, 170, 177
"Divinity School Address," 51, 56-58, 82, 130, 131, 150, 162, 180, 188, 211, 217, 248
Dostoevski, 60
Dugard, Marie, 44, 46b, 242
"Each And All," 76, 80, 81, 82, 86
Eckhart, 115
Economics, 186-194
"Education," 68, 176-178
Edwards, Jonathan, 60, 102, 128, 130, 162, 196
Eliot, C. W., 177, 206b
Eliot, George, 240
Eliot, T. S., 253
Elliott, G. R., 70, 89, 104b, 219n, 255b
Ellsler, Fanny, 101, 201
Emanation, 54, 61, 212, 215
Emerson, B. K., 46b
Emerson, Charles C. (brother), 6, 7, 8, 11, 17, 23, 24, 73

Emerson, Edward B. (brother), 7, 8, 10, 11, 73
Emerson, Edward W., (son), 3, 44, 46b, 51, 82
Emerson, Ellen Tucker (wife), 11, 22, 23, 73, 133
Emerson, Ellen T., (daughter), 189
Emerson, Lydia Jackson (wife), 22, 23, 28, 70
Emerson, Mary Moody, 5, 22, 68, 73, 195
Emerson, Ruth Haskins (mother), 4, 5, 6
Emerson, Waldo (son), 11, 12, 23
Emerson, William (grandfather), 4
Emerson, William (father), 5, 6, 8, 73
Emerson, William (brother), 7, 10, 28
Engel, M. M., 23n, 47b
*English Traits,* 51, 65-66
Erskine, John, 55, 104b
*Essays, First Series,* 58-61
*Essays, Second Series,* 61-62
Evil, 13, 124, 143-152, 169, 241, 245, 247
Evolution, 54, 179, 181-182
"Experience," 12, 53, 61, 62, 67, 74, 76, 86, 109, 119, 145, 148, 177, 178-186, 243
"Fable," 81
Falk, R. P., 217n, 255b
"Fate," 66, 211, 212, 245
Fields, Annie, 49b
Finland, 251, 252
Firkins, O. W., *43*, 47b, 51n, 52, 56n, 62, 76n, 80n, 144, 149, 182, 204
Flanagan, J. T., 104b, 192, 193n, 206b
Florida, 38, 144
Foerster, Norman, 96, 104b, 204b
Forbes, W. H., 189
"Forebearance," 81
Formichi, C., 251, 255b
"Fortune of the Republic," 41, 150, 157, 161, 163
"Fortus," 79
Fosdick, H. E., 238
Foster, C. H., 44, 105b, 154, 162, 206b
Foster, Grace R., 246n, 249n, 255b
Fourier, C., 37, 186, 190
France, 241-243
Francke, Kuno, 244, 255b
Franklin, Benjamin, 109, 165, 194, 222
free verse, 95
French, D. C., 2
Freud, S., 249
"Friendship," 21ff., 58, 60
"frontier," 155-158
Frost, Robert, 83, 236
Frothingham, O. B., 124n, 128, 204b
Froude, J. A., 240
Fruitlands, 31, 37, 38, 134, 186
Fugitive Slave Law, 68, 189, 193
Fuller, Margaret, 23, 24, 26, 32-33, 37, 38, 66, 71, 73, 101, 133, 201, 218, 221, 231
functionalism, 99
Furness, H. H., 22n, 24n, 79n
Furness, W. H., 22, 24, 71
Gandhi, 193, 251
Garnett, R., 47b, 96, 239
Garrison, W. L., 39
Gay, R. M., 47b
"Genteel Tradition," (see Puritanism), 33, 127, 200-203
geology, 180
Gerber, J. C., 36n, 187, 193n, 206b
Germany, 244-249
Gilman, M., 242n, 243n, 255b
"Give All To Love," 80, 85, 230
Glicksberg, C., 18n, 49b
Goddard, H. C., 128, 204b
Goethe, 32, 65, 201, 209, 217, 221-222, 225, 232, 244, 245
Goggio, E., 251n, 255b
Gohdes, Clarence, 58n, 72, 103b, 105b, 226n, 239n, 240n, 241n, 255b
"Goodbye, Proud World," 6, 13, 81, 94, 223
Gorely, Jean, 105b
"Grace," 89, 197, 219
Gray, H. D., 166n, 176n, 207b
"Great Chain of Being," 181
Greeley, Horace, 16, 18, 28, 33
Greenough, Horatio, 100
Grimm, Herman, 24, 34, 71, 244
Guernsey, A. H., 47b

"Gulistan," 72, 86, 212
Gundersen, O., 252n, 255b
Guyau, 241n, 243
"Hamatreya," 80, 83, 94, 211
Hafiz, 212
Hamilton, Alexander, 188
Hamsun, Knut, 251
Haroutunian, J., 112n
Harris, W. T., 19, 52n, 62n, 77, 82, 87n, 105b, 183, 186, 207b, 212, 225, 256b
Harrison, J. S., 214, 222n, 256b
Harte, Bret, 4, 157
Hartwig, G. W., 25n, 49b, 58n, 105b, 217n, 256b
Harvard College, 7, 27, 28, 69, 72, 79, 188, 197, 198, 213
Harvard, Mass., 37
Haskins, D. G., 47b
Haskins, John, 4
Haskins, Ruth (see Emerson, R. H.)
Hastings, Louise, 17n, 18n, 49b, 72
Hawthorne, N., 33, 37, 40, 66, 130, 135, 155, 229, 230-231, 232, 233
Hazard, L. L., 157, 204b
Hedge, F. H., 132, 168
Hegel, 19, 168, 225, 245
Henney, T. G., 83n, 85n, 94, 97n, 105b, 110n
"Heroism," 63
Hicks, Grenville, 71, 105b
Hildebrand, Hedi, 58n, 245, 256b
Hill, J. A., 47b
"Historic Notes . . .," 62, 68
"History," 58, 119-120, 185, 245, 246, 248
Hitler, 137
Hoar, Samuel, 20
Hoeltje, H. H., 20n, 30n, 31, 44, 47b, 49b
Holmes, O. W. Sr., 3, 4, 6, 20, 24, 44, 47b, 52, 55, 61, 91, 123, 134n, 155, 200, 229.
Holmes, O. W. Jr., 166, 172-173, 209, 229, 235
Homer, 123
Hopkins, V. C., 99n, 100n, 102n, 105b, 222n, 256b
Hotson, C. P., 49b, 53n, 105b, 220n, 256b
Howard, B. D., 242n, 256b
Howe, J. W., 189
Hubbell, G. S., 105b
Huggard, W. A., 149, 207b
"Humble-Bee," 80, 81, 83, 84, 94, 233
Hume, 198
Hummel, Hermann, 245n, 246, 247n, 248n, 256b
Hutchinson, Anne, 162, 196
Iamblichus, 215
"Identity Philosophy," 121
Idealism (see Transcendentalism, Platonism)
"Illusions," 67, 89, 119, 183, 184, 211, 212
Imagist, 94, 97
India (see Orientalism), 250-251
Inge, W. R., 142
Ingenieros, J., 252n, 256b
"Initial, Daemonic and Celestial Love," 60, 85, 236
instinct, 126, 142, 248, 249
intuition (see "Reason")
Italy, 251
Jackson, Lydia (see Emerson, Lydia J.)
Jackson, S. L., 252n, 256b
James, Henry, Sr., 18, 34, 168, 170
James, Henry, Jr., 47b, 71, 77, 96, 143, 144
James, William, 61, 69, 101, 114n, 116, 165, 166, 167-175, 182n, 200, 202, 204b, 210, 221, 235, 244
Japan, 111, 250
Jeffers, Robinson, 85, 237
Jefferson, Thomas, 147, 164, 188, 202
Jesus, 64, 110, 129, 142, 146, 152, 162, 217, 218
Jones, Rufus, 113, 114
Jones, Joseph, 243n, 256b
Jordan, L. E., 105b
Jorgenson, C. E., 144n, 146, 147n, 207b
*Journal of Speculative Philosophy*, 19
*Journals of R.W.E.*, 4n, *passim;* and 69-70, 72-73
Jugaru, B., 250, 256b
Kanda, N., 250

Kant, 110, 125, 126, 128, 130, 135, 168, 169, 198, 199, 224-225, 245
Karma, 212
Keller, Hans, 241n, 243n, 256b
Kennedy, W. S., 87n
Kern, A. C., 207b
Kingsley, Charles, 241
Kirkegaard, 252
Koht, H., 256b
Koran, 213
Kreymborg, A., 105b
Kronman, J., 103b
Kurtz, Kenneth, 63, 105b
Ladu, A. I., 157n, 158, 187n, 189, 207b
Lamb, Charles, 77
Landor, W. S., 25
Lane, Charles, 31, 37
Langer, Susanne, 97, 98n, 110n
"Language," 53
Lathrop, J. H., 129n
Lectures (of R.W.E.), 71ff.
*Lectures and Biographical Sketches,* 67
*Letters of R.W.E.,* 70-71
*Letters and Social Aims,* 67
Lewis, A. E., 176n
Lewisohn, L., 101, 106b
Lincoln, A., 40, 88, 189
Lindeman, E., 9, 172n, 175, 185n, 207b
Lippmann, W., 59n
Locke, 125
logic, 109-110, 169, 174
Longfellow, H. W., 155, 186, 229
"Lord's Supper," 68, 71, 130
"Love," 21ff., 58, 60, 85
Lovejoy, A. O., 136-137, 181n, 204b
Lowell, Amy, 97
Lowell, James R., 1, 17, 20, 29, 47b, 55, 56, 113, 155, 229
Lyceum, 16, 177
Lyche, N. T., 251
McDowell, T., 79n, 106b
McEuen, K. A., 92n, 106b
McGiffert, A. C. Jr., 15n, 47b, 71, 73, 103b
MacMinn, G., 243n, 256b
McNulty, J. B., 49b, 60n, 106b
McQuiston, R., 47b, 188n, 207b
MacRae, D., 100n, 106b
Maeterlinck, M., 210, 241n, 242, 243, 256b
Maitra, H., 250n, 256b
Mali, Marie, 243n
"Man the Reformer," 51
Mann, Horace, 176
"Manners," 61
Manu, 213
Manuscripts (of R.W.E.), 72-73
Marchand, Ernest, 49b, 157, 207b
Martineau, Harriet, 239
Masters, Edgar Lee, 238, 256b
Matthews, J. C., 218n, 256b
Matthiessen, F. O., 75, 83n, 88n, 100n, 106b, 135, 148, 204b
Maulsby, D. L., 87n
*May Day,* 79, 86
Mazzini, 251
Mead, E. D., 176
Melville, Herman, 135, 164, 229, 231-233
Mendenhall, M., 176n
"Merlin," 86, 93, 94
Metaphysical Club, 172
Metaphysical Poets, 222
Michaud, Régis, 3, 48b, 96n, 106b, 235, 242, 246n, 256b
Michelet, 242
Mickiewicz, A., 241
Miles, Josephine, 92n, 106b
Miller, Perry, 41, 57n, 106b, 112, 130, 131n, 196, 205b, 207b, 220n, 223n, 256b
Milton, 4, 69, 89, 146, 147, 217, 218-219, 223
*Miscellanies,* 68
Montaigne, 2, 28, 64, 77, 217, 219
Montégut, E., 242
Montez, Lola, 16
Moody, M. M., 38n, 39, 49b, 207b
Moore, J. B., 27n, 28, 49b, 226n, 227n, 229n, 256b
moralism, "moral law," 59, 64, 70, 102, 112, 128, 140-141, 169, 181, 192, 194-203, 248, 249
Müller, Max, 240
Münsterberg, H., 244, 257b
Myers, H. A., 136n, 162, 179, 205b
Mysticism, 59, 61, 64, 65, 70, 85, 101, 102, 108, 112, 113-124, 165, 171, 185, 203, 209, 210, 212, 214,

215, 218, 221, 243, 249, 253
Napoleon, 21, 64, 65
*Natural History of Intellect*, 69, 186
*Nature*, 28, 30, 51-54, 57, 59, 77, 84, 94, 95, 96, 99, 101, 121, 126, 141, 151, 170, 177, 178, 180, 183, 184, 216
Nazism, 245-248, 251
Neilson, W. A., 56, 106b
Neoplatonism, 54, 61, 64, 98, 115, 125, 210, 212, 214-216, 225, 232
"New England Reformers," 37, 60, 61, 62, 85
Newcomb, C. K., 35
Nietzsche, F., 13, 85, 146, 210, 244, 245, 246-249
Nihilism, 187, 192, 248, 249
"Nominalist and Realist," 111
Norton, Andrews, 57, 128, 131
Norway, 251
Novalis, 225
Noyes, Alfred, 96, 241
Nye, R. B., 49b
"Ode" (to Channing), 40, 80, 85, 109
"Ode" (Concord), 87
Oliver, E. S., 88n, 106b, 231n, 232n, 257b
Oltramare, 241n, 243
optimism, 108, 113, 123, 139, 141, 143-152, 163, 193, 209, 218, 235, 245, 253
organic theory, 98-100
Orientalism, 82, 87, 108, 110-111, 112, 113, 115, 119, 121, 134, 183, 209, 210-214, 215, 250
Ossoli (see Fuller)
Otto, R., 115, 205b
"The Over-Soul," 58, 59, *61*, 116, 118, 122, 151, 162, 199, 211, 212, 215, 249
Overstreet, H. A., 59n, 238
Owen, Robert, 186
pain (see Tragedy), 10
pantheism (see Romanticism)
Parker, Theodore, 57, 58, 133
Parkes, H. B., 253, 257b
*Parnassus*, 79
Paul, Sherman, 207b
Peabody, Eliz., 11n, 176
Peirce, C. S., 69, 127, 165, 166, 168-172, 174, 175, 186
Pericles, 123
Perry, Bliss, 2, 10n, *44*, 48b, 54, 56, 69, 70, 87, 91n, 106b, 207b, 235, 243, 252, 257b
Perry, R. B., 34n, 168n
"Persian Poetry," 212
Pettigrew, R. C., 219n, 257b
Phillips, G. S., 239
Phillips, Wendell, 16
"piety," 112, 128, 195, 196, 197
Pittsburgh, 18
Plato, Platonism, 32, 35, 64, 65, 75, 81, 85, 87, 98, 111, 112, 122, 125, 165, 172, 173, 181, 210, 213-214, 231, 232
Plotinus, 2, 54, 61, 115, 180, 214, 215
Plutarch, 64
Pochmann, H. A., 19n, 48b, 73, 106b, 225, 257b
*Poems*, 79, *81*, 91
"The Poet," 61-64, 75, 76, 82, 95, 97, 102
"Poetry and Imagination," 67
"Politics," 61, 62, 186ff.
Pollitt, J. D., 257b
Porphyry, 215
"Power," 66, 67, 247
Pragmatism, 54, 69, 110, 112, 113, 114, 117, 126, 127, 164-178, 202, 203, 209, 210, 249
Presbyterianism, 19
Princeton, 57
Pritchard, J. P., 213n, 257b
"The Problem," 80, 81, 82, 83, 90, 91
Proclus, 215, 216, 225
"progress," 150-152
Protestantism, 114, 115, 120, 128
psychology, psychologists, 59, 97, 110, 120, 175-176, 182, 183, 184
Puritanism, 3, 13, 68, 89, 102, 112, 120, 125, 128, 130, 131, 135, 181, 194-203, 210, 213, 218, 219, 221, 249
Quaker, 120, 130, 196
Quinet, Edgar, 241
Quinn, Patrick, 114n, 207b
"Ralph Waldo Emerson Memorial Association," 72

"Reason," 110, 116, 125-127, 128, 139, 153, 169, 197-199, 224, 249
Reed, Sampson, 220
Reid, Thomas, 198
Renan, E., 242
*Representative Men,* 51, 62-65, 217
"Rhodora," 80, 81, 83, 92, 94
Richmond, H. L., 50b
Ripley, Ezra, 5, 6, 68, 195
Ripley, George, 37, 57, 133
Robinson, E. A., 236
Romanticism, 113, 120, 121, 124, 135, 136-143, 144ff., 197
Roosevelt, F. D., 194
Rousseau, 12
Rusk, Ralph L., 8n, *passim,* 41-42, 48b, 70-71, 73, 103b, 257b
Ruskin, John, 241
Russell, Bertrand, 116, 119n, 120, 127, 185n, 186, 205b
Russell, George, 241
Russell, Phillips, 3, 48b, 165
Russia, 251-252
Ryder, Arthur, 87
"Saadi," 86, 212
St. Louis, 18, 19
St Louis Philosophical Society, 19, 225
Sainte-Beuve, 28
Sakmann, Paul, 245
Sanborn, F. B., 48b, 92, 189n, 227, 234, 257b
Sandeen, E. E., 154, 158, 159n, 163, 207b
Santayana, George, 127, 154, 182, 196, 200, 205b, 208b, 238, 245
Sartre, 243
*Sartor Resartus,* 26
*Scarlet Letter,* 33, 230
Schneider, H. W., 165n, 194, 205b
Schottlaender, R., 245, 246n, 247n, 249n, 257b
Science, 127, 169, 178-186, 209, 211, 220, 253
Scott, E. B., 50b
Scott, Walter, 201, 222
Scudder, Townsend, 25n, 26n, 33n, 34n, 48b, 50b, 65, 241n, 257b
Searle, 48b
"Self-Reliance," 51, 54, 55, 58-59, 61, 74, 81, 141, 199, 247
Sermons (see McGiffert), 71ff.
Shakespeare, 30, 64, 65, 102, 147, 201, 217-218, 219, 245
Shaw, C. G., 187n, 208b
Shepard, Odell, 31n
Sherman, Stuart, 96, 235
Shih, Hu, 251
Silver, Mildred, 150-151, 157n, 208b
Simon, Julius, 244n, 245, 246n, 257b
Singh, M. M., 146n, 210, 212, 250n, 257b
Skard, Sigmund, 251, 257b
Smart, G. K., 208b
Smith, H. N., 31n, 50b, 56n, 106b
Snider, D. J., 48b
"Snow-Storm," 80, 81, 83, 94, 99
socialism, 190
*Society and Solitude,* 67
Socrates, 214
Spencer, Herbert, 182, 240
Spengler, Oswald, "Preface," 245
"The Sphinx," 81, 82
Spiller, R. E., 102, 185, 205b
Spinoza, 232, 245
"Spiritual Laws," 58, 60, 83, 120, 227, 248
Spurzheim, 16
Steinbeck, John, 237
Sterling, John, 24, 33, 71
Stewart, Dugald, 140, 197, 198
Stewart, Randell, 50b
Stovall, Floyd, 236n
Strauch, C. F., 72, 87, 89n, 90, 91, 106b
Style, 74ff.
Sullivan, Louis, 100
Sumner, Charles, 40
Sutcliffe, E. G., 106b
Swedenborg, Swedenborgianism, 34, 53, 63, 64, 89, 113, 146n, 212, 217, 220-221, 243
Swift, J., 126
Symbolism, Symbolists, 94, 95-98, 110, 112, 216, 241n
Tagore, R., 251
Taine, 242
Takahashi, G., 250
Tasso, 218
Taylor, Thomas, 214, 215
Taylor, W. F., 205b
"Temperance," 38

"Terminus," 79, 80, 89, 91
Thayer, J. B., 48b
Theosophical Society, 251
Thompson, F. T., 25n, 50b, 107b, 223n, 224n, 257b
Thoreau, H. D., 21, 24, 27-30, 31, 33, 68, 70, 73, 84, 133, 135, 136, 156, 192, 209, 225, 226, 229, 251
Thorp, Willard, 16n, 17n, 18n, 20n, 50b
"Thought," 89
"Threnody," 12, 81, 84, 86
Ticonderoga, 4
"time," 119, 185 (see History)
Todd, E. W., 198n
Tolstoi, 251
Townsend, H. G., 166n, 171n, 205b
Tragedy (see Evil), 10, 13, 69, 122, 144, 147-149, 233, 236, 237, 249
Transcendentalism, Transcendentalist, 24, 31, 33, 51, 52, 57, 70, 98, 109, 110, 113ff., 121, 124-136, 137ff., 171, 173, 181, 184, 189, 193, 203, 214, 220, 223, 232, 241
Transcendental Club, 132, 172
Trueblood, D. E., 57, 107b
Tucker, Ellen (see Emerson)
Turgenev, 242, 251
Turpie, M. C., 68n, 107b, 130n, 208b
"Two Rivers," 80
Tyndall, John, 186, 240
*Uncollected Writings*, 69
Underhill, Evelyn, 114, 115n, 204b
Unitarianism, 3, 13, 52, 71, 129-131, 135, 180, 188
"Uriel," 57, 80, 82, 145, 219
"Uses of Great Men," 63
Van Buren, Martin, 36
Varona y Pera, 252n, 257b
Very, Jones, 35, 133
Virginia, 20
*Vishnu Purana*, 83
Waggoner, H. H., 237n, 257b
Wahr, F. W., 65n, 107b, 221n, 222n, 257b
"War," 38, 149-150
Ward, S. G., 23, 24, 71
Ware, Henry, Jr., 57
Warfel, H. R., 32n, 50b
Warren, Austin, 34n
Wasung, C. J., 50b
Wayman, V., 176n, 208b
"Wealth," 194
Webster, Daniel, 7, 39, 189
Wellek, René, 224n, 258b
Wells, H. W., 96n
Wendell, Barrett, 10
*Western Messenger*, 81
Whicher, G. F., 233, 258b
Whicher, Stephen, 57, 61, 150, 208b
Whig, 187, 190, 191, 193
Whitefield, 6
Whitman, Walt, 27, 33, 94, 95, 100, 116, 135, 136, 147, 200, 201, 202, 209, 213, 225, *226-229*, 233, 234, 237, 241, 243, 251, 252
Whittier, J. G., 16, 84, 156, 229, *230*, 234
Wicke, M. F., 117, 140, 141, 208b
Wilkinson, L. A., 145n, 208b
will, (see Reason), 249
Winters, Yvor, 3, 35n, 126n, 138-142, 197, 205b, 227n, 237n, 253, 258b
Wolfe, Thomas, 238
"Woman," 38
Woodberry, G. E., 2, 10, *43*, 44, 48b, 52, 58n, 79, 85, 111, 146, 149, 182, 204, 235
Woodbury, C. J., 48b
"Woodnotes," 80, 81, 84
Wordsworth, W., 25, 65, 222, *223*
"Works and Days," 67, 88
Wright, Frank L., 100
Wright, Henry, 31, 37
Yeats, W. B., 241
Yogi, 122
Yohannan, J. D., 212, 213n, 258b
Young, C. L., 64n, 107b, 220n, 258b
"The Young American," 51, 191
Zink, H. R., 217n, 258b